Inner Space Philosophy

Why the Next Stage of Human
Development Should Be Philosophical,
Explained Radically (Suitable for Wolves)

T0243756

Inner Space Philosophy

Why the Next Stage of Human
Development Should Be Philosophical,
Explained Radically (Suitable for Wolves)

James Tartaglia

IFF
BOOKS

Winchester, UK
Washington, USA

CollectiveInk

First published by iff Books, 2024
iff Books is an imprint of Collective Ink Ltd.,
Unit 11, Shepperton House, 89 Shepperton Road, London, N1 3DF
office@collectiveink.com
www.collectiveink.com
www.iff-books.com

For distributor details and how to order please visit the 'Ordering' section on our website.

Text copyright: James Tartaglia 2023

ISBN: 978 1 80341 358 7
978 1 80341 359 4 (ebook)
Library of Congress Control Number: 2023936074

A CIP catalogue record for this book is available from the British Library.

Design: Lapiz Digital Services

UK: Printed and bound by CPI Group (UK) Ltd, Croydon, CR0 4YY
Printed in North America by CPI GPS partners

We operate a distinctive and ethical publishing philosophy in all areas of our business, from our global network of authors to production and worldwide distribution.

Previous Titles

A Defence of Nihilism, co-authored with Tracy Llanera
London: Routledge 2021. ISBN 978-0-367-67845-6.

Philosophy in a Technological World: GODS AND TITANS
London: Bloomsbury 2020. ISBN 978-1-350-18501-2.

The Meaning of Life and the Great Philosophers, co-edited
with Stephen Leach
London: Routledge 2018. ISBN 978-1-138-22095.

*Nihilism and the Meaning of Life: A Philosophical Dialogue with
James Tartaglia*, edited by Masahiro Morioka
Saitama, Japan: University of Waseda 2017.
ISBN 978-4-9908668-2-2.

Consciousness and the Great Philosophers, co-edited
with Stephen Leach
London: Routledge 2016. ISBN 978-1-138-93442-9.

Philosophy in a Meaningless Life
London: Bloomsbury 2016. ISBN 978-1-350-01751-1.

Mind, Language, and Metaphilosophy: Early Philosophical Papers
(by Richard Rorty), co-edited with Stephen Leach,
foreword by Daniel Dennett
Cambridge: Cambridge University Press 2014.
ISBN 978-1-107-61229-7.

Richard Rorty: Critical Assessments of Leading Philosophers, edited
collection in four volumes
London: Routledge 2009. ISBN 978-0-415-49005-4.

Rorty and the Mirror of Nature
London: Routledge 2007. ISBN 978-0-415-38331-8.

Contents

This book is dedicated to the memory of Lord Executor (Philip Garcia, 1878–84–1952). One his many classic calypsos was "Gambo Lai Lai before the Court", recorded in Port of Spain in 1939—it's so good that most folk nowadays can't hear it. After a lifetime of cutting 'em down, the Lord Executor died poor, blind and forgotten.

Introduction

Imagination and Presentation

Imagination has woven the most durable threads in the history of philosophy. The ideas each passing generation are most likely to consider, deepen, dispute, reinterpret, dismantle, make their own, or slander, are the ideas most readily traced to acts of imagination, to new ways of looking at things, to visions. Otherwise they would not have been so startling in their time; otherwise they would not persist in capturing imaginations; otherwise they could not be reimagined. In philosophy, as in most walks of life, the best ideas simply come to us, once we have prepared the ground. And it is not only in the genesis of ideas that imagination has distinguished the history of philosophy, but in presentation too. Parmenides, at the beginning of the Western canon, set down an enigmatic poem about a Goddess who wanted her views judged by reason, rather than taken on trust: "judge by reason the battle-hardened proof which I have spoken," she tells him, during his visit to her house in the sky.[1] In this new form of inquiry, then, reason, truth and imagination were to reside in harmony.

If imagination is valuable in philosophy, then it is certainly worth attending to the manner in which philosophical ideas and arguments are presented. The importance of presentation is obvious in other areas where imagination is valued, after all. A novelist with a good story cannot simply publish their notes and leave it at that, both because the manner in which imagined situations, personalities and narratives are presented to the reader is integral to the value people find in novels, and also because novelists need to develop their ideas in the process of writing. Presentation matters to philosophy for parallel reasons, namely the reasons people have for reading philosophy, and

1

the close relation between presenting philosophical ideas and arguments, whether to yourself or others, and the process of philosophising itself. Imaginative presentation inspires both the consumer and producer of philosophy, which are strongly overlapping categories. It is no accident that the history of philosophy is marked at key points by poems, dialogues, allegories, neologisms, meditations and aphorisms, in addition to treatises of dry, argumentative prose. The latter approach has also been an integral part of the history of philosophy, of course, and can trace its pedigree to the *Corpus Aristotelicum*. But these surviving works of Aristotle's are generally agreed to consist in notes for use within his school, as opposed to the lost works he wrote for publication; the latter probably followed the Platonic model of philosophical dialogue, and were considered by Cicero to be of even greater literary merit than Plato's.[2]

Concerns about imagination and presentation are unfamiliar within today's academic philosophy, where presentation is standardized, and any mention of philosophy being imaginative is most liable to bring to mind a specialised application of imagination, namely the thought experiment, in which hypothetical situations are imagined to evoke intuitions, and thereby test philosophical theories against those intuitions. Thought experiments have become a controversial methodology these days, however, despite the fact that philosophers have used them since ancient times, as indeed have scientists such as Newton and Einstein.[3] One reason the controversy runs deep is because some of the most influential philosophy of the last sixty years has revolved around them, with prominent examples including Gettier's Smith and Jones cases, Foot's trolley, Searle's Chinese room, Parfit's teleporter and Chalmers' zombies; remove the thought experiments from those sixty years and you have to wonder whether the debates they relate to could have otherwise transpired. Even regimented into the narrow role of generating possible scenarios for us to think about, then, it seems imagination has retained the power to inspire philosophical reflection; and yet exactly because of this narrow association, imagination has come to seem like a controversial ingredient in philosophy.

The standardized presentational style of mainstream contemporary philosophy is not particularly distinctive, in that broadly the same format is to be found throughout the social sciences and humanities. The prose is plain, clear and concise (or supposed to be), referencing conventions adopted from the sciences are employed, and the general expectation is that within a standard word limit, the author must demonstrate familiarity with the relevant literature while arguing their points with reference to that literature. It is a format which often resembles a scientific paper recording new experimental results in the context of previous results, or, in the case of monographs, an interconnected series of such papers. The reason for this resemblance seems clear enough, namely that science has become the model for academic inquiry in general; and recognising this helps explain why thought experiments have become a nub of philosophical controversy, namely because they are liable to appear unscientific.

Concerns about the standardization of a science-modelled presentational format in philosophy have been voiced from opposite ends of the philosophical spectrum. At the conservative end, Roger Scruton reported being,

> struck by the thin and withered countenance that philosophy quickly assumes, when it wanders away from art and literature, and I cannot open a journal like *Mind* or *The Philosophical Review* without experiencing an immediate sinking of the heart, like opening a door into a morgue.[4]

Similar concerns have arisen from the radical traditions of continental philosophy to which Scruton was most vehemently opposed. Byung-Chul Han, reflecting on Alcibiades' speech in Plato's *Symposium*, about being intoxicated and driven wild by Socrates' reasoning, concludes that, "Logos is powerless without the force of eros" and that, "Philosophy is the translation of eros into logos".[5] For Han, the god Eros represents a kind of seductive otherness which leads our thoughts down new, previously untrodden paths, and which is being crowded out of our world by calculative, data-driven reasoning. His target is broader than Scruton's, then, but it seems safe to assume that he would not find Eros's touch much in evidence on the pages of *Mind* or *The Philosophical Review*.

The force of these concerns depends on what purposes you have in mind for philosophy. If Scruton did not think philosophy most valuable when united with art and engaged with public affairs, then he would not be so inclined to judge the professional journals he mentions as lifeless. For those who view the advancement of technical philosophical debates within a scholarly community as the priority, however, the contemporary model is liable to seem highly effective, which is an impression that can be reinforced by browsing some of the anthologies that increasingly proliferate within contemporary philosophy, and which are designed to offer cogent routes through decades of debate via selections of influential papers. One's reaction to a model of presentation for philosophy, then, is bound to turn on one's conception of what constitutes good, valuable philosophy, to which that model will seem either appropriate or inappropriate. As such, questions about how philosophy ought to be presented implicate a host of contentious metaphilosophical issues about the nature, value, goals and criteria of success for philosophical inquiry.

There is as much disagreement on these metaphilosophical issues, however, as there is on first-order philosophical issues in metaphysics, epistemology or ethics. Given such diversity of opinion on no less a matter than the soul of philosophy, then, what is problematic about today's standard presentational model is not the model itself, which may be the best available for tackling a wide range of philosophical issues, but rather the pressure its dominance exerts towards metaphilosophical conformity. To accept the standard model of presentation as obligatory—something you are obliged to work with whatever your metaphilosophical views might be—is to have already made a crucial concession in the struggle to determine how philosophy will develop in the future. Argue that philosophy is not like science in a science-like journal article and the medium undermines the message.

Another reason to be concerned about the standardization of presentation is that it turns its back on something very distinctive and appealing about philosophy, namely the diverse and imaginative ways in which it was presented over the prior course of its history. Imaginative presentation might have been used to widen the appeal of philosophical reflection while distinguishing it from other forms of inquiry, but standardization has instead narrowed its appeal while homogenizing it. This was not inevitable and is not irreversible. Consider the 19th century stylistic experiments of Kierkegaard and Nietzsche; consider Heidegger inventing his own philosophical language, or Sartre seamlessly integrating his philosophy with experimental novels and plays; consider Wittgenstein's aphorisms, which get endlessly reproduced as direct quotations within the homogenized prose of today, like magic spells. It was only in the second half of the 20th century that the standardization set in. It has created an atmosphere in which it is now assumed that serious, original and new philosophy must always be presented in the standard model, and that any other kind of presentation indicates popularization, or, at least, less than fully serious philosophy; the only real challenge to this assumption comes from continental philosophers like Han. But this is a historical aberration to be challenged by all philosophers who value imaginative presentation alongside analysis, clarity of expression and rigorous argument, as Plato and Aristotle did.

There is also a problem generated by the particular model that has been standardized, to the extent it marginalises others, and this is that it is an essentially specialist-to-specialist presentational model, akin to a scientific paper. As such it creates pressure towards insularity, and insularity in an academic discourse is liable to lead to questions about its value, both from outsiders and insiders alike. This is rarely a problem in science because such concerns are mitigated by the prospect of technological and other practical applications, primarily, and also by a growth in the general store of human knowledge which can be communicated to the public via popular science. There are no technological applications of philosophy, however, and since its practical applications tend to be societal or personal influences which are gradual and typically only recognised in retrospect, and for which there is only impressionist evidence even then, the justification for pursuing philosophy in an insular, specialist-to-specialist manner must turn more heavily on the possibility of communicating simplified versions of this knowledge and understanding through popular philosophy.

Whereas popular science is a thriving industry that effectively conveys today's science to an interested public, however, most popular philosophy concerns either the big ideas of imaginative philosophers who died long ago, or else is produced by outward-looking philosophers who apply their expertise to issues of perennial or topical public interest. It very rarely consists in relating to the public what is going on in the journals at the moment, and this seems to be reflective of key differences between philosophy and science. Interest in science is centred on discoveries, and when new ones are made, on the back of years of specialist-to-specialist communications, they can be announced, explained, discussed and generally marvelled at. Interest in philosophy, on the other hand, is centred on ideas, ways of thinking, and unfamiliar questions that become increasingly gripping the longer you dwell with them. As such philosophy is massively contextual in a way that science is not, so while popular science can relate a new discovery about black holes, for example, you cannot convey even a grossly simplified understanding of the latest philosophy of language to somebody who has never got to grips with the problems in that area; and without a knowledge of related philosophical concerns they are unlikely to find those problems interesting anyway—a black hole, by contrast, is a huge and mysterious thing in the sky.

These concerns—about unearned pressure towards metaphilosophical conformity, maintaining philosophy's distinctiveness, and insularity—all strike me as good reasons to explore different ways of presenting philosophy, and also, crucially, to resist any suggestion that to do so is to leave the fold of serious, cutting-edge philosophy. What counts as the serious stuff depends on what you think philosophy is supposed to be doing, and thus on your metaphilosophical commitments. If you think of philosophy along scientific lines, as a community of inquirers with shared assumptions and methodologies trying to make incremental progress on agreed problematics, then the standard presentational format of today's philosophy makes good sense. There are other ways to think about it, however. One which I find both attractive and realistic is that philosophy is a creative enterprise of producing ideas to remove us from the goals and presuppositions of everyday human life, not by redirecting our attention to something else, such as dinosaurs, black holes, or fictions, but by recognising the strangeness of what we naturally take for granted so that we can question it and come to understand it differently. This is a conception of philosophy as thinking-outside-the-box, although not to find novel approaches to presupposed goals, which is the usual idea behind the phrase, but rather because there is value in such thinking for humans, just as there is in music, love and laughter.

We may end up thinking differently as a result, and this may have practical consequences, even world-historical ones, but it would be philistine to offer this justification.

Once you start thinking about philosophy in this kind of way, namely as essentially a matter of trying to give people valuable new things to think about, then the case for exploring different forms of presentation becomes more compelling still. Standard presentation in essays and monographs focuses on making a case: here is my understanding of the issue, here is what I think, here is what others think, and here are the reasons I am right. But if the purpose of philosophical writing is to provoke and inspire thought, your own and that of your readers, then there are other things you might want to do. You might want to juxtapose different ideas, or make contrasting points that both seem relevant, but without taking on the artificial burden of explaining why in convoluted connecting prose. You might prefer to leave it to the reader to join the dots on any number of matters, in fact, or else leave them wondering how you joined them. You might want to imagine yourself into a different philosophical outlook—past, present, future, imaginary, or one rooted in reality but adjusted. You might want to leave a thought hanging, perhaps to come back to it later, perhaps to imply it was not worth pursuing. You might want to work with, rather than ignore, the emotional side of philosophical viewpoints. Or you might simply want to find new and more interesting ways of expressing philosophy, in recognition of the fact that any written presentation is a reconstruction of the messier reality of thinking that takes place over the considerable period of time it takes to write a book.

I have called this book *Inner Space Philosophy* for two reasons, both of which follow on from themes of my previous book, *Gods and Titans*. Firstly, I think the dramatic turn we have made towards computers and online life in the last few decades indicates a future in inner space—in making human consciousness enclose virtual worlds, rather than transporting its physical housing to distant planets. Rather like Mark Zuckerberg, I think this is in the cards, and although Mark and I may be wrong, the philosophical implications need to be thought through now that this future has emerged as a live option. The second reason for the title is that whatever kind of future we face in a world of technological transformation, I think we will need more philosophy in the inner space of the human mind to cope with it; neither religion nor science can preserve our collective sanity, but philosophy, neutral between the other two as a mode of thought, may have that potential.

My initial idea for *Inner Space Philosophy*, once I decided on a non-standard presentation, was to try my hand at writing a book of aphorisms. The main reason for this, I do not mind admitting, was that I love reading Nietzsche—despite rarely finding much to agree with him about. What Nietzsche's writings do best, in my opinion, is inspire new philosophical thoughts, of all kinds, and frequently ones that are unlikely to have occurred to him, or so his legacy suggests to me at least. And apart from the inspiration of Nietzsche, I was also encouraged by John Gray's *Straw Dogs* (2002), which demonstrates, if nothing else, that the idiom still has the potential to capture people's imaginations, as well as by John Stuart Mill's reflections on the value of using aphorisms to convey philosophical ideas, in which he writes that,

> If aphorisms were less likely than systems to have truth in them, it would be difficult to account for the fact that almost all books of aphorisms, which have ever acquired a reputation, have retained it; and, we apprehend, have generally deserved to retain it; while, how wofully [sic] the reverse is the case with systems of philosophy no student is ignorant.[6]

Mill said this in a review of Arthur Helps' book of aphorisms entitled *Thoughts in the Cloister and the Crowd*, which apparently did acquire a reputation at the time, but which I had certainly never heard of before. Not long after embarking on my new book of "aphorisms", however, I began to entertain doubts about my understanding of the term. Some definitions make it a pithy embodiment of a general truth, especially one gleaned from experience, in which case aphorisms would constitute only a tiny fraction of Nietzsche's output; "What does not kill me makes me stronger", perhaps, except that Nietzsche calls this a "maxim", which is also the term employed La Rochefoucauld, who provides perhaps the purest example of this kind of writing.[7] The way Nietzsche typically writes, however, as do other paradigmatic philosophical aphorists, such as Cioran, is really just a kind of disjointed, notebook-like style, for which the main recommendation seems to be the freedom it provides for abandoning academic conventions of argumentative and narrative transition. In practice, it amounts to the production of visually standalone short sections of text, usually consisting of a single paragraph of very variable length, sometimes very short, sometimes very long (for a paragraph), although they can also consist of more than a paragraph, albeit typically no more than two or three. These short sections do not necessarily follow one another in the manner of an argumentative, thematic or expositional development, and may switch topic abruptly; having said that, however, Nietzsche does quite often continue the previous train of thought from one section to the next in much the same manner as standard academic prose.

Having assured myself that writing in this manner was all that was required to be said to be writing aphorisms, or writing aphoristically, as it is sometimes more cautiously phrased, I began to feel that even these looser presentational constraints were not necessary. I felt I was splitting up short essays into sections for no other reason than to conform to the style, and that there were other things I wanted to do with the text, such as imagine myself into different philosophical perspectives, or write dialogues, which would be hard to describe as "aphoristic" no matter how loosely that description is employed.

Ornette Coleman, the radical Texan saxophonist and composer who originated the freeform style of jazz, called "free jazz", found that the standard jazz practice of improvising with a predetermined chord sequence was restricting his creativity, so he started improvising without chords, famously remarking that, "If I'm going to follow a preset chord sequence, I may as well write out my solo".[8] I have tried to write this book without predetermined presentational constraints. Like Coleman, who has been an inspiration since I was a teenager, I wanted to make space to be guided more by imagination and less by convention. Coleman was never radical for the sake of it, unlike some of the musicians he inspired. The core of his art was always melodic, he was an improviser of folk melodies, I sing along with his solos—and, *mutatis mutandis*, that is how I like philosophical writing to be, too.

This book makes a case for the next stage of human development being philosophical, that is, for the human race to become a philosophical people. I previously argued this case in a conventional book, *Gods and Titans* (2020), where the focus was on replacing materialism with a different metaphysical understanding less antagonistic to philosophy, and hence more conducive to its growth. The philosophical awakening I envisage, however, will obviously not result from a change of consensus in the increasingly marginalised discipline of academic philosophy. Something much, much bigger would have to happen before a widespread philosophical awakening could possibly come to seem like a practical and prudent goal. Well, as it so happens, something of that much, much bigger kind is indeed going to happen before very long: thoughtless technological development will transform human life in the 21ˢᵗ century in some manner or another, that much is for sure, and based on the current evidence, I and many others think the most likely direction of travel is to inner space. I want philosophy to reinvent itself so that it can follow us inside. I think we will need it there in abundance, and I have written this book to inspire thought along these lines.

In Chapter 1, "Everyday Life Is Real", the focus is on the nature of philosophical inquiry, examined through the concern that philosophical language has fallen out of step with our sense of reality, such that it has become almost impossible now to give anything more than empty lip service to philosophical ideas.

Chapter 2, "Thoughts Not Stories", is a book-within-a-book, in which the reader hears from a chronological procession of philosophers, starting with Plato and ending in the distant future. They are all philosophers for whom philosophy could hardly be more real.

In Chapter 3, "Destiny and the Fates", I note some revealing contrasts between how we think about the fate of individual people and how we think about the fate of the human race.

In Chapter 4, "The First Thinker of the Meaning of Life", I provide a new theory of "meaning in life", that being the special ingredient supposedly required for an individual's life to be, well, meaningful! I was dismissive of this notion in *Philosophy in a Meaningless Life* (2016) but since it seems to be very popular I have found a way of working with it. Once modified to accord with my metaphysical and ethical scruples, I place it at the heart of the case for philosophical development.

In Chapter 5, "Gambo Lai Lai the Cynic", I relate the life of a fictionalized version of Gambo Lai Lai in a style loosely inspired by Diogenes Laertius's *Lives and Opinions of Eminent Philosophers*, a biographical work which was probably written in the first half of the 3ʳᵈ century. Gambo, who lived in Trinidad during the golden age of calypso music in the early 20th century, was an impeccably dressed eccentric who harassed passers-by with barbed comments delivered in a deliberately antiquated and florid English—his "old anglé" or "big English". When I was struck by some possible resemblances between Gambo and the Cynic philosophers Diogenes of Sinope and Crates of Thebes, I realised there were certain home truths which only he could comfortably tell us.

Finally, in Chapter 6, "Once More with Feeling", we welcome back Zemina, the philosopher from the distant future who we first encountered in Chapter 2. This time she is hosting a virtual reality discussion of this present book between two people who know it exceptionally well: Barney, who loves it, and Cuillin, who hates it. As they review the book, chapter-by-chapter, we see how their interpretations and appraisals differ.

Anyway, that'll do for the introduction, I'll say no more, if I give too much away in standard prose then I might as well have carried on that way. If you've enjoyed this first instalment of *Inner Space Philosophy*, please hit "like" and subscribe to my "Philosophy Wolves" channel ... Hang on, I haven't got the presentation wrong simply by writing a book, have I? No, I most certainly have not.

Endnotes

1. Parmenides (5th century BC), in J. Barnes (ed.) *Early Greek Philosophy*, 2nd edition, London: Penguin 2001, p. 82.

2. C. Shields, *Aristotle*, 2nd edition, London: Routledge 2014, chapter 1, p. 25 on Cicero.

3. For an overview, see M. Stuart, Y. Fehige and J. Brown (eds.) *The Routledge Companion to Thought Experiments*, London: Routledge 2018.

4. R. Scruton, "Confessions of a Sceptical Francophile", *Philosophy*, vol. 87, 2012, 477-495, p. 478.

5. B-C Han, *The Agony of Eros*, trans. E. Butler, Cambridge, MA: MIT Press 2017 (original 2012), p. 52. Han's book has a foreword by Alain Badiou, one of the continental philosophers whom Scruton attacks at length in his *Fools, Frauds and Firebrands: Thinkers of the New Left*, London: Bloomsbury 2015, pp. 239-259.

6. J.S. Mill, 1837, "Aphorisms: Thoughts in the Cloister and the Crowd", in J. Robson and J. Stillinger (eds.) *Collected Works of John Stuart Mill, Volume 1: Autobiography and Literary Essays*, London: Routledge 1981.

7. Nietzsche wrote this in the opening section of *Twilight of the Idols* (1888), which is entitled "Maxims and Arrows". Dr. Johnson defined an aphorism as a maxim, however; see G.S. Morson, "The Aphorism: Fragments from the Breakdown of Reason", *New Literary History*, 34:3, 2003, 409-429, p. 409 on Johnson.

8. M. Williams, *The Jazz Tradition*, 2nd edition, Oxford: Oxford University Press 1993 (original 1970), p. 237.

Chapter 1

Everyday Life Is Real

Section 1: Appearance, Reality and Lip Service

Maybe things aren't as they seem — where would we be without that thought? Philosophy plays with it endlessly, sometimes dressed as religion, sometimes as science, and like the rest of us it's more influential with its clothes on. The aim is to believe that everyday life is an illusion, which is very, very difficult; or to prove it's not, with a proof that will be doubted now and forgotten later; or just to get people thinking about whether it is or not, yourself included, and maybe yourself only. Everyday life goes on day after day after bloody day, each followed by the next, and that's how we like it, that's why "life is short" is a disconcerting thought. But maybe it's just a test taking place in the blinking of an eye for an immortal soul, a soul which only has an eye while it's unlucky enough to be lumbered with a body — funny that version of "maybe things aren't as they seem" would hold so much appeal to human beings. Or maybe souls are superstitious nonsense. Maybe everyday life is an evolutionary illusion, as real to us as pollen to a bee, but hiding a reality of waves our physicists found out about, more real than the sea. Or maybe it's the kind of illusion we've only recently become familiar with, a computer simulation. Personally I think everyday life is real.

§

Confident as I am, given that everyday life contains things like weddings, military invasions and hospital appointments, I know very well that it all depends on what you mean by "real", what you mean by "illusion" ... it depends on what's been meant by so many words, meant by so many different people, mostly dead. It depends on what has been meant, what should be meant, what could be meant ... and sooner or later that's going to bring in what's meant by "meant". A complex historical discourse called "philosophy" cannot be avoided if you want to say "everyday life is real". Philosophy is that special place where you're allowed to make a claim like that—but only if you know your stuff.

§

You wouldn't want to say that everyday life is real at the checkout of a supermarket, would you? It's only ever tempting in that niche area of life called "philosophy", where statements like that have gained an extra significance to attract us—where an everyday context has been created to allow us to say them with seriousness. At the checkout, the only remotely viable context would be a joke ... and I wouldn't want to try it, I don't think many people could pull it off. For most people, the extra significance which makes it OK is like that of a story, one you like to think about and discuss, albeit with an interactive element, namely that the philosophers thought what they were saying was true, and you're supposed to decide if you agree. For the philosophers themselves there's also professional significance. Suppose the professor is derided by an audience of her peers for offering only naïve support to the claim that everyday life is real—that'll hit her like a brick. In both cases, everyday life easily gets the upper hand in the discourse that questions its reality, and that's because everyday life has domesticated it. But there's what you say, what you feel, and what you should say given how you feel. If something like "everyday life is real" is worth saying, it ought to be able to hit you like a brick—like discovering that house prices have doubled in your area, or that your partner's having an affair. That's the kind of statement it ought to be, one with the force of everyday life but attuned to its actual content.

§

Even the monk most sure of the illusory nature of his existence here on earth would have stopped thinking about that kind of thing when a fly persisted in buzzing around his head; and the thought would have left him for much longer if he heard that soldiers were on the way to ransack his monastery. Wittgenstein said philosophy is about showing the fly the way out of the bottle, but was anyone ever a fly? Wasn't the inner turmoil some philosophers apparently felt—worrying they were the only soul in existence, or that they couldn't be sure of an external world— tied to their need to contribute to a debate, to be taken seriously, to prove that person wrong, advance their reputation, alleviate boredom—wasn't it a product of everyday life, rather than genuine doubt as to its authenticity? If it wasn't, weren't they mad? I don't know, I think I must be failing to imagine how different some inner lives have been—and still are, perhaps. I can see how having doubts about the reality of everyday life might amount to making certain kinds of philosophical statement in public, with their sincerity affirmed to yourself in fragmented inner monologues, but I struggle to see how it could attain equivalence with doubting that he'll take less than £2000 for the car. Consider: I think he might take less than the asking price of £3000, but it's very doubtful he'll go below £2000, despite the fact that you're insisting that I try. I think it's going to insult him—it's pointless and I don't want to do it, it's embarrassing. I struggle to imagine doubting the reality of everyday life being anything like doubting that he'll say, "Sure, mate, £1800 is fine, the car's yours!" You can start thinking philosophically about reality by thinking about how unreal philosophical discourse can seem.

§

I don't think you can cut through directly, like a Zen master who shocks you into immediately seeing what he sees. I don't doubt that kind of thing happens, but it must need a shared life, you couldn't do it with a book. But maybe philosophy can hunt like a wolf pack.

§

To say everyday life is real is significant because it's been denied so much, but the explicit denials of the philosophers aren't the most telling, it's the mass phenomenon of being prepared to accept words to that effect and not caring. It's being prepared to pay lip service to everyday life not being real, but only when pressed, dutifully, if that's what you have to do to make it go away. There's nothing that won't be denied to make it go away, not even your own existence. The everyday significance of needing to say the respectable thing has become stronger than the significance of the words.

§

If everyday life was an illusion, how would you react? That's the first question that occurs to me when faced with this proposition and it's a natural one: you find yourself in a situation you weren't expecting to be in, so what do you do? If I was kidnapped and dumped in Rio de Janeiro with only the clothes on my back, the first thing I'd ask myself is: what do I do now? So let's assume your whole life isn't what it's seemed to be, and to make the suggestion concrete, let's go with the currently most popular version: it's a computer simulation. That's popular because we've recently started living with computers; if chariots were the new big thing, it'd probably involve being whisked into the sky on one, as Parmenides was. So, the scenario goes like this: as soon as you were born, you were connected to a virtual reality machine and everything since then has been a simulation. That might be true right now, presumably, but if so then it's only one of billions of idle possibilities, like there being buried treasure in your garden, so you obviously wouldn't do anything about it. To make the situation interesting we need more than it being true, we need to know it—otherwise nothing happens, you carry on oblivious, it's nothing to you. You could ask how we know it's not true, and, admittedly, that's been the usual path philosophers have taken, but I don't find that so interesting. How do I know it's not true right now? I don't know, but you'll struggle to persuade me to take the prospect seriously, especially since it involves computers; I remember when mine had 32 kilobytes.

So let's say you have hard evidence. You suddenly discover, in some incontrovertible fashion, that you've been living in a simulation your whole life. What are you going to do? I think that depends on whether your discovery has public ramifications. If I found out I was living a simulation then the first thing I'd do is talk to my wife. If I initiated that conversation right now she'd think I was joking, obviously, but if I persisted for long enough I'd eventually persuade her of my sincerity. At that point she'd have concerns about my mental health and want me to see a doctor, but then I'd back off, and at the end of a long and difficult process, I think she'd learn to live with the realisation that I genuinely believed these things. The extra, everyday significance of philosophy would save our relationship: philosophers do have some whacky ideas, there really are philosophers who say that we live in a computer simulation, and even though I'd have spilled the beans about that special, incontrovertible way in which I'd learned the truth, I guess it still wouldn't really matter, she could dismiss it as an eccentricity. Maybe I have gone a little mad, she might think, but there are lots of people like that, and it's appropriately compartmentalized—it might even come to seem endearing. That's a realistic way I can imagine it panning out on that front. Don't forget that I'm the one who's right in the situation we're imagining.

Meanwhile, I'm probably going to tentatively test the ground with some other people. If they're reacting in the same kind of predictable, everyday manner, then I'm quickly going to realise that what I've learned has no place in the simulation—that it's a private thing with no public ramifications. And after that, I think I'd gradually learn not to care so much. I'm always going to think about it from time to time, and I'll probably develop differently in the long term, but I wouldn't pointlessly ruin my life by acting like a lunatic. It isn't that I'm stuck in the simulation, it's that my life is there. Granted, I'll know I'm talking to empty shells, and that'll be disconcerting when I think about it—but there's nothing I can do, so it'll become academic.

The situation is transformed, however, if there are public ramifications. Suppose that when I talk to my wife she tells me she already knows, and it becomes clear that I'm talking to a simulated intelligence from another dimension—"we thought the time was right to reveal this to you, but you needn't worry, etc." In that case I'm going to want out—what I'll want to do is get out pronto. I'll start playing around with the simulation, testing it to see what happens, and whatever does happen will determine the direction my life goes in. I'd be trying to make contact with a soul in a life that's real, that's what I'd mainly care about. I'd want to learn everything I could about the situation outside. Even if I became convinced there was nothing like me outside, only machines whirring, and that there was no way out in any case, I think I'd still want to play around with the simulation, rather than live the make-believe set in place for me. That way I'd be exercising my freedom on reality; the public ramifications I'd seen would show me I could. Living the make-believe couldn't be real for me once I knew I had other options, it could only be an act undertaken for comfort and pleasure— and even if that did seem like my best option, I might not be able to suppress the mental turmoil well enough to keep up the act and benefit from it.

In the end, then, I think that if you believed everyday life was an illusion, and could do something about it, you'd try to live the outside life that was real, as best you could. The loneliness would force you to try, just in case, even knowing it was pointless. If you couldn't, on the other hand, as in the former case where there are no public ramifications, then sooner or later you'd only be paying lip service to the idea that everyday life is an illusion.

The fact that whether we can do anything about it makes so much difference to our sense of reality shows that we only pay lip service to the idea that everyday life is an illusion. Things are changing, however—philosophy is moving things on.

§

If philosophical statements could acquire the force of everyday life, but attuned to their content, then it wouldn't feel like finding out the price of your house doubled, or that your partner's having an affair. I just meant that the intensity and reality should be much greater. Making a statement to the effect that the whole of reality, absolutely everything, either was or was not created by a god shouldn't be like saying that you forgot to buy frozen peas. I don't want the waver in the voice of an evangelical preacher, but it's a nod in the right direction, when it's genuine. For a context suited to that kind of content, you might think of standing on a mountain in the driving rain as the night sky takes on unearthly colours. But that's to forget that there's both outer and inner space. It's what's going on inside that counts—the voice can be calm and the lighting electric.

§

In any profession you're going to end up paying lip service to things, not attending to the resonance of their content. "We've really got to make sure we're keeping to our billing targets," says the businessman—but that sort of thing won't sink in until they hit financial rocks and jobs are at stake. It becomes a background concern, rather as the ultimate nature of reality, or the difference between right and wrong, can become a background concern for a philosopher. It has to, since everyday life rolls on day after day and intensity requires contrasts. Is it true that in philosophy, unlike in business, there's no prospect of an event occurring which draws its statements out of the background and makes them sink in?

Section 2: Is Death the Answer?

Some philosophers like to talk about death, it's a tradition. Remembering that it's a fact, no joke, that your inner space is heading for oblivion gets you into philosophical areas sharpish, and everyone knows it's for real—it's something you don't have to try to take seriously because you already do. It's a short-cut borrowed from various schools of ancient Greek philosophy, most notably Stoicism, which was then adapted by Christianity, and then adapted again for atheists by 20th century existentialist philosophy. It's a tool that's always available: the businessman only has potential disaster to give his words force, and if he manages things well it'll stay like that, but the philosopher always has the real thing.

§

In his book, *The Black Mirror*, the philosopher/doctor Raymond Tallis, who specialised in geriatrics during his medical career, sets the scene for a philosophical investigation of everyday life

by means of a grim imagining of the day of his own death—
Tallis tells us how the hospital staff will set about dealing
with his warm corpse, for instance. In a review entitled "Why
can't we stop for death?", John Gray, the philosopher/political
commenter, says that the fault with the book, "lies with the
hopes the author has invested in philosophy", for according
to Gray's reading, Tallis thought philosophy would assuage
his fear of death, but there are tell-tale signs on the pages
that it didn't serve him well.[1] This is revealing about Gray's
philosophy, not Tallis's. Tallis's book is a detailed reminder
of what everyday life consists in, with death used as a device
to break the spell of our daily preoccupations so that we can
more easily see how the details add up to a whole, rather as a
mirror breaks the spell of the world we gaze into so we can see
ourselves; Tallis uses death in the regular existentialist manner,
then. There's no suggestion that he sees philosophy as a remedy
for fear of death—this is an attraction of religious faith in an
afterlife, or course, but Tallis is an atheist. So why does Gray
misread the book so completely? Why assume that any book
connecting philosophy and death must be looking for comfort
through understanding?

Gray's philosophy revolves around a conception of human
nature according to which Darwinian evolution has made
us irreparably flawed and contradictory beings. Part of our
contradictory nature, as he sees it, is to both fear death and
long for the transition it offers to a better existence, a religious
instinct which can't be overcome, only suppressed. Since he
sees philosophy as a futile attempt to address mortal fears and
anxieties with reason, he interprets Tallis's project accordingly.
And yet Gray himself thinks death is "no big deal", as he
puts it in the review, despite his view that it is part of human
nature to fear death. On the assumption that Gray is neither
contradicting himself nor speaking as an extraterrestrial,
he must mean that he's realised his fear is irrational. That'd

make sense: reasoning taught me I shouldn't be afraid, I still am because that's unavoidable for humans, so it didn't help. And yet there's no fear and trembling in Gray's writings, as you'd expect from the bravado of "no big deal". The reason, I think, is that unlike Tallis, Gray actually does hold out hope for overcoming fear of death—but not through philosophy, rather through attacking philosophy. He hopes that by recognising its futility we might become carefree, like a cat, as suggested throughout his enjoyable book, *Feline Philosophy*; a book that is very special to him and which he'd always wanted to write, as he revealed in an interview.[2] But cats don't think about these things, philosophers do, and philosophers must avoid contradiction to defend any view, including the view that philosophy is futile.

§

I don't think it's necessary to talk about death. Philosophy shouldn't need anything to happen to draw it out of the background. Philosophy draws reality out of the background. We just need to remember what philosophical statements are saying, which shouldn't be hard when they say what they say, but it is now. Since things are going to change, we need to remember while it's still academic.

§

The operative philosophies in our world are all very old. Christianity and Islam are the youngsters. Buddhism and Materialism, the science philosophy which currently dominates our destinies, both originate around the 4th century BC. Hinduism, the world's third largest religion, is the really old one. They all deny that everyday life is real.

§

Keep death always in mind, says ancient wisdom. Heidegger, one of the few philosophers to think that everyday life is real, considered it vital that we reclaim this ancient wisdom. Every gamer knows it now. You always have to be thinking about death, and how to avoid it, because it sets you back in the game; it's only worth it for special reasons, such as if there's giggles to be had from a particularly spectacular death, lol. While some dream of beating death with science, culture has naturally developed to show how boring we think that would be. There's massively more death around than ever before.

Section 3: Materialism and Anti-Philosophy

The word "obscene" has taken on new life. It used to be most appropriate to matters of a sexual nature, nicely capturing the disgust people felt. It's still used that way, although to describe an act or image as "obscene" is taking on something of a jokey edge these days; it can be used to condone while condemning the prudes who wouldn't. The new natural home of the word is to describe the super-rich: individual people who are wealthier than a whole nation of millions of people. Their wealth is obscene in the way that exposing too much flesh used to be — it offends people's taste by stepping outside the boundaries of decent behaviour. That explains the use of the word, but we must simply be paying lip service since we keep doing business with these people. Someone openly condemned for obscenity in Victorian England wouldn't be invited over for tea.

§

Doubts about the value of philosophy become conspicuous as soon as philosophy does. Socrates was satirised in

Aristophanes' bawdy comedy, *The Clouds*, then Plato hit back by portraying the playwright as a drunk. These days the doubts are gnawing away at a lot of philosophers and its symbol is, of all things, the *armchair*. It's like the symbol of the cross: a reminder of the sins of philosophers. The idea behind it is that philosophers lounge around on expensive armchairs, pontificating about matters they couldn't possibly know about, given that they haven't left their armchairs to find out—unlike the action-men and -women of science who put in the legwork required.

This doubt has reverberated throughout the profession to a degree that never ceases to amaze me. I'd be interested to see research into the number of times the word "armchair" has appeared in philosophy books and articles over the last couple of decades, as well as the number of printed images of armchairs used as book covers or illustrations. It's become a cliché for philosophers giving a research paper on anything to do with metaphilosophy or philosophical methodology, to use an image of an armchair on one of their PowerPoint slides—it provides their cue to mount a defence against the (to them) self-evident objection that they're wasting everyone's time. I've even seen an armchair-image on the opening slide of an introductory talk for incoming philosophy students—young people choose to spend three years of their lives studying philosophy, and the first thing they're confronted with is the image of the armchair. The symbol is almost always accompanied by a defence of philosophy against what it represents, of course, but I do often wonder if these philosophers are genuinely convinced by their defences and don't instead feel like a small, cornered band of fighters who've decided to make a last stand against the vast approaching army. Are the chairs they sit on to do their work similar enough to armchairs that they can't escape the symbol of their shame? Plato had the right idea, put it down to booze.

§

American philosopher Richard Rorty found that doubt about philosophy was the defining feature of his life's thought. In his autobiographical essay of 1992—when he was 61 and now able to speak as a public intellectual—he says that he'd spent 40 years "looking for a coherent and convincing way of formulating my worries about what, if anything, philosophy is good for".[3] A philosophical prodigy if ever there was one, Rorty arrived at university to begin his undergraduate degree on the day before his 15th birthday, but it seems that he spent his career worrying that the philosophy he'd loved since childhood was useless. This is largely explained by his allegiance to Pragmatism, America's home-grown philosophy that begins, long before Rorty, in a similar kind of doubt—that the ancient European philosophical tradition Americans had inherited was useless, that it wasn't going to help Americans, that something useful was needed. American culture has been the dominant one of our world for the best part of a century now, so no wonder the symbol of the armchair has arisen. It's a misunderstanding, however. What's not being realised is how useful philosophy is, now and always. The real problem is how useful it is while its sense is domesticated.

§

If you're looking for evidence of philosophers having a direct influence on the everyday life of the world, then there's Aristotle and Alexander the Great, Marx and Lenin, and you might add, as Bertrand Russell did, Nietzsche and Hitler.[4] There's some major transformations of the ancient and modern world, most obvious because they invoke death and destruction, things we talk about in a highly domesticated manner. (In today's drama, they have to keep upping the realism to bring the craved shock and excitement—or else downing the realism by upping the extravagance, if it's to remain fun. One day, finding yourself sweating and injured in the perfect reality of a virtual battlefield might not be good enough.) The transformations get bigger when we allow philosophy to dress. There's Plato and the Christian philosophy, Buddha and Buddhism, there's Galileo, Francis Bacon, and the Science philosophy ("materialism"). In none of these cases did people discover a new way of looking at things by going out to have a look. Where new evidence was a major factor, beyond what you pick up by being part of everyday life, it had to be thought about. Since nobody would have listened to a peasant, and never would have if non-peasants hadn't started thinking about their lot, there were probably lots of armchairs involved; fine chairs, in any case. People tend to sit to think, and for writing, where the thought expands and refines, it's hard not to. So it's easy to see that philosophy has no problem with usefulness, nor indeed armchairs. Philosophy is a dangerous thing, as Nietzsche realised.[5] If people start to think differently about everyday life, that can change everything. Everyday life is real, and denying that, among other things, has transformed it. A philosopher looking to see the usefulness take effect, however, so they can reap the personal rewards of feeling useful, has gone into the wrong business.

§

(Our drama keeps upping the realism of violence.) Suppose that's right, and that eventually the perfect virtual battlefield wouldn't be enough. It wouldn't be enough because you'd know it wasn't real, the biggest feared consequence, death, wouldn't be there. To up the realism they'd have to trick you. You'd have to forget that everyday life is real. In that case there wouldn't be anything you could do about it on that virtual battlefield, namely wait it out, so your life would be there for the duration.

Technology would have taken you to the same place everyday life has taken people throughout our history, a venerated and horrifying place that drives our drama and which people chat about incessantly. Would that be upping it to the limit we're aiming for, namely heaven for *Homo sapiens*? (Or perhaps just for the males of the species.) Afterwards: "Wow, that was intense to the max!" When it happened for real, when there was no afterwards, was the consolation of a peaceful heaven the ultimate self-deception?

§

As filmmaker and "Master of Suspense" Alfred Hitchcock explained, if the audience is oblivious to the time-bomb ticking away under the table, about to blow up all the characters you've come to know over the course of the film, then there's no chance of suspense. One minute you're listening in on their conversation, the next—BOOM—it's all over. If the audience knows about the bomb but the characters don't, however, then suspense can be generated; and if the characters know about the bomb they can run away or defuse it. People all over the world take materialist philosophy as a matter of common sense without even knowing what the word "philosophy" means— whenever a child is taught that the world is made of atoms, without any philosophical qualification being made, then they're being taught materialist philosophy. There's suspense involved in wondering how science and technology will transform our lives next. Are we all going to move into virtual reality? Are we going to live among robots?

§

Materialism arrived in the 20th century like a new empire—as the Christian philosophy was fading, materialism's creativity and energy soared. Professional philosophy took a while to catch up, but after WWII it became progressively more materialist, and more dominated by American philosophers, until the 1960s when the process was complete—a period of professional philosophy was inaugurated which continues to this day. Although the profession's favoured philosophy was transforming the world, however, it didn't get the role as its official spokesperson, which was taken by science. For science to become the spokesperson for a philosophy required much ignorance about the nature of philosophy, but the new professional philosophy had little interest in remedying this.

§

American philosopher W.V.O. Quine (1908–2000) is venerated in contemporary professional philosophy as one of the most important and influential philosophers of the 20th century, and yet it's very unlikely that anyone will have heard of him unless they're a philosophy graduate—and lots of those won't either. Like the European philosophers who founded the analytical philosophy movement in the first half of the 20th century, most notably Frege, Russell and Wittgenstein, Quine's focus was on highly technical issues concerning logic and language, but unlike them he was also a materialist and had a certain sympathy for pragmatism. It was Quine, more than anyone else, who set the mould for Anglophone professional philosophy in the second half of the twentieth century and ever since.

§

Quine was an imaginative thinker and a distinctive stylist. Of all the original and controversial ideas he had, his argument that translation is indeterminate is probably the best-known, his trademark claim. Imagine explaining that to someone who doesn't know any philosophy; someone with an office job, say, or a plumber. I think I could get the gist across. At the end, they might say it was interesting, if we were getting along well, but they wouldn't really find it interesting. Again, depending on how we were getting along, they might be a little more candid and ask, "So what?" —and then I'm stuffed. All they'll remember by the end of the day is the novelty of having had a chat with a philosopher.

§

"But if translation is indeterminate that's something that needs to be known."

"It's not known. It's just something that some professional philosophers discuss. The ones that discuss it agree or disagree with Quine to a greater or lesser extent."

§

Quine thought of philosophy as continuous with science. In a letter to a journalist who was writing a piece about American philosophers, Quine says the question of what counts as philosophy is only a concern for librarians, who need to decide which books to group together on the shelves.[6] The question of the nature of philosophy is a trivial one, that's basically what he was saying. Ancient Greek philosophy, in its various schools, was preoccupied with "spiritual exercises", as Pierre Hadot puts it.[7] Members of Plato's Academy, which lasted some 300 years before Sulla put a violent end to it, would recite idealised rational dialogues in order to try to refine the inner space of their everyday lives.

§

Quine rose to prominence at a time when educational standards were soaring, atheism was becoming acceptable, and people needed philosophy that wasn't coming from the church. The profession didn't step up to the task, it barricaded itself away. These social changes were driven by the materialist philosophy which, on the whole, the profession was inclined to agree with — wholeheartedly, in the case of Quine.

§

Meanwhile, Rorty was worrying about philosophy being useless, so he spent his career trying to make a connection between what the most highly respected professionals, like Quine, were talking about, and what he wanted to talk about — namely the development of culture, preventing conflict, reducing cruelty in interpersonal relations, people living together happily, equitably, peacefully, sustainably. Over the course of those 40 years he mentioned in his autobiographical essay, he did find a story to connect the dominant professional philosophy of his time with social and political issues, thereby making philosophy seem publicly useful, at least to him. (Rorty gave central place to Quine in his story, but Quine didn't appreciate it.[8]) The essence of the story was that if everyone gave up on the idea of objective truth, which Quine and others had shown to be untenable (says Rorty), then a major source of conflict would be removed from the world, thereby encouraging more toleration and expanding human solidarity. That message seems very out-of-date now, given how much misinformation there is on the Internet, and given all the damage and danger this has caused — the idea of objective truth now seems more valuable than ever. You could defend Rorty by saying he meant something different, by making a subtle distinction, but why bother when his philosophy has become so completely off-message? Maybe there was a time, back in the swinging '60s, when truth seemed too authoritarian—but materialism and its technology have since reminded us of its value.

§

Quine saw philosophy as a kind of science and was the most influential figure in enacting its 20th turn to materialism, the science philosophy. It is a great irony, then, and a surprisingly unremarked one, that he found his way into the Sokal Hoax. In 1996, physicist Alan Sokal, infuriated by the misuse of science in postmodernist philosophy (the kind that tends to reject objective truth, like Rorty), wrote a deliberately nonsensical article which was accepted for publication in a leading postmodernist journal. He then wrote a book with another physicist, Jean Bricmont, in which they work through quotations from leading postmodernists to show that they haven't a clue about the science they're talking about. Nestled in the middle of these discussions, however, is a critique of Quine's philosophy of science. After quoting from Quine's most famous paper, "Two Dogmas of Empiricism" (1951), widely regarded as a classic of 20th century philosophy, they ask, with the kind of muted scorn to be found throughout their book, "What can one reply to such objections?"—almost as if Quine were objecting to science itself.[9] In the following chapter they're quoting Luce Irigaray saying that $E=mc^2$ is a "sexed" equation.[10] Quine's own scorn of this kind of postmodernist excess would surely have been equal to theirs, at least, and if he'd written his own critique it would have probably been more effective. (Sokal and Bricmont score their points primarily from being physicists and from the quotations themselves.) To these scientists, however, Quine and the postmodernists were much of a much: philosophers talking crap about science.

§

Rorty's mistake was to assume that the professional philosophy of his time must have social relevance, it being his job to find out what exactly. But the world's new materialist philosophy, with its overwhelming social relevance, simply didn't have a use for the profession, despite its loyalty; being more influential dressed as science, materialism never wants to be reminded of the philosophical frailties beneath. Rorty was looking in the wrong place for the usefulness of philosophy, then, and so overlooked how the materialist philosophy—which he only half-hearted supported as a professional doctrine—was out there in the world changing his life again and again, via technology. He was right to want to connect the profession with everyday life, but once you see that the usefulness is already out there, then the task transforms. It's not a matter of getting the public to listen to the professionals, perhaps through the science-model of producing simplified accounts. It's a matter of reviving the force of philosophical statements, so they're available in undomesticated form to enter people's lives as more than a quirky hobby. Once that's done, the profession will be useful again, not because it made itself useful, or demonstrated its usefulness, but because people recognised philosophy and found they had a use for it.

§

The symbol of philosophy modelled on science is the armchair—a symbol of arrogance, laziness and absurdity. The symbol of science modelled on philosophy could be one of obscenity—the mushroom cloud, perhaps, a symbol to torment the profession and create an obsession with justifying itself. But it could also be a symbol of hope, something to remind us that only science offers a future in which all our problems can, in principle, be solved. Science offers both heaven and hell, whatever they are for *Homo sapiens*, which is one reason it's become so hackneyed to say that we treat it as a religion. But it doesn't enter into the inner space of our everyday lives and change how we see it, in the way that the philosophy of a religion can. The main connection is that materialism and atheism are seen as a united package. This connection has always been one of materialism's main selling points, and can be traced back to ancient times. What it's come to mean now is that if you're an atheist, which is a resonant choice within a person's inner space, then you naturally acquiesce in materialism. You become unaware of your right to decide your own philosophical views, so there's a sense in which you have a faith—not faith in science, exactly, but rather faith in materialist philosophy, a faith produced by not recognising it as a philosophy. If the connection between atheism and materialism can be broken, it will help philosophical statements regain their force.

Section 4: Communist Materialism Lost, Invisible Materialism Won

The word "materialism" has both a popular and metaphysical sense. The popular sense is knowing the price of everything and the value of nothing. The metaphysical sense is that reality is built up from the smallest things science can discover; back in ancient Greece, Democritus simply worked out that the atoms must be there, from his fine Greek chair, but these days scientists use instruments to observe them. These two senses correspond to the two new obscenities. Both the obscenities and the popular sense derive from the metaphysic of materialism. There was a deep metaphysical bond between the USA and the Soviet Union. They also had one of the obscenities in common, with which they faced off against each other and worried about ending our civilisation, quite possibly the human race. They didn't have the other one in common because the USA had a much better plan for harnessing the atoms and distributing them among people— far more atoms flowed, although not fairly, hence the second obscenity emerged. Popular materialism is simply a practical application of the metaphysic.

§

Another way to see how the popular and metaphysical senses connect is to recall the discussions of the professionals, which started as soon as materialism had its 20th century renaissance. These discussions have naturally centred on conscious experience, because that's always been the hardest thing for materialists to account for, ever since ancient times. Conscious experience gives things value—finding something valuable is a conscious experience. But materialism says all that really exists when we think we're having conscious experiences is atoms in the brain. So the value doesn't really exist, only the atoms you can count and measure. Hence: knowing the price of everything and the value of nothing.

§

Materialism is the driving philosophy in our world, but it doesn't have anything to say about ethics. Philosophy always needs both metaphysics and ethics—a view of reality and a view of what we should be doing in it. This problem was solved, rather haphazardly, when materialism aligned itself with utilitarianism, the big-hearted Victorian philosophy of trying to spread happiness, an ethic which goes well with Dickens novels. The combination is awkward, however, because if materialism puts consciousness in trouble, then that applies to happiness too; the unconscious are never happy. It's doubtful there could be any happiness in a materialist world.

§

The professional discussions about consciousness weren't concerned with ethics, however, and the standard example chosen for these discussions wasn't happiness but pain—it was asked whether the property of pain might be the same as a physical property of the brain, or the same as a functional property of the brain, or whether a particular pain might be the same thing as a brain during a particular period of time, or whether pain might be a property that depends for its existence on brain properties without being the same as any of those properties. One option, which materialist philosophers have been coming back to ever since the 1960s, is that pain doesn't even exist, it's just an illusion created by the brain. There's been nearly 70 years of these dispassionate discussions of pain now. If we're not even sure whether pain exists, why follow the utilitarian philosophy of trying to minimalize it?

§

Despite these metaphysical difficulties, materialism did manage to pick up its utilitarian ethic nonetheless, at least in the sense of establishing a firm association. Still, to look at the ethic as one of trying to minimalize pain and spread happiness does seem a bit dutiful these days; it can appropriately gnaw at us, but sounds too much like the ethic it is. What's really popular is the idea of maximising pleasure, which isn't necessarily the same thing. Was the Satanist Aleister Crowley's "Do What Thou Wilt" an ethic? It does tell you what you should be doing in the world...

§

What's it like to think something, when it's sound or sight that you're thinking? If nobody's around at the moment, or you don't mind being heard anyway, then try singing out loud the first few lines of a song you know really well. Now sing the same thing silently, just in your mind, but taking up exactly the same amount of time, the same rhythm, the same melody and words.

§

Something happened in real time the second time, but did you actually hear it? Were you simultaneously aware of both the silence in the room and the song, in which case how could you be hearing something while not hearing anything—and in the process of not hearing anything, being aware of the silence? Is it that you didn't hear it, you just grasped the same significance you grasped when you actually sang it, but without hearing anything this time? So the idea's that in the first case when you sang it out loud you both heard and intellectually grasped it, and in the second you only grasped it. Or is it rather that you did indeed hear it during the silent rendition, just in a different way that isn't like hearing something in the room, and can somehow coexist with awareness that it's silent outside? Sometimes when you're lying in bed with your eyes closed you can definitely see things—you can also, sometimes, make yourself see whatever you like, although the control isn't as good as that suggests, it takes effort to even get into the right ballpark … sometimes the details are surprising and sometimes it doesn't work at all. But I doubt it's the same for everyone. Now we're talking about inner space.

§

Everyday life is real, but the idea that things aren't as they seem has been operative throughout our history. It seems, however, that there never was a Real World beyond the everyday one, we were only imagining there was, just as Nietzsche said we were in the famous section of *Twilight of the Idols* called "How the 'Real World' at last Became a Myth". Maybe that's why philosophical statements have lost their force, namely because we can't believe they take us beyond the everyday anymore. But what if everyday life becomes a product of imagination? What if the reality that fills our waking lives becomes a virtual one facilitated by technology? How can everyday life remain real when the reality in question has changed? In such a life, if philosophical statements referred beyond everyday life to a new Nietzschean "Real World", then we'd have been plunged into a collective dream—technology would have enacted a new Fall upon our souls. Our focus on experience, and the technological manipulation of it to fulfil our desires, would have made appearance diverge from reality, but the cost of restoring the force of philosophical statements in this manner would be our collective sanity. This can only be avoided if the operative philosophy in our world is, by the time we reach that point, no longer materialist.

§

If that's a realistic possibility then we ought to prepare for it. The last time we were haphazard with our philosophical development we ended up with nuclear bombs, now we're stuck with them forever.

§

That's enough for now, we can ease off a little. Try not to lose sight of the pack, enjoy the chase, and dart if you catch the scent.

Endnotes

1. R. Tallis, *The Black Mirror: Fragments of an Obituary for Life*, London: Atlantic Books 2015. Gray's review is in *The New Statesman*, 1 September 2015, and is available online; it covers two books, the other being *The Worm at the Core: On the Role of Death in Life*, by S. Solomon, J. Greenberg and T. Pyszczynski, London: Allen Lane 2015.

2. J. Gray, *Feline Philosophy: Cats and the Meaning of Life*, London: Allen Lane 2020; the interview is on *Ideas with Nahlah Ayed*, CBC radio, broadcast 6 May 2021 and now available online.

3. "Trotsky and the Wild Orchids" in *Philosophy and Social Hope*, London: Penguin 1999, p. 11.

4. See Russell's passionate denunciation of Nietzsche in *A History of Western Philosophy* (book 3, chapter 25), a book written during the war and published in 1945.

5. "The *ascertaining of 'true'* versus *'untrue'*, in general the *ascertaining* of facts, differs fundamentally from creative *positing*, from the forming, shaping, overwhelming, *willing* which is of the essence of *philosophy*."—Nietzsche, 1887, italics in the original; *Writings from the Late Notebooks*, edited by Rüdiger Bittner, Cambridge: Cambridge University Press 2003, p. 150.

6. "A Letter to Mr. Ostermann", in *The Owl of Minerva: Philosophers on Philosophy*, edited by C.J. Bontempo and S.J. Odell, New York: McGraw-Hill 1975.

7. *Philosophy as a Way of Life: Spiritual Exercises from Socrates to Foucault*, translated from the French by M. Chase, London: Blackwell 1995.

8. Quine, "Let me Accentuate the Positive", in *Reading Rorty: Critical Responses to Philosophy and the Mirror of Nature (and Beyond)*, edited by Alan Malachowski, Oxford: Blackwell 1990, pp. 117–9; the barb in the title is that Quine struggles to find anything positive to accentuate within Rorty's

reading of his work, as he impatiently lists what he regards as misunderstanding after misunderstanding.

9. *Fashionable Nonsense: Postmodern Intellectuals' Abuse of Science*, New York: Picador 1998, p. 66.

10. Some have doubted whether this most infamous of Sokal and Bricmont's quotations is genuine. Thanks to some excellent detective work by a blogger called Dan, however, we know that it is — see "The Hunt for the Sexed Equation", 4 December 2016: http://zetetical.blogspot.com/2016/12/the-hunt-for-sexed-equation.html.

Chapter 2

Thoughts Not Stories

Encounter 1: Plato

Plato (c. 427–347 BC) was a philosopher from Athens, Greece. He was the student of Socrates and the teacher of Aristotle. He'll be along shortly.

§

Everyday life is real. You can decide freedom is an illusion, that everything you've ever done was predetermined before you were born. You can decide objects like tables, chairs and human beings don't exist, that only swarms of invisible particles in largely empty space do. You can decide you live in William James's world of pure experience, with the difference between physical objects and mental states just a matter of context. You can decide morality is a fiction. You're still going to have to pay the garage to get your car back tomorrow; they've been deceitful, opportunist, cynical, they've done it all with a contemptuous sneer, but you'll have to pay the bastards anyway. Is philosophical interest in our mysterious reality sustained by the hope that there's a way out? Maybe if you had a proper understanding of what reality amounts to you could locate the exit.

§

Stories don't just happen, we narrate them. We either narrate the whole by playing around with materials from everyday life, or, with true stories, we pick out bits our thoughts like to linger over and then connect them in a sequence our thoughts like to run over. If I tell you about a chap sitting in the jungle, eating his sandwiches and preparing his equipment, then turning up at the gentlemen's club to drink a large glass of Tawny Port, I've missed the story where he steals the ancient artefact and evades the evil genius. If I made a story of my life, I wouldn't mention today—it's fine, I'm writing, the final product might make the narrative, today won't. (As I read that a few weeks later I've already forgotten that day, and I'll forget this one too—but never my wedding day.) Thoughts are not stories. They're not something you think about, they're what you think—although thinking needn't mean endorsing, that's a deeper level of self, it might only mean entertaining. Just like stories, thinking may require us to pick out the significant bits, but not for narration, only to focus our minds on what's true. Or significances may transfix us to provoke thought, sometimes never resolved. In stories, we either know the answer or the storyteller hasn't told us, perhaps deliberately, perhaps because they never made the decision. We haven't got to the important difference between thoughts and stories yet.

§

Socrates was a hard man—tough, a warrior. He drove his sword into the breast of many a man—just imagine that gargoyle-face staring down at you, desiring of your fate, as your blood runs into the sand and the lights fade over a sea of pain. Terrifying! I'm no wimp myself, I was a very good wrestler, a contender. You learn something about toughness when you're facing off against another man, stark naked, your cock and balls shrunken firm, the sun frying your oiled skin, sand rough on your feet, chest expanded. I was thrown down so hard the blood flowed from a wound in my head, but I wriggled free, broke the fellow's arm, won the match. Glorious!

It was man fighting man in emulation of gods. Socrates was at that one—he gritted his teeth when I was down and let out a mighty bellow when I turned it around. We all loved him, sent by the gods and he knew it. It gets exaggerated, but he did look a bit like the Sileni—you know, those weird half-men that accompany Dionysos in his festivities, at least as our artists represent them; maybe they get it right sometimes. I guess he looked a lot more normal than that suggests, to be honest, but definitely hard and definitely not beautiful. There was nothing normal about his soul, that's for sure; not except for the hardness, and even that was well above average in this nation of warriors.

§

I wouldn't normally talk about him like that, what's the point? I'd certainly never write it down. I write about the ideal Socrates, a Socrates others can learn from. The only people you write about naturalistically are the losers, the corrupt, since there's nothing ideal about them, no lessons to be learned—it's just that recognising their habits causes disgust in good men, so it's a useful reminder, like the smell of sewage. When I say "naturalistically" I don't mean "real" of course, I just mean: talking as we do in the illusion. In that sense it wouldn't be right to say he was exceptionally ugly—a stranger wouldn't remark on it as he passed in the Agora, that's all. He looked like the grisly old warrior he was, and he certainly had the old warrior's lust for boys who came under his influence—very strong in him it was, well into old age. But I detected the spirit of love often enough to see the ideal in that obsessive behaviour. Oh yes, and his wife Xanthippe was an exceptionally beautiful woman, the flower of Athens, our very own Helen.

§

I don't know why these things interest you—not that it matters in here. It'd be different in a book, writing books is always a risk since you never know who'll read them, what curiosity they'll stir up. Your own curiosity isn't so bad—a distraction, I'd have to say, but life is full of distractions, some of which raise the spirits. One thing that particularly worries me about writing is that if people are still reading my books in a hundred years' time, then my name may become associated with all kinds of harmful views, simply because corrupt men didn't use them as intended. They'll flick through the pages until they see words that agitate their undisciplined souls, then they'll talk about "Plato's view" on this or that. Others similarly indisposed to philosophy will accept it without their fingers even touching a book, and while all this nonsense buzzes around the hive, nobody'll notice that the "views" were voiced by my Socrates, who says that all he knows is that he knows nothing! (I came up with that, by the way—naturalistically speaking, he never said it.)

§

Socrates was opposed to writing. Apart from practical necessities he didn't do it at all until near the end, when he turned his hand to poetry; I still have those poems, can't make head nor tail of them. Never try to write philosophy down, he'd say, it has to be improvised. Improvisation is of the essence of philosophy. Learn to spontaneously reason within yourself soberly and you'll have a well-cultivated inner space. Reason with others to bring out the best in them, show them the way, learn from them too, it's the same improvisational mastery, philosophical mastery, you'll be living the philosophical life.

§

If you're trying to teach the philosophical life of good reasoning with yourself and others, as Socrates saw it, then the first thing you do is identify a man with the will and aptitude—it could also be a woman, in my opinion, but I doubt he'd have agreed ... my student Aristotle doesn't. Or you might pick on someone you don't expect to learn, but whose views need to be publicly shown wanting, there's another task. Or you could just try your luck with someone you happen upon in the street—Socrates would do that, he was fearless. Anyway, once you've chosen someone, you talk to them and test their views. They'll probably be rash, too sure of themselves, since spirit overflows in youth, even in the mildest of souls, and those who age without philosophy become set in their opinions, finding it hard to change them unless they sense immediate advantage. The good philosophical educator will make them think again. What needs to be said—to shake their confidence, make them see the need for better reflection, show them by example what good reasoning amounts to—that all depends on what they've just said; just as, within your own inner space, it depends on what you've just thought. Facial expressions can do a lot of work, a well-timed wink, a gesture of the hand, a step backwards; people notice these things when their minds are changing. But you won't change their lives without love and respect, that's something Socrates would always insist on. Without that they won't consider what you say in the right way, namely as something they themselves, maybe just maybe, ought to think. The words of a stranger, if they dazzle with enough knowledge, might kowtow you into acceptance out of fear of being hurt, and if confusion is evoked by a good philosopher that can be instructive to onlookers. But love and respect are needed to change how a person thinks, that's what he thought. He didn't like writing because the author of a book is like a statue and their stone words can't adjust to the moment. A writer can never say the right thing because they don't know who they're talking to—if they knew the thoughts their last sentence prompted then they might say something different with the next, but never can. So Socrates just talked. Some of his words made it into my writings, not many, although I did capture the essence.

§

He had a wonderful way of taking the student's burden upon himself. The fall into awareness of ignorance can be quite a shock, and it's daunting when you see that the best path ahead is constant questioning, a life of open-mindedness, no more certainties to put thought at rest. So when Socrates sensed distress in the student, he'd take up the argument himself. "OK, we're not getting anywhere with this line of reasoning," he'd say, "let's try another one"—and when he ended the failure was his, blamed on his own shortcomings. He didn't have to act, that's for sure, he was a true philosopher—always bewildered, always trying, thoroughly at peace with it. The student's pain of beginning on the path of thought was soaked up by him, absorbed until bearable. It's just like when you're at a wrestling match and the one poor fellow is taking an awful battering. He gives you a hangdog look, he's bloodied, panting and raw, so in sympathy you undress. "Look," you say with your nakedness, "compare my physique to yours and imagine what'd be happening to me!" It's the only decent thing to do. Naturalistically speaking, Socrates did that when we first met.

§

My brother Glaucon introduced us when I was just 14, my soul full of wrestling and mathematics. I knew of Socrates only as a renowned warrior who'd become active in public life, not a philosopher. He asked about my interests and I talked about geometry. "Aren't you more interested in living well?" he inquired in a warm, gravelly voice, no smile. Before I could answer, he asked what I'd been learning in geometry recently. I'd been doing a lot of work with triangles so I talked about that, trying to impress. "What is a triangle?" he asked — which stopped me in my tracks because he didn't seem to be testing my knowledge, as is normal when talking to a boy. The look on his face was one of genuine puzzlement. Not knowing what to think, I grabbed a branch and drew a triangle in the sand to illustrate the definitions I gave, which were good. "If you're so confident in your words, boy," said he, "why ruffle up the sand? I see nothing to match your words." He looked and sounded angry — Glaucon instinctively stepped back. In my soul there was a whirling, dizzy feeling, as I stared at the unsteady, uneven excuses for lines which I'd drawn, impressions made even more unsteady by the sun churning the air. Seeing my distress, Socrates whipped off his toga, revealing terrible battle scars, and he looked at me with a calm sadness. I cried, as did he, and I loved him from that moment on.

§

With the philosophical life now before my eyes, I developed very quickly. I became one of the gang who followed him around. He didn't want to teach us; you could tell because he never objected when Xanthippe chased us off with a stick. No good teacher ever wants to teach, just as no good ruler wants to rule — but Socrates knew it was his duty. He told me how proud he was of my development, how he thought I'd become a great philosopher, and I'm pretty sure he didn't say that to the others.

§

While I was learning from his conversations, I was also learning from philosophers who wrote, especially Parmenides, my favourite. He was a Greek from Italy, in case you didn't know. I've practically shredded that man's book over the years; there's a bit at the end of the scientific speculations I really like where the goddess tells him to consider what she's said as a ladder to be discarded once climbed, or a makeshift raft to be abandoned once you've crossed the river. Very memorable. Anyway, Socrates knew I read philosophy books, of course he did, but he didn't care. I never agreed with him about writing, not really. Well, he was right that for the purposes of teaching someone how to live philosophically you can't beat conversation. A book will always be second-best, just like the rule of law—if you don't have a teacher make do with a book, and if you can't trust your rulers make do with legislation. But you can write down model dialogues for students to practise with when you're not around, as you can't always be. And I also think people I've never met could get in good practice with my books, if they're prepared to put in the effort. I like to make them long drawn out, lots of classification and subclassification, not just because you need plenty of practice in that kind of thing if you're going take control of your inner space, but because it puts off those just looking for a quick fix: "Did Socrates really think that?" "Did Plato really think that?" Away with you, I say! Yes, written dialogues can serve similar purposes to spoken ones, they're just much less effective. But writing can do other things too.

§

You can make images with words, like a painter makes images with paint. The philosopher learns, through painstaking practice in attentiveness, classification and subdivision, to think about the general forms themselves, the true reality. You can make images to direct people's minds towards those forms, or at least to direct their actions in a manner according with them. Conveyed through writing, the images can help a stranger see the nature of justice, or just induce them to act more justly, even if they don't understand why. I used words to make an image of Socrates: an image of the just man, the true philosopher. I looked at him and what he did, naturalistically speaking, and that helped me define and redefine in order to get the occasional glimpse of justice itself. Then I looked back at him, then at justice for a little longer this time, then back at him ... the results are there on the page, available to everyone, an influence on the world I can't adjust anymore, but I'll bet it does more good than harm. You've got to try. A philosopher can't just wallow in the ecstasy of thinking about the forms, that doesn't make sense once you've an awareness of what they amount to. You've got to try to make the world a better place, steer it a little.

§

You want to know about the ecstasy of the philosopher? You can't imagine it? Well, recall what it's like when you're listening to master musicians, the spirit of the music and the atmosphere of the event combining with their hard-won virtuosity; there's expert dancing breaking out spontaneously, like at an orgy, and the pipe player wails a dazzling pattern in the Locrian mode. I have my students debate the political merits of that kind of thing, but all I'm doing here is showing you what I've got in mind, something you'll recognise. Well, that pipe player's face distorts, doesn't it? It becomes a mask of emotional strain, grotesque if considered out of context, like a theatrical mask. That's an outer sign of the musical ecstasy he feels inside. There's no short-cut to that. Those with musical talent, after

years of painstaking work, will come to know that ecstasy—
and they'll naturally seek out more. Why else do you imagine
his face goes like that? Contemplating the forms is a different
kind of ecstasy, with a different path to attainment. I can't tell
you more than that, any more than the master musician can tell
his student about the ecstasy his mastery brings him. But you
can follow the philosophical path and know it as I do. Don't
mistake ecstasy for intoxication. Pouring from a jug is the
path to that. What will the intoxicated man do? Think inane
thoughts, perhaps debating which of the fictional sorcerers
our poets invented is the most powerful? Grab up a musical
instrument and sound ridiculous? Those who haven't followed
a hard path can't experience ecstasy, only induce its side-effects
through intoxication—then find themselves at a loss. Even sex
is mere intoxication for a layabout.

§

Philosophy is the highest music and Socrates was a master
improviser.

§

You get why the forms are the ultimate reality, right? The
illusion around us reflects reality in its way, but that we're able
to think about mundane things, like rocks, trees and tables,
shows that the reality being reflected is general, just like our
thoughts. Rocks aren't general, they're particular things, so
they're not real. You can't think about that rock over there—see
the one?—not without using the general idea of a rock that's
indiscriminately applicable to all rocks, or else using other
general ideas less specifically applicable, such as size, shape
or colour—just try it, you'll see. You need those general ideas
to think because that's how reality is, general, as opposed to

rocks, trees, even your own body. Those particular things can't be the reality persisting through the whirling, inconstant, ever-changing illusion you experience, because if they were you wouldn't be able to think about them; your thoughts wouldn't catch anything in their net, the holes'd be too big. We're all dreaming for the duration of this life, surrounded by illusions, but philosophers can think through them to know the general forms of reality. We're the ones who woke up. Still, knowing that's one thing, making contact with the forms is something else: ecstasy.

§

Did they kill him, the bastards? No, he wanted death, he was old and tired, he longed for the afterlife. They just gave him an opportunity to turn it into a magnificent final lesson, thereby making him want it all the more. I wrote about his death because its essence is so powerful no-one can miss it—he died for what he believed in: philosophy. I included his last words, naturalistically speaking, which were a request for a dedication to be made to Asclepius, the god of medicine. I've regretted it ever since because some thought he was condemning life, making a final statement of pessimism—as if he were saying that life is a disease for which hemlock is a medicine. Socrates was incapable of thinking something so grotesque! The truth is that a very old man, who'd wanted to die long before the poison touched his lips, was now looking for the gods to end it quickly. His irony made him express his piety that way, his irrepressible spirit shining on through the terrible effects that had begun ... and they can go on for quite some time. A sick man who's taken medicine dedicates to Asclepius in the hope the medicine will be effective. Socrates made his final ironic statement by calling hemlock "medicine"—it was a potion imbibed by a man anticipating imminent death, in normal circumstances it would indeed have been a medicine — and yet his hope in dedicating to the god was perfectly ordinary. Unfortunately it isn't a terribly effective poison, but it's the best we Greeks have.

§

There's a problem with the power of books that's even worse than the chance the good ones will be misused. It's the bad ones. That fellow Democritus, he really is the worst, but his books are everywhere. I'd be doing the world a favour if I set my students the task of buying them all up and burning the lot. Can you believe that someone who styles himself a philosopher would set out to reinforce the most ignorant prejudice of mankind? "Oh yeah, I can pick it up in my hands, it's solid to the touch, it's real" — it doesn't get much dumber than that. Yet Democritus takes that thought as the starting point of his metaphysics, finding tangible particulars to be built from smaller, intangible ones called "atoms", like little bricks making up a big wall. There's me trying to wake people up while he's finding reasons to snooze on — the man's a walking soporific!

§

Where did your atoms come from, Democritus? What set them in motion? Did they pop out of thin air, already moving? Soul provides our only model of the initiation of movement, acts of free will. Sir, the beginning of everything is hardly a minor issue for your materialist theory, is it now? What's going to happen if people take you seriously? They certainly won't experience reality, and they won't get any closer to it in their thinking either — but that's what they'll think they're doing. They'll end up modelling the little bricks with mathematics, of course, since that's the only way they'll get precision about what they've been led to suppose — by you, Democritus! — is the nature of particular things. Then our crafting powers will start multiplying, because you can always get smaller. If the architect could model his design not just at the level of blocks, but fractions of blocks, right down to the tiniest grain, then he'd have far more power to create. Before long we'd be making robots like Talos to hurl giant rocks at our enemies. With this kind of thing passing for interest in the nature of reality, philosophy would wane and the power we acquired would be misused. True philosophers would argue back, but the followers of Democritus would have the basest instincts of humanity on their side, as well as the incentive of lust for the products of his philosophy. While Democritus' philosophy was leading the world on blindly, philosophic discourse would become nothing more than an endless dispute between his followers and the rest, happening powerlessly on the side-lines. If that process begins it's hard to see a way out for us, unless...

§

Twelve thousand years ago, the ancient civilization of Atlantis was at its prime. A massive island it occupied, rising from the Atlantic Ocean, closest to the shores of Portugal and Morocco but equally far removed from both. That was long before its fall into corruption, which ultimately roused heroic Athens to bring her to her knees, with the gods finishing the job by sinking the island deep into the ocean, never to be seen again. Back in the halcyon days of which I speak, however, one of the kings of Atlantis heard tell that the titan Prometheus, recently rescued by Heracles, was residing in the Caucasus Mountains and prepared to take visitors. The king took the arduous journey to the East, bearing a gift of orichalch, a metal nobody alive today has set eyes upon, although Atlantis was rich in it—dazzling red it was. "Let me improve on your gift and teach you to do the same," said Prometheus, as he crafted the orichalch into a magical mirror, then settled down to teach the craftsmen in the king's party how he'd done it.

§

On the return journey, the king didn't notice when his ship first came in sight of Atlantis, he was too busy looking at his mirror. His men had to guide him back to his palace, lest he trip on some obstacle in the road, since he refused to look up from it. They sat him on his throne, and there he sat for three days, gazing. On the fourth day, he called for his most trusted advisor, and ordered as many orichalch mirrors to be made as possible; a noble man, he wanted his people to share in his own good fortune. The craftsmen struggled so the process took longer than expected. When one hundred mirrors had been made, the king's patience was at an end. He ordered that one hundred good men and women be taken down into the deepest cave on the island, sat comfortably, then given a mirror each, with slaves to attend to their bodily needs. He ordered that a report be made to him daily on their situation. It wasn't long before these people, deep underground, were all gazing at their mirrors, just as the king still was. Although seated closely in rows, they quickly lost interest in communicating with each other, or in initiating any bodily contact whatsoever, even lovers. But then it was reported that some had found a means, by touching the mirrors with their fingers, of communicating by writing. What was written on one mirror appeared on another, and in this way they started conversing again. They learned to see each other in the mirrors too, and this allowed them to interact in something akin to the old manner. Then they found they could do much more than this. They could see the outside world in the mirrors, albeit without its vivid colours, nor its aromas. They could create imaginary worlds of their own, dreams in which they could take part, like a human in the human drama, but safer—they could not die, their bodies were in the cave, but there was imaginary death in the dream which could be reversed in an instant, thereby spurring them on towards the semblance of risky behaviour. Their notions of bravery, boldness, excitement, pleasure, hospitality, justice, even truth, came to be moulded by the reflections in the mirrors.

§

Hearing of this, the king despaired: "My people have been made timid! I have become timid! When the other kings hear of this, they'll take my kingdom for themselves!" Rising from his throne with mighty resolve, he handed his mirror to the advisor, saying, "Cover this in cloth so that you may never gaze into it, then go down to the cave to collect the other mirrors and throw them into the ocean." The advisor did as he was bid. Those in the cave lacked the stout heart of the king, so when their mirrors were taken away they fell into despair, weeping and wailing as at the death of a loved one. Eventually some found the resolve to leave the cave and the rest followed. Dazzled by the light of the sun, to which they had become unaccustomed, they huddled together in their misery, before the wisest of them made an address. "The lesson of this episode," he said, "is that experience is what we care about most. Let us live philosophical lives and cultivate inner space, recognising ourselves and our reality for what they truly are. Then we'll know how to use the mirrors, if we ever choose to craft them again. Or we may make something quite different, more suited to who we are and the lives we want to live. Either way, we must always think hard before we craft."

§

The Atlantean civilization flourished for another three thousand years after that ... what'll it be three thousand years from now ... the 27th century! We might still be here. Even if things do take a decidedly unphilosophical turn, there'd still be a way out.

§

That's what I reckon, anyway, and who's going to argue with Plato?

Encounter 2: Plotinus

Plotinus (c. 204–270) was a philosopher from Roman Egypt. He was the student of Ammonius and the teacher of Porphyry.

§

The important difference is that a thought, but not a story, can characterise your inner space. If you think something and endorse that thought, then that's a difference between you and someone who doesn't. If you endorse a thought you didn't yesterday, you've changed. If it's a thought that endures you've developed; seeing nothing wrong with that thought, you'll think it again if the occasion arises. A story isn't like that. It's just content to think about, if you want to. Even if the story is about you, it still doesn't characterise your inner space, not in the relevant sense. Suppose you tell yourself that certain events in your life were the most significant, the most defining of how you became who you are today; or perhaps someone else tells your story, it makes no difference. It's still just content. If you think the story hits on something true then it can change you by inspiring new thoughts, but any content can do that. The fact that it's your own story is no boon, quite the opposite. Thinking your tough childhood formed your entrepreneurial spirit is less defining of your inner space than thinking you're part of the universal spirit. The former uses content from your life, and given that life, provokes an obvious thought. But the latter, if you're not just paying it lip service, is a distinctive thing to think—especially for a successful entrepreneur who had a tough childhood, requiring of much thought.

§

Telling stories about yourself can be fun, and useful too, but you're kidding yourself if you think it's the key to enlightenment. There are more productive ways to take an interest in yourself—such as by wondering why you keep telling stories about yourself.

§

If you've just been talking to Plato I don't know what you're bothering with me for. I don't know anything he didn't, I'm a teacher of his ideas, and quite frankly I find your suggestion that I might have something new and original to say a little insulting. But ... I suppose that if you didn't make the most of your time with the master then I might be of some use to you. Just don't expect me to talk about my life, that's all. What? He told you about his life? That does surprise me, let me think it over. Please don't fidget while I'm thinking. OK, I think I see what he must have had in mind ... after all, we are in a most unusual situation. OK then, what do you want to know?

§

It wasn't easy for an Egyptian lad to get hold of philosophy books back in Lycopolis, but I did my best, and was always very studious. It wasn't until my mid-twenties that I came across Plato's *Laches*. Socrates discussing courage with the generals Laches and Nicias, that image changed my life! The generals point out that a great warrior like Socrates ought to know something about courage if anyone does, but it turns out he doesn't. Condemning his own failure to define it, since to act courageously without knowing the nature of courage is part of the inferior, unphilosophical life, Socrates resolves to go back to school. What a call to philosophy that was! A few years later, once I'd put my affairs with my father in order, I headed off to Alexandria to find my own Socrates to learn from.

§

Ammonius had great physical presence—very tall, with a clean-shaven head and thick black eyebrows that cascaded down to cloudy brown eyes. It drew my attention as he towered over me, since I was very inexperienced in philosophy back then, but by the end of my decade with him it was only his soul that concerned me. And what a soul it was! He knew the whole Platonic tradition, stretching back some six hundred years to the great man's death, and Ammonius saw it as his task to purge that tradition of extraneous elements that had crept in. He placed particular emphasis on the teachings on Numenius, whom I studied closely, since of recent writers he considered him the purest. But Ammonius also knew Indian philosophy, having studied with Eastern sages as a young man, and these doctrines illustrated Plato's in a most vivid fashion. It was Socrates he identified most closely with. Alert to the tension in Plato's writings about Socrates' disdain for writing, he knew there were two callings for teaching the philosophical life. His was that of Socrates, so Ammonius never wrote a thing. I thought mine might be too, for a while, but it turned out to be that of Plato. You might wonder, as I once did: what's the point of writing when we have Plato's books? Well, six hundred years is an awfully long time. New audiences need new presentations, you have to write for your time to keep truth alive. I never read anything I've written—never will, don't need to. It flows directly from my inner space to the paper, and there it stays, instructive to others, I hope.

§

Ammonius started dropping hints that it was time for me to move on; I was getting on for forty, after all. So when I heard the Emperor Gordian was planning an expedition against the Persians, I saw an opportunity to seek out an Eastern sage, in the hope of learning more about Indian philosophy. It was easy enough to get an invitation to the civilian camp which would follow the army, since I had political connections of my own by that time, with no more need to rely on my father. So I headed off to Antioch in Turkey from where the march was set to begin— and what a cesspit I found! The prostitution and drunkenness in that camp was brazen and I found it hard to find anyone worthy of conversation. I was glad when we finally headed off, but the journey across Syria, then deep into Iraq, was very hard. I'd learned well from Ammonius, so was mainly able to keep external circumstances at bay—but the few opportunities I had to try to seek out a sage came to nothing.

§

We dispersed among the border towns of the empire when the army began its march on Ctesiphon, the Persians' capital, waiting to rejoin them on their triumphant return. Then we heard of the terrible defeat, that Gordian Caesar himself, aged only nineteen, had been killed. There was widespread panic as the Persians rampaged through the territory, but the money I possessed proved enough to secure passage back to Antioch. The time seemed right to take up one of the many invitations I'd received over the years to move to the capital.

§

I've lived in Rome ever since, leading my own philosophical school in the beautiful house of the lady Gemina, one of my best students; her daughter, also called Gemina, is progressing nicely too. It's a good job it's such a very large house, with all the orphans we keep taking in! My school and I are well known, and it was an honour when the new Emperor, Gallienus Caesar, took an interest in my philosophy. I've come to know him and his wife as friends, I kiss them whenever we meet, and he's agreed to allow me to establish a city of philosophy in southern Italy, which I shall name Platonopolis. It'll be designed to Plato's plan, right down to the very last detail, and that's where I'll spend the remainder of my days. It isn't fair that in this matter, at least, I seem destined to succeed where he failed, but I'm sure he'd have approved anyway.

§

And there you have it, a reminder of the life I spent trying to forget. My real life, the only one worth remembering, was in inner space. My Lebanese student Porphyry, an impetuous fellow but very clever, was always keen to write about my life—to produce an image of an image, an even more doggedly persistent one. I knew he would eventually, no matter how much I discouraged it. And discourage I did. Whenever he was around I'd harp on about my lack of interest in it, its complete irrelevance. Again and again I'd drive the point home so that it was bound to make it into his book, but I also gave him the details he craved, the ones I've just told you; a snippet here and there, as if let slip by accident within the commotion of embodied life. You can't make things too obvious, you see, not if you want to inspire reflection. Anyway, now that nonsense's over can we please get down to business?

§

You'll have learned from Plato one thing, at least, namely that the central question of philosophy is: what the hell is my soul doing stuck in this body? And hopefully you'll have also realised that the aim of the philosophical life is not to answer questions, nor ask them—that's just the route—but rather to leave your body far behind in states of ecstasy. I'm pretty good at it but they're still stubbornly infrequent, I'm sure he was much better. Please don't think there's anything selfish about spending your life seeking these states, you'd be missing the point on so many levels. When you reluctantly return to the illusion, as you must, you'll have moral fibre, you'll know what you're talking about in practical matters, you'll know what to do. The reluctance to return and participate is crucial, because you don't want to be a do-gooder, someone who wants to do the right thing, whose desires are set on this world of illusion. They're useless, they'll do more harm than good unless they're lucky—because they don't know the good. To seek the good is to seek the ecstasies, so the otherworldly are the ones to trust.

§

I'll tell you the answer to The Big Question straight away. You won't understand it, not until you've felt it, and that's the point anyway—the point is to feel the truth by transforming your inner space. You naturally ask yourself: why is my beautiful soul stuck in this relatively ugly body? Well, it's not actually there, you just think it is, it's an illusion. You fall for the illusion, can't help yourself, because you haven't taken control of your inner space. Your inner space is unfocused, continually distracted by what you take to be a body in a physical world. You're stuck in the middle, looking down at the lowest part of the soul—and please don't interpret that as an ego observing its body or you'll raise pointless questions. No, what you need to do is learn to look up! Keep your attention fixed on the higher part of the soul and you'll be in the vicinity of goodness and love. The illusion of the body will still be there—feeling it is an inferior part of your soul—but once you don't believe in it, it won't distract you anymore ... not so much, anyway. It'll become an irrelevance, like a stone in the shoe when you're having the time of your life! Your soul will be experiencing its unity with all things, and if you're trying to do that all the time then you're living the philosophical life. You'll rarely manage it, not if you're anything like me, but you can always be trying. Get used to looking up because there's no looking down when you're dead. Get yourself a little slice of heaven while you're still here by feeling the true reality you emerged from and will return to, the universal soul.

§

That sounds like mystical nonsense to simple folks; "men of the world" they call themselves, I call them "lost souls". You try to help, but there's only so much you can do if they're set on ridiculing you. They won't take you seriously because they've not experienced it and won't try, or, sadder still, because they had a glimpse, usually through intoxication at a ceremony, but refuse to give credence to what they saw. The latter are like dreamers who wake and are so startled that, putting it down to intoxication, they snooze on. They assume it's the other way around, of course, because they're just so sure the dream is real; and in the dream they did indeed intoxicate themselves. If you get there through disciplined thinking, however, that thought'll never tempt you. When you can change how you feel with how you think, you're fully assured that the radical new feeling is simply your soul's hard-won self-awareness. You've been through all the arguments, there are no decent replies to the good ones, so you've convinced yourself with level-headed, passionless reason—and that's what makes it happen, the passion and the ecstasy. You don't know you're right when you're there, you don't know anything – not at highest attainment, when you're merged into The One—but you do when you return, you've received the definitive verification.

§

Once you get the hang of it you'll be like a frog. You'll swim through the slimy water like the rest of them, but with eyes always fixed on what lies above. You've been up there, to that wonderful world you can glimpse past the surface, distorted and fragmentary as you're seeing it now, to be sure, but glimmering and enticing nonetheless. You've hopped on land and think always of returning. The others won't notice where you're looking because you'll glide so elegantly, you'll be a good, practical, effective frog in the water, even though you'll never feel at home there, knowing that you're not. Everyone remarks on what a thoroughly decent chap I am, even lost souls who think they're fish.

§

Once, when Porphyry started a heated debate about philosophy's value with one such man, a builder by trade, Gemina remarked to me that he was "grilling the fish"!

§

You mustn't let your inner space get too cluttered up with stories because you'll never find enduring love for yourself if you do. They're so enticing—Plato knew how to use them well for educational purposes—but they won't do you any good if you internalise them. Suppose the Emperor changes his mind about building Platonopolis, or, as is more likely, political realities force his hand. Well, that little story would have found itself an unhappy ending, so it'd be a good job I never identified with it. I'd feel the disappointment in the lower part of my soul and it'd be nothing to me. The problem with stories is that so many are possible, and the possibilities change as time passes. Find a place for yourself in one, a place you can love, and it might prove untenable; and even if it doesn't you'll still never be able to persuade yourself it was the right story, among all the other options. Better to focus on thinking and think up to what you are—that's real, that's trustworthy.

§

You're in the middle, as I said, a frog swimming near the surface, with deep waters below and endless skies above—and if you take my advice, you'll be the kind of frog that's always looking up, waiting for an opportunity to break out. It's mixed up in the middle, divided, that's what consciousness does. When you're reading you're not usually aware you're reading, not as a conscious theme, not unless you make it one—or the author does. Reading works best without that kind of self-reflective attention. It's better when you're lost in the thoughts of the words, at one with them, and many other activities are like that too—running down stairs, for instance, if you're too self-aware of what your feet are doing you're bound to come a cropper. For conscious beings like us the potential for division is always there, since consciousness splits self-awareness of soul from whatever the soul happens to be attending to. Memory makes this point particularly vivid, for the self-awareness is happening now, but what you're attending to is in the past, so the split could hardly be more evident.

§

The division in the middle explains both why we frogs can be so reluctant to leave the water, and why we're so reluctant to come back again once we have. Gain awareness of the higher things, the world of pure forms, and consciousness loses itself in them, transfixed. It's just like when you're engrossed in a book, or running down stairs, but this time you're lost in something infinitely more alluring. All self-awareness of the lower part of the soul, your body and the rest of the material world, is gone. You'll feel like the soul you are, that's the only self-awareness you'll have. You can go even further, to the unity beyond the divided forms, that's as high as it gets, and then you'll feel at one with the universe, there's no self-awareness to be had anymore, only unity. It can be scary, feel as if you're losing yourself, losing your mind, so people naturally back away. In actual fact you're finding yourself, your true nature. But then, once you're used to it, find you love it, when you're exhilarated to be soaring with goodness itself ... now you won't want your consciousness to split into self-awareness again, won't want to come back down. But alas you must, for we're irredeemably conscious beings. The potential for the split was always there, the potential for awareness of the lower part of the soul. The fear you felt at regaining self-awareness was the beginning of the split, for there's always the fear and what frightens you, two things. You start thinking in your old patterns again, your concentration's broken ... thud!

§

But what you've learned from the experience, what there is to think about now! Plenty to keep your eyes fixed skywards until you rise again, and, hopefully, the new paths of thought will lessen the wait—should do.

§

If you're reassured by the inevitability of return you've far to go. You're not at home with yourself yet, when you are it'll be a source of disappointment. That's what Ammonius had in mind when he'd say that philosophy prepared him for death—sounds morbid if you don't understand, but it's anything but.

§

Lost souls sometimes say they don't like the sound of the philosophical life. A good friend of mine once said to me, "That sounds great for you, mate, but it's not for me ... no way!" My response was: if you can't even imagine it, you can't really knock it, can you? The conversation was then cut short because I saw Porphyry entering the room and I didn't want him giving the fellow a hard time—I saw immediately that it wouldn't help and it'd be better to leave the fellow thinking over what I'd just said. I maintain some hope for him, he's certainly interested.

§

It's true, though, isn't it? If you can't imagine it you can't knock it. Can you imagine my life? I sleep as little as possible because it's a waste of time, you can't think about philosophy while you're asleep. When I awake my first thought is a longing for the ecstasy of contemplating the forms, a homely thought for the soul I am. While I'm having my morning massage and eating a well-balanced breakfast, my inner space will catch up with the philosophical train of thought I was pursuing the night before. I'll continue with it the rest of the day if I get a chance, but more often than not I'll have duties to attend to. I enter into these with great reluctance and no-one can tell. People greet me with a smile as I go about my business with outward enthusiasm, although inside I'm always looking up. I'll pursue these goals with all the energy and efficiency I can muster because I want to return to philosophy, it's true, but also because I act in accordance with the good in all matters. The two motivations are complementary, I assure you; I'll snatch a moment of philosophical contemplation when there's a lull in the commotion and it won't harm, not otherwise, but I've got the right attitude always, a background readiness and eagerness for the higher. Everyday life is an illusion but a beautiful one, as it would be considering the reality it reflects. Within that illusion, justice and happiness are always to be preferred to their opposites—real souls are still affected, so you do what you can to help. But the beauties, splendours and goodness of outer space are nothing to what's inside, a place where nothing's required of me because everything's already perfectly good. It's a reality in no need of justification, because it transcends the idea of justification, so you certainly won't find yourself wondering about the meaning of life. I know I'm a soul of the true reality, so I live like one. Now, can you *really* imagine being like me?

§

I thought not, not beyond basic comprehension of the words I spoke, with perhaps the addition of a couple of images of your own. Humdrum stuff that doesn't amount to imagining yourself into a way of life, and with mine you've found you can't ... not yet. Still, you get the general idea, that's all we ever have to start with.

§

There's an aspect you still might be overlooking, something that might particularly appeal to you. You go about your daily life much like me, working towards goals of one kind or another. Even if you enjoy your work, which many don't, you won't always enjoy it, and you'll often long for leisure time, it's perfectly natural. So the reluctance of the philosopher in practical affairs isn't as alien as you might at first have supposed, don't you see? But then, what do people do with the leisure time they long for? They get carried away by conversation; they intoxicate themselves; they make up new goals to replace the work ones, "hobbies"; if they're alone they may find some endless series of novelties to distract themselves with (you could build machines to do that); maybe they just sleep. It won't be terribly memorable, you won't be able to regard it as terribly significant—the pleasantness will be largely unconscious, the satisfactions of the zombie. Wouldn't it be wonderful if the time you longed for was what you regarded as your real life, the time of your greatest acuity, the time for development and progress, with absolute success an ever-present possibility?

§

You won't know until you try. But trying a life isn't like trying a new food or sport, I'm afraid. You can't just "give it a go", secure in the thought that if it doesn't work out you'll quit—you may as well not bother if you're thinking like that, you'll quit for sure. No, if you want the philosophical life you have to commit. People say they want the best life possible for themselves—it'd be odd to meet someone who said otherwise. I'm telling you what it is.

§

Where do you start? Get a good teacher and start reading Plato's books; mine too if you like, they certainly won't do you any harm. A good topic to begin with is your nature—assure yourself you're a soul that doesn't belong here. That's easy enough. You already know you're a thing that thinks and feels, and you know you've got a body. Ask yourself: how are soul and body supposed to unite into one entity, a human being? The only way to account for that, the only way there'll ever be, requires coming to the realisation that the physical world is illusory, a product of soul. Once you're secure with that thought, start to reflect on how the unity of your soul unifies your body and the rest of the physical world. Begin by looking at the beautiful physical world out there, the stars shimmering above our planet. Train yourself to strip it of its physicality in thought: look for the forms that underlie it, forms like roundness and redness—rounder and redder than anything you'll ever see with your eyes. That'll lead you to the forms which unify your soul, just as your soul unifies your body. Eventually you'll get to the highest unity of all, the unity of the single reality you're part of. That's the end point, but you can't rush these things—it's a whole life of thinking we're talking about here.

§

The number of us living the philosophical life remains small but it's growing; when the Emperor builds my city then that's bound to accelerate the process. Sooner or later, the widespread realisation will dawn that our shared destiny is in inner space. The realities awaiting the trained mind are just so startling, so much more marvellous than anything the senses could ever present to a body—no matter how far that body travelled, to whatever strange lands. And inner marvels can be abided with in full satisfaction, while the outer ones always leave us searching for more—insatiable because we're away from home. Even ordinary folk who know nothing of the higher feelings instinctively prioritise inner space, without realising the implications, for they care most for their own feelings and those of others. It can only be a matter of time until the human race progresses to the next level of self-consciousness.

§

That's what I reckon, anyway, and who's going to argue with Plotinus?

Encounter 3: Xuanzang

Xuanzang (602–664) was a philosopher from Luoyang, China. Wu Cheng'en's Journey to the West *(1592), one of the traditionally designated Four Great Classic Novels of Chinese literature, is a fictionalized account of Xuanzang's pilgrimage to India.*

§

Your life isn't a story and you can't make it one.

§

So you want to hear about my life? Hardly surprising, it must be one of the most exciting ever lived. You'll mainly want to hear about the pilgrimage, my great adventure. It took 16 years and you could narrate endless captivating stories from it. I wrote my own, the Emperor insisted. It's aptly entitled *Record of Western Lands* and comes in 12 volumes. But you're mainly here for philosophy, that's a sentiment I can empathise with. Still, you'll not want to completely miss out so I'll give you a little taster, then you can follow up in your spare time. When you do, choose wisely, because each recounting is a different story—mine is quite factual, the one by my assistant, Hui Li, provides more of a story, and with those two you can be sure they stem directly from the man who actually made the journey: me. Well, by "actually" I only mean "naturalistically speaking", but the important matters can wait for now.

§

I was a prodigy—no point in modesty when the facts speak for themselves. I was given the best possible start by my father, an important Confucian philosopher and politician, and when I followed my elder brother into the monastery it was like bringing a fish to water. I was giving lectures at 13 and was fully ordained at 20. Monks three times my age would take me for an authority on Buddhist philosophy because they'd mistake my knowledge for wisdom. Sure, I could recite millions of words of scripture and never make a mistake, which others thought a superhuman ability. Sure, I understood what the leading Chinese philosophers understood by those words (better than they did, I'd often think), so I could explain and illuminate their disputes. But what the Buddha meant, what his most talented Indian interpreters meant … I didn't know that, so I didn't understand Buddhist philosophy. Nobody in China did, we couldn't, we just didn't have the books. What we had was incomplete, a fragment that contradicted itself like crazy; and since the contradictions didn't ring true there was no point trying to resolve them—it was obvious the texts had been corrupted over the years. Chinese philosophy wasn't going anywhere fast until we had more and better books. That thought really started to sink in when I got into Yogacara philosophy, best represented by that brilliant duo from Gandhara, Asanga and Vasubandhu. When I found out Asanga had written a comprehensive overview of Yogacara, I gasped: "That's *exactly* what we need." Better head off to Gandhara to pick up a copy, then! But that's in Pakistan, a bit of a daunting journey, to say the least. Still, Faxian managed it, over 200 years ago. He went in search of Western sages and succeeded, I could do the same; plus he got to visit the important Buddhist sites, just imagine that! First I'd have to master some languages, in particular Sanskrit ... but—you guessed it—that didn't cause me much trouble.

§

It wasn't hard to find like-minded young monks to travel with. We applied for permission through the official channels, but it never came, and while we were waiting it was publicly announced that the roads had been closed to all but essential business, since the empire was under attack by the Blue Turks. Well, finding out the truth about reality struck me as essential business, so I was determined to go anyway. The others weren't having it—"If they catch us they'll execute us," said they. "What of it?" said I. So I'd be going alone, then, and as a fugitive. They left me at the frontier of the empire, where I met a shifty-looking Buddhist who wanted to swap horses with me. It seemed a terrible deal because my horse was fine, whereas his, grandly named White Dragon, was old and scrawny—but the man assured me it had experience of traversing the Gobi Desert, and he was very insistent. So, in the dead of night in my 27th year, I set off on White Dragon to pass through the Jade Gate and onwards along the Silk Road to the West.

§

My troubles began as soon as I entered the desert. I wasn't prepared for the heat ... or cold ... or ever quite sure if I was going the right way. As the days and nights dragged on I saw skeletons in the sand of previous foolhardy travellers. Then I made a mistake that almost cost me my life. I'd been warned the army had sentry towers in the desert and I saw one, so was careful to steer clear—but I also saw there was water nearby and I'd almost run out. So I waited until nightfall then crept down to the water—but they spotted me. An arrow glanced my knee, nothing serious, but others were whistling through the air all around—in panic I cried out that I was a monk. The arrows stopped and the soldiers took me into custody. Luckily, their captain was a Buddhist. He thought I was crazy to think I'd make it to the oasis town of Hami, still over 300 miles away. But he released me nonetheless and set me on the right track—although it didn't take long to get lost again. I just couldn't keep my bearings in the seas of shifting sand; and when I stupidly dropped my water bag and it all drained away, I fell into despair. For five days I was slipping in and out of consciousness, and I was on the verge of death when White Dragon finally led us to water. Once I'd recovered, I decided to just let him go his own way—I had no idea where we were anyway, but he evidently did, for we eventually arrived in Hami.

§

I recuperated in a small and friendly Buddhist monastery until I received a summons from the King of Turfan, a devout Buddhist, who sent a party to escort me to his kingdom. The king was a wonderful man who placed great stock in my teachings—a little too much, I soon discovered, for he was expecting me to stay for life. It was difficult to extract myself, but when he did eventually concede, he supplied me with letters of introduction to other rulers along the route, plenty of supplies, and a party of men to ensure my safe passage— including hardened warriors. As we set off I promised to return one day, but alas it was not to be, for I later heard that the king crossed the line in his precarious dealings with both Turks and Chinese, perishing as a result.

§

On the long road to the Celestial Mountains, where China meets Kyrgyzstan, we were sometimes set upon by bandits—vicious men, untouched by Buddhism. Our warriors were well-trained in the martial arts, but they were often outnumbered, and if it weren't for the presence of a certain remarkable fellow then I'm sure we'd have been overwhelmed. Rugged and hairy, he'd leap from his horse at the first sign of danger, seeming to float to his feet in an unearthly manner before charging our assailants with his heavy iron cudgel. Once accustomed to these encounters, confident we'd win through, I'd watch him in action before properly attending to my prayers—his ferocity was breathtaking, I was glad he was on our side! He never told me his name, preferring that I refer to him as "disciple". When we finally parted company this was indeed an appropriate form of address, for he'd travelled far on the path to Buddhism, after his own fashion.

§

We lost a third of our company crossing the mountains—we all froze and starved, but with them it was to death. We then proceeded along the shores of an enormous lake in Kyrgyzstan, in which I sometimes saw dragons emerge from the depths, before continuing deep into Uzbekistan. The welcome received in the vibrant Persian culture of Samarkand was hot, then cold, then warm … let me explain. First we were set upon with firebrands by Zoroastrians, a very unpleasant start, but the king had the perpetrators punished. Yet when I first met with the king he was distinctly frosty … and he remained so until he heard me preach the Buddhist message, after which he became most congenial. Some think this transformation was a cynical ploy stemming from his political advisors—he did seem keen to get on the good side of the Emperor of China. But I disagree, for everyone is capable of recognising the truth when they hear it.

§

With our company and stocks replenished, we travelled on to New Monastery in Afghanistan, an important Buddhist centre, with some 30,000 monks studying there when I visited. We stopped so I could spend time working with Prajnakara, a master of Theravada Buddhism. It was never my thing, really, with its obsession with personal salvation—I prefer Mahayana, which teaches monks to try to help everyone ... but you've got to know all the interpretations to argue for the best. Moving on, the route to Gandhara took us through the Hindu Kush mountains—a second daunting mountain range to cross, although we fared much better this time—and then past two enormous statues of the Buddha, carved into the face of a mountain and adorned with gold. When we finally arrived in Gandhara ... well ... I'm sorry to report that I was disappointed; that land's certainly seen better days, I can tell you. No chance of picking up the Asanga book among the ruins there. But no matter, there were excellent sites to visit, such as a house where Vasubandhu once lived, and my philosophical horizons were broadening by the day.

§

India was full of cities of philosophy and we stopped in many. It wasn't always Buddhist philosophy, in some it was only a minority interest, if that. Some of these cities were populated by naked ascetics, who covered their skin with ash and wore headbands of bone—to me they looked like cats who'd slept in the chimney, but never mind, I'm always interested to hear people's thoughts and engage them in debate, whatever they look like. Finding out about the philosophies of other religions turned out to be very important, in fact, because some of the Buddhist books we'd had back in China had been referring to them and we just hadn't realised. I even heard tell of philosophy in the extreme West, where they venerate a philosopher called Plato—the one you talked with, right? I think I'll leave that journey to somebody else!

§

India was also full of tigers, venomous snakes, stiflingly humid jungles, diseases … and hostiles. On one occasion, while boating down the Ganges River, we were accosted by pirates and overwhelmed. They tied us up and the pirate captain decided to sacrifice me to Durga, the Hindu goddess. As higher powers would have it, however, a typhoon blackened the skies while they were sharpening the sacrificial blade—I was on the makeshift altar they'd built, in lotus position, reciting names of bodhisattvas. They were terrified by this omen and wanted to know who I was. When one of my guides explained (in a rather exaggerated fashion, I must say), they begged my forgiveness, which I granted. They vowed to become Buddhists, which I took with a pinch of salt, but at least we were saved—there's nothing more precious than life.

§

Nalanda University was always on my itinerary—it's the most important centre of Buddhist philosophy in the world; Asanga and Vasubandhu had worked there, also Dignaga, the great logician. I ended up settling down and it became my base for further expeditions in India. Our arrival was unforgettable. The moment we caught sight of the enormous temples looming in the distance we were met by an escort, and when we entered the compound we found the entire community waiting to greet us: thousands, to the sound of huge, booming gongs. I was presented to none other than Silabhadra himself, the great Yogacara philosopher. I was overjoyed he was still alive, since I'd been told he'd have to be 104 — well, he certainly was remarkably old and frail. I prostrated myself and kissed his feet, but all he cared about was where I'd come from. When I told him I was Chinese he started to weep, and, unable to speak through the tears, he gestured to his nephew to explain. Apparently, three years ago he'd been stricken by a terrible illness, so had decided to starve himself to death. His mind was changed by a dream, which told him he was being punished for misdeeds in a previous life, but that if he carried on teaching he'd recover, and then in three years' time a Chinese monk would arrive. Me! Well, as soon as Silabhadra became my master I realised how little I'd understood before. He cleared away my misconceptions and answered my deepest questions — or rather, taught me how to answer them myself. I'd found my Western sage! And Buddhist philosophy wasn't all they did at Nalanda, by no means, they also had masters of mathematics, astronomy, and much else besides, I lapped it all up.

§

When the pile of books I'd collected was looking complete, or complete enough, I knew I'd have to return to China, it was my duty. But just as we were making the preparations, the king of Assam called for me and I couldn't really refuse. I stayed at his capital city for a couple of months and finished writing a book, my third in India. Then we heard that Emperor Harsha, the most powerful man in India, was most displeased — because he wanted my company instead! The king of Assam was so concerned by this development that he personally escorted me to the Emperor's capital, where we were met, on a starry night, by Harsha himself—heading an army, and with hundreds of drummers coordinating their beat to his footsteps. It turned out that he was planning a Great Debate in which I was to be the central attraction.

§

There were all manner of wildly extravagant ceremonies and processions to open the Great Debate, which was attended by thousands of Buddhist, Hindu and Jain scholars, and witnessed by 18 vassal kings. It began with my lecture, arguing for the superiority of Mahayana Buddhism, and, in particular, Yogacara. I then proceeded to defend my views against objections for five long days. I'm sorry to say that it all became rather nasty after a while—which certainly wasn't my fault, I'm always calm and reasonable. I was continually insulted and serious threats were made against me, to which Harsha responded by decreeing that anyone who harmed me would lose their head, and anyone who insulted me would lose their tongue. When he finally declared me the winner, a Buddhist temple was set ablaze and an attempt was made on the Emperor's life; it was chaos, until Harsha settled things down with a very heavy hand. Well, if I'd felt some reluctance to return to China before, then I certainly didn't anymore—I wanted out! Harsha sent me on my way on the back of an unusually large elephant, one of his personal favourites, and with a military escort to ensure safe passage.

§

The journey back was hardly uneventful ... but I'm only giving you a taster, remember? The defining moment happened early on, when a storm caught us while crossing the Indus River and

50 of the books were lost. Well, I couldn't have that, so we sent back for replacements and waited in Gandhara; when most had arrived, not all, we needed to press on. Crossing the Hindu Kush on my elephant was quite an experience, I can tell you, but sadly I wasn't destined to ride him all the way home. He was lost at the mountainous border between Kyrgyzstan and China—bandits ambushed us, causing him to stampede and drown in a river. After that tragic loss, we made base in Khotan, in the deserts of northern China. We stayed eight months, both to wait for the remainder of the books, and to give me time to write to the Emperor, since I was still a fugitive back home. Well, the books arrived and the Emperor wrote back to say that all was forgiven—it was still the same Emperor too, Taizong. When we finally arrived home I was amazed to find myself a national hero! There were great processions and cheering crowds; the kind of thing I'd become accustomed to in India but never expected in China. Still, I had travelled over 10,000 miles on a 16-year epic adventure, and most importantly, I'd brought back 657 classics of Buddhist philosophy.

§

No such excitement for me anymore, only the better kind, the philosophical kind. With my own monastery and a large team of monks to assist me, I spend my days translating the books into Chinese. I doubt I'll ever finish, the task is too vast, even for me; and with students flocking from all over China, as well as from Japan and Korea, it's increasingly hard to keep up. And that's how I like it: immersed in the truth and doing everything I can to spread it around. You mustn't forget the reason for my adventures: to find better books, to find better teachers, to learn. Can you imagine going through all that simply for the sake of it? In the spirit of discovery, from a sense of adventure, for the sheer experience … such reasons are given with a straight face, no? I can't think of anything more shallow.

§

Anyway, now you've had your taster, let's get into it! I hope I won't be saying anything original, I don't think I do that anymore but you can never be sure.

§

So, do you think that if it's incredibly natural to believe something, then it must be true? Of course you don't, you wouldn't be talking to philosophers if you did. I doubt anyone really thinks that, it's just that they don't think. They've always believed these things without question, everyone they know does too, so the beliefs start to seem unquestionable rather than just unquestioned. They wouldn't want to hear about the reservations of philosophers, and if they did they'd dismiss them out of hand. If you were trying to reconstruct their reasoning, you might think they were working on the premise that whatever's natural to believe must be true, but that's not it at all. They just haven't thought about it and want to carry on like that—carry on as if their dream were reality, despite the suffering it causes them.

§

Here are two things that are incredibly natural to believe, the crucial ones. The first is that you're something that endures— that continues to exist from one moment to the next—and the second is that you live in a physical environment that endures. Both are false and you need to get over them to have any chance of thinking correctly. And I mean *really* get over them, as in, not just say you don't believe because you like the idea of being a Yogacarin, but disbelieve in the depths of your heart. If you can get there—and nobody's saying it's easy—then you're on the path to salvation.

§

Give it its due, endurance makes sense of the evidence in an easy way. You shut your eyes, open them again, and the horse is still there; you bolt it in the stable, go about your business, and you know where to return when you need it. So the horse is an enduring object but your experiences aren't, they're fleeting. But the fleeting experiences must belong to something enduring, namely you, otherwise they wouldn't be yours rather than another person's. So enduring selves and objects make easy sense of how experiences connect up, and you need to understand those connections to live and prosper. Imagine someone who didn't: there's a horse experience (was it mine?), there's another (was that mine too? was it of the same horse?) ... that person's not going to last long!

§

Endurance does the job ... but really badly, as the Buddha was first to realise. That's because if you think in terms of enduring things, then everything you care about will inevitably cease to endure and you'll suffer as a consequence. Your loved ones, pleasures, and sources of pride will transform and perish, and you'll live in fear of transformation and perishing yourself, right up until the moment you perish. Overcoming selfishness will always be a battle, in which some will fare better than others and some won't even try, because it's only a short step from metaphysically privileging a particular object as "me", to caring about it more than anything else. A self-centred conception of reality promotes self-centred lives. From the point of view of morality, individual well-being, and social cohesion, I'm afraid I'd have to say that belief in endurance is nothing less than a total disaster.

§

But how will you view reality once you've purged your thinking of endurance? You'll view it as only consciousness. You'll view it as specks of experience that momentarily appear only to disappear the very same moment—appear as they disappear, disappear as they appear. They're always being replaced, and the way they're replaced fools us into believing in endurance. Imagine a succession of tiny dots of coloured light that appear and disappear so quickly on a screen, and in such an orderly procession, that it makes it seem like you're watching a horse running across a plain. Well, the specks we're talking about aren't just colours—they're specks of all kinds of experience, whether sounds, the roughness of running your hand over rock, bodily feelings, emotional feelings, or what it feels like to think. And the screen is an infinitely subtle container consciousness that you never experience. The specks appearing within the container create the appearance of a physical world with you situated within it, but it's all only consciousness.

§

I like that slogan, "only consciousness", but be careful not to be misled by it, since the last thing you want to do is replace your attachment to illusory enduring things with an attachment to consciousness. The point is that it's only consciousness making you think there's enduring things, not that consciousness is the ultimate reality. The specks are just illusory appearances, like horns on a rabbit or flowers in the sky. They're so fleeting you couldn't form an attachment to them, and that's where the moral value of the teaching begins. It's true that consciousness is more real than physical objects and selves, that's for sure, because at the level of conventional truth, the only kind our words are fit for, it's the reality causing the illusions. But consciousness is expressible in language—I'm talking about it now and you understand me—while the ultimate reality isn't. The enlightened ones who attain consciousness with no object might say that the ultimate reality is consciousness, isn't consciousness, both is and isn't consciousness, or neither is nor isn't consciousness. They might say the same about whether it exists—that it does, doesn't, both does and doesn't, etc. It's all the same, it doesn't really matter at that level.

§

Language is always an expression of dualistic thinking: say the apple's red and you contrast it with things that aren't (duality: red and not red), say the self isn't real and you contrast it with things that are (duality: not real and real). That's fine for ordinary purposes, but it won't work when you're trying to talk about absolutely everything—and what's "ultimate reality" if not absolutely everything? So you can't grasp the ultimate reality with dualistic thinking ... and you can, and you neither can nor can't, if you catch my drift? But you can still reason yourself along the path to where ultimate reality transcends reason.

§

One of the biggest obstacles to that path is that at some level, deep down, it's hard not to feel that there must be enduring objects, and that any reasoning suggesting otherwise just has to be trickery. And yet endurance is only an idea for explaining the connections between our experiences, that's easy enough to see. So why cling so doggedly to an explanation? Why the deep-down feeling that an explanation in terms of endurance must be right, and that we're not at liberty to explain the connections between our experiences in another way? I'll tell you why, it's because endurance is an explanation that says you have a self, and you've been clinging to that your whole life.

§

It's started to rain. Look at that cherry tree over there. We're seeing it through the whitish descending flecks of rain—the pattern's always changing, but it's always descending in distinct lines; you couldn't say how many lines in a given moment, except that it's lots. That's a reminder of what experience is like, inconstant and beyond words, but for now just focus on the cherry tree. So, if we walked over there we'd see the cherry tree's other side, and if you were to climb it you'd see the top from close-up; if you dug away at the soil you'd see roots that aren't currently visible. The idea of an enduring cherry tree explains all those experiences, possible and actual—it explains which ones you'd get in which circumstances, and why you would. The idea explains all that, and yet here's the thing: *it's only an idea*. You're not focusing your mind on reality anymore, only on your own explanatory construction—don't you see? The enduring tree is only what you're reasoning *must* exist in order to explain experiences. The cherry tree isn't something that *just* exists, like the experiences do, it's something that *must* exist—*must*, but only according to the explanatory system of endurance. It's like dreaming of eating cherries, and then reasoning, within your own dream, that there must be a tree they were picked from—your mind's looking away from reality to focus on an unreal intellectual construction.

§

The point's even clearer when you turn from outer objects to the inner one, the self. Unlike with the cherry tree, there aren't even any experiences to mistake for a self. Nobody mistakes thoughts or tickles for selves, they just reason that selves must exist because they're what have the thoughts and tickles. Reasoning like that just *screams*: intellectual construction! So easy to see the error, so hard to let go of it.

§

How much have you already lost by allowing your mind to look away from reality to focus on an unreal intellectual construction? When I was a boy I'd often get caught up in reliving times when I'd been unjustly harmed, rehearsing in my mind how I might have reacted better to the injustice, and regretting that I didn't. While these recurring loops of bitterness dominated my inner space, I was lost to experiences happening right now. It's all only consciousness, but you're missing opportunities in the moment if you allow your mind to wander towards the suffering of attachment.

§

A mother and daughter hold hands while climbing stairs. An angry mother drags her crying daughter up the stairs. In both cases stairs are climbed.

§

Consciousness has existed since beginningless time in a state of continual transformation. It's evolved through the power of karma, with each moment of transformation a vast array of mutually dependent experiential events conditioned by a vast array of earlier ones, the earlier conditioning events spread throughout beginningless time. The karma which builds up in the evolution can be good or simply neutral, but some is bad. The bad karma caused experiential events to aggregate together by attaching themselves to the illusory notion of self, as if they'd become separate to the rest of the flow — and that's where we come in. For once this happened, there seemed to be individuals having their own experiences. Since all these experiences were conditioned by the same vast history of evolving consciousness, they cohere in a manner we can think of as: people experiencing the same world from different perspectives. They cohere in this manner because of bad karma, because it reinforces attachment. And that's why we can so readily understand the world in terms of endurance.

§

Think back to the cherry tree. Did you really need the theory of endurance to know what kind of experiences you'd have if you climbed to the top of the tree? Of course you didn't, you knew that instinctively, the theory just made sense of what you already knew from long experience. Well, so does Yogacara, but with consciousness only, instead of the false intellectual constructions which consciousness encourages. I can't go into detail about the alternative explanation here, but I've already given you a taster, and you can find some very fulsome discussion in my books. Very, very fulsome indeed, the product of a lifetime of study and debate, and with answers to all the objections I've ever come across; the ones worth mentioning, that is. I spent five days replying to objections in the Great Debate and by the end they'd run out of steam, all they had left was their scowls and grimaces.

§

It does make me laugh when people are sceptical because they think it's not a very practical philosophy—you get a lot of that kind of thing in China, people who think it's worldly to believe in endurance ... maybe they'll pick up a big rock and tap it with their knuckles to prove its solidity, poking fun at us "head in the cloud"-types with our preference for fleeting experiences. Well come on ... I mean ... *honestly*! I was an explorer, mountaineer, leader of men, cultural ambassador, diplomat, politician ... how much more worldly can you get? If I ever hear that suspicion voiced by someone half as practical as me then I promise to take note.

§

I'll tell you what's practical: remaining perfectly calm when pirates capture you, haul you onto an altar, and start sharpening the knife ready to cut your throat. Panicking wouldn't have helped me, if my time had been up it would've just made my last moments awful. As things turned out I think they'd have probably killed me if I'd believed in endurance—that sudden typhoon wouldn't have seemed so significant to them if they hadn't already been struck by my serenity.

§

You should think about our chat about the cherry tree when you're meditating. All you have to do is sit on the floor, it couldn't be easier, at least to start with. That simple act establishes that you're doing something, meditating—that you're going to open yourself up to the present moment of your experience. At first you'll have what we call "Monkey Mind"—you'll think about some issue that's been bothering you, wonder what you're supposed to be doing, what's supposed to happen, how long you've been going, notice your toes don't feel comfortable ... But if you keep at it you'll settle down and wake up to the moment, see that it's only consciousness—consciousness just happening, doing its thing, unfathomable, caused by innumerable factors you'll never know about. You'll really notice it, attune with it, and eventually become at one with it. Once you can think like that when you're not meditating, when you're out and about in the world, then you'll act in the common good both effortlessly and unselfconsciously—doing the right thing will be like adjusting your pillow in the middle of the night.

§

That's what I reckon, anyway, and who's going to argue with Xuanzang?

Encounter 4: Nana Abena Boaa

Nana Abena Boaa was a 17th century Akan queen from Offinso, Ghana, but beyond that nothing has been remembered about her. Ghanaian philosopher Kwame Gyekye (1939–2019), who sought to reconstruct Akan philosophy from its oral traditions, argued that it should be regarded as the product of individual philosophers whose names were not recorded.

§

Are you preferring the stories or the thoughts? Honestly? That last story was particularly good, I'm not so sure myself.

§

You spend your life thinking, but about what kind of thing? Of the thoughts you have, do the ones you endorse have anything noteworthy in common? And what about the ones you don't? What about the kind you wish wouldn't even cross your mind, that make you uncomfortable when they do? Can you work out what you're like from such reflections—about what you mainly think about, endorse, reject, wish had never occurred to you?

§

Well yes indeed, I'd love to talk to you about philosophy! It'll be so refreshing to be treated as a philosopher rather than the queen. Yes, yes, they call me the philosopher-queen, and I still engage in debates, but nowadays they just can't help thinking of me as, first and foremost, *queen*—some pretend better than others but you can always tell. They can never relax, they're watching their words, and you just can't have a proper discussion like that. I don't know why—it's not as if I'd put them to death for disagreeing with me, you'd think they'd know me better than that. But there's nothing to be done about it, whatever I say they'll only humour me, it'd only change how they pretend. I guess it's one of the lesser burdens of sitting on the royal stool. I made my name as a philosopher on my own merits, you know, nobody disputes that, but attitudes started to change when I married the king. Then, when he died and circumstances obliged me to become leader of our people, well … after that, things were never the same again. Talking with you will be wonderful, just like the good old days—I'm not your queen, so you haven't even got a reason to pretend. Not that I think you would anyway, for some reason I trust you, maybe it's something to do with this place.

§

I've not heard of any of the philosophers you spoke with. Since the most recent of them died a thousand years ago that's hardly surprising—you wouldn't expect their names to be remembered. The ideas of philosophers join the collective wisdom of a people, together with some of their maxims in exceptional cases—and that's all that needs to be remembered. I know the names of philosophers who died in living memory but it's not something you pass on. You pass on the names of kings and queens to preserve your people's sense of history, but philosophy is about understanding reality, not at this time or that, but how it is always. It doesn't matter who spoke the truth so long as it's recognised and remembered. If other peoples are doing these things differently, as you seem to be suggesting, then I think they ought to watch it: they'll end up turning philosophy into a historical hall of fame.

§

There's great wisdom in laughter—it's an expression of joy in living, but one you don't have to try to take seriously.

§

Isn't excitement better than happiness? It's unmistakable in the moment and looks forward, while happiness is most easily recognised by its absence now and presence in the past.

§

The philosopher who instinctively focuses on morality attracts reasonable suspicion. Perhaps they just want to help. Perhaps they seek deeper understanding, clarification, the precision of theory, the resolution of acknowledged dilemmas. But if morality strikes them as an obvious mystery, take a broader view of their conclusions.

§

I can't say I loved my husband. I felt nothing similar to what I feel for my children. It was a surprise when I heard we were to be married; not so much that I'd be first among his wives, the reason for that was obvious. He was very insecure about his intelligence, and in his mind, at least, nobody could think he was stupid if he married the famous philosopher. That's all I was to him, a symbol, and when we married he soon found he didn't like me. Thinking made him uneasy and so did I, but he had other wives he loved—and they all hated me, of course! Well, after we'd been married a while he started asking my opinion on political matters—reluctantly, and only because he knew he could trust me, that nobody'd find out that he never knew what to do, that it tormented him. Since my suggestions usually turned out well he started seeking my advice more often, until eventually I became his chief political advisor, not in name but in reality. He valued me for that at least. I wasn't sad when he died, his spirit was released and he'll be happier now. I was excited to become queen. I knew I was the best option our people had at that time, and although I never sought it, you must always give thanks for opportunities sent by the higher powers, then do your best to reward their trust.

§

Seeing is believing, unless reason intervenes. Reason must be monitoring the situation, then.

§

There's spirit all around—*sunsum*, we call it. It's deep in you and me, in the animals, the plants, the sun ... not absolutely everywhere, not in a rock or a log, you'd be crazy to think that, but it's all around like the breeze and the birdsong. *Sunsum* is in all living things. It's in our souls before they depart this world, the free spirits that roam the skies are pure *sunsum*, and greatest of all is the holy spirit in the beyond ... I don't mean beyond our lands, I mean she's beyond outer space.

§

There's nice a story we tell about why god is transcendent — you need simple stories to introduce children to philosophical concepts because sooner or later they'll start getting curious. The story goes that one fine day, not long after she'd created the human race, god was watching some women grinding grain when they started attacking her with their pestles — they didn't like being watched — so she ran away to a transcendent realm. Our ancestors had a great sense of humour, don't you think? There's another one about sex — when people were first created they didn't know how to reproduce, so god sent a python down to earth to teach us!

§

Feel the joy of the sun's spirit as it resonates with your own, warming your skin. But if you stay out in the sun too long he'll beat you small. Too much joy and you're a fool, but only as much sadness as befits how your fortune's scaled to your people's — that's as true for washerwomen as for queens.

§

What's it like to be the sun? It doesn't feel like anything, his joy isn't centred in inner space, only outer space. He's got a centre somewhere up there, that's for sure — he's a fiery ball and all balls have centres! But the sun's a purely spiritual being, like god herself, so he hasn't got a soul. Only people have souls, they centre the world in an inner space infused with spirit. Souls come from the spirit of god, like everything else, and they contain our spirit during life on earth. Your spirit can leave your soul, it does every time you dream, but it always comes back while your soul has a body. When you die and your soul doesn't privilege part of the physical world anymore, your work on earth for god and the spirits is over—let's hope you served them well. With no more body to centre its inner space, the soul now opens up to everything, the one reality, while still holding the memory of what you were—the souls of our ancestors retain enough active spirit to help us from time to time. The spirit of the sun doesn't have a centre in inner space because it's a joy at one with the universe.

§

The invisible is more real than the visible. You can't have everyday life without invisible time and can't have anything without invisible god.

§

One of the many philosophical maxims that's been passed down to us is, "you can't see the seeing eye", and it was at a debate about its meaning that I first made a splash, so to speak. Ano was there, Offinso's most venerated philosopher in living memory—he was over 100 years old, they say, I'd just turned 20. Until I spoke there wasn't any debate as such, since some of the elders thought they already knew what it meant and everyone else was just listening. They thought it was referring to how spirit emanates from the eyes to envelop the thing seen—so that when you're looking at a tree, for instance, spirit leaves your soul through the eyes to wrap around the tree and make an image to guide the body. You can't see a seeing eye, they said, because you can only see where the spirit lands, and a seeing eye is always sending spirit away from the eye. That sounded completely wrong to me; I mean, where do you start in criticising something so confused? I noticed Ano wasn't saying anything, although it was wishful thinking on my part to think he'd be on my side; his wrinkly old face was inscrutable by the light of the open fire, you couldn't even tell if he was awake.

"How's covering a thing with invisible spirit supposed to make it visible?" I blurted out—and they all went quiet and stared. I was haughty in those days, I wasn't afraid, they had to be respectful of the views of somebody from my family, that's what I thought—I'm much more modest now I'm queen, isn't that funny! Anyway, having caught their attention, I went on:

"You're thinking of seeing as like throwing a pail of water over something—it's the drenching theory of perception!"

One of the younger men laughed out loud at this—he'd smiled at me earlier so I ignored him, assuming there were ulterior motives behind his moral support. I then explained what the saying means. It was a bit of a long-winded explanation, I can do much better now.

§

You see that boulder at the top of the hill? I'm going to look at it while you watch me—just look at my eyes, I'll ignore you, my eyes'll be fixed on the boulder. The eyes you see are eyes seen by you, so in that sense they're seen eyes rather than seeing eyes, right? Yet it's my seeing eyes you're looking at—I'm seeing with them—so they're both seen eyes and seeing eyes. And in that case you can indeed "see the seeing eye", so the maxim must be wrong ... are you happy with that conclusion? I certainly hope not, maxims like that could be centuries or even millennia old!

Don't worry, I know you're expecting there to be more to it, I already said I trust you.

§

Notice how they're not seen eyes and seeing eyes in the same sense—because they're seen eyes for you, but seeing eyes for me. You can't see my eyes as seeing eyes for me, you can only ever see things as they are for you ... and you can't see them as seeing eyes for you either because they're not, they're seen eyes for you. So you can't see seeing eyes, after all, just as the saying tells us. You know they're seeing eyes for me because you know I'm seeing with them—but there are plenty of things we know but can't see.

§

You're still not getting it ... let's get you thinking about your own eyes rather than mine, that'll help.

§

When you look at yourself in the perfectly still waters of a lake, can you see your own seeing eyes? The only eyes you see are on the surface of the water, so if you could you'd be in the water looking up, not gazing down at your reflection.

Now you're getting confused because we're talking about reflections, so let's switch the example again.

What if a powerful spirit pulls out one of your eyes—it floats in the sky in front of your face and the two eyes look at each other ... surely now you can see the seeing eye ... two of them, in fact!

§

OK then, let's think hard about this. One eye's floating in front of your face, the other's still in the socket—what image are you seeing? There's the image of your one-eyed face coming from the floating eye, and there's the image of an eye floating in the air coming from your normal eye, how do they fit together to make what you see? The only way I can imagine it is as a picture with a line down the middle ... or something like that, some kind of division within a unified scene. Let's stick with the divided picture, that makes it easy—so on the left is one view and on the right is the other. Alright, so where's the picture? Is it in your head or hovering behind the floating eye? It has to be one or the other because the soul is a unity, just like reality, just like the creator—that's why you can't imagine it being both at the same time. (Try if you don't believe me.) Let's suppose it's in your head, it doesn't matter which one we choose, the point's the same. In that case it's like normal seeing except for the visual field being split—on one side you're looking forwards at the floating eye and on the other you're looking back at your face. Well in that case you're still only aware of seen eyes. When you focus on the floating eye, that's an eye seen by the normal eye, and when you focus on the normal eye that's an eye seen by the floating one—you can even take in the whole at once, if you like, you'll still only see two seen eyes, never any seeing ones.

§

So if seeing your own seeing eyes doesn't make sense, even with the help of powerful spirits, why should seeing mine make more sense? We both have physical bodies with physical eyes, and physical things are visible, of course, but ... and here's the point you missed the first time ... your soul is invisible to itself, just as my soul is invisible to you. And that's because souls are invisible, there's nothing else to it. The seeing eye is the eye of my soul—so it's invisible. Within my soul I'm aware of my eye looking at that boulder on the hill, or looking at a reflection on the water, but I can never see it, it's an awareness of something invisible.

§

As I came to the end of my explanation, I saw that the men who'd defended the "drenching theory of perception" (as it's been known ever since that night) were eager to butt in with their objections. I didn't let them.

"Uh, uh," I said, "I need to talk about religion ... the maxim hasn't been explained until I do." Ano's eyes popped wide open, otherwise he remained motionless. Noticing this, the others let me carry on, although they clearly weren't happy about it.

The maxim isn't really about seeing at all, I explained, it's about god. The ancestors are pointing out that just as seeing is the touchstone of our reality, despite the invisibility of the seeing eye, so god is the invisible source of all reality and understanding. They're telling us that although we naturally believe what we see, unless reason tells us otherwise, our belief is always rooted in the invisible—in the seeing eye, and, ultimately, in the creator god who made everything we see, and without whom nothing would make sense, nothing could make sense, and there'd be nothing to make sense of.

§

Ano leaned forward and raised his finger close to the fire, which cast a flickering shadow across me; it was a dramatic motion for such an old man, everyone knew it meant strong approval. When he eventually sat back again and the silence he'd created was broken, I bowed my head, then walked briskly home, leaving the others to debate my contribution—it was an arrogant gesture, I know, but I was young. The next time the philosophers met I was asked to lead the discussion, and the maxim chosen was, "One is not born with a bad head, one takes it on the earth"—I explained its meaning in the abstract, carefully avoiding any suggestion of the personal criticism which had obviously been intended. That debate went really well for me too, so for the next six years, until that fateful day when the king made me his bride, I was never allowed to miss a meeting. Sometimes my own maxims were chosen for the discussion; they regularly come up these days, of course, but it's only because I'm queen; it pisses me off.

§

You'll have noticed our symbol of the crossed crocodiles, it's painted and carved all over town. Two crocodiles join in the middle to make one strange creature: it's got two heads, two tails, eight legs, but only one belly. The maxim that goes with it is: "two heads fight over food that nourishes both"—they snap at each other to be the one that swallows the food, but the food goes down into the same belly either way. Nothing better sums up our ethics, or *suban*, as we say—it's slightly different from your word because it means a kind of character, an ethical or moral one. If you don't have *suban* you don't have any morals, but if you do then you won't snap at the other heads, you'll be thinking of the shared belly.

§

Whether you have *suban* depends on your deeds, on whether you act in a way that serves the community. You're not born with *suban* and you're not born without it either. No, you're born neutral—everyone who's spent time with a baby knows that, they don't have a good or bad character, they're completely unproven; as the maxim says, "One is not born with a bad head, one takes it on the earth". So you're not born with or without *suban*, then, but everyone's born with *sunsum*, and it can be weaker or stronger—as mothers know, some babies are more wilful than others. Well that's going to affect the development of *suban*, because if *sunsum* is weak you'll tend to laziness so have to try harder, while if it's strong that might make things harder too, you might have to overcome impulses to self-gratification or self-aggrandizement. Still, anyone can develop *suban* if they put in the work—every time you serve your community it grows a little stronger, a little more natural, more instinctive. Morality's essentially the same with gods and spirits, even the creator god; we tend to reserve the word "*suban*" for people, but it's still true that what makes gods and spirits good or bad is the acts they perform for our communities. If we ask for their help and they don't come through then it makes sense to stop worshipping them, at least for a while—and if they fail badly enough it might even be reasonable to hold them in open contempt, just as you would a human who let the community down. In really extreme cases we may even apply our ultimate punishment for a god or spirit, which is to completely forget about them, refuse to pass their names down to the next generation—serves them right.

§

The creator god is pure goodness because she only ever does good things for us and never harms the innocent; none of the other gods and spirits are like that, unfortunately. Helping the community makes gods and spirits good, just as it develops a person's *suban*, so we're all working for the good across metaphysical boundaries: human and spiritual, visible and invisible, united in a common cause. A man who commits a crime against his community may be punished by good people, gods and spirits alike — maybe we'll chase him with sticks, jeer as he walks down the street, boycott his business ... but it's the gods and spirits he needs to fear most, his roof's going to fall down, it might be worse. It's not always easy to do the right thing, as everyone knows, so the threat of both human and supernatural punishment is a great help. But there will always be some who fail, and even those completely lacking *suban* at least have the consolation of death — whatever terrible punishments they've been suffering for their crimes, it all ends when their soul leaves the earth. What then? Nobody knows, nobody could, life continues in a transcendent reality beyond our understanding. I don't know my husband's happier now, but he had such a miserable time when I knew him I'd have thought he's bound to be, I'd have thought it's all relative.

§

Doing the right thing is acting in the best interests of your community, but it can be very hard to tell what that is. Here's a story Ano told me, it brings out the difficulties nicely.

§

Once upon a time there was a hunter named Agyenim who was hoping to bring home a duiker or bushbuck for his family. It'd been a long, hot day and he had nothing to show for his efforts, so he sat on a log and looked down despondently at his hunting bow. He noticed a small spider crawling across it and instinctively flicked the creature off — when the spider landed on the floor, however, it immediately transformed into Ananse, the trickster god, who now stood before Agyenim in all his splendour.

"How would you like to be able to feed your family all the duiker and bushbuck flesh they can eat? And not just your family, the whole community! You'll never have to hunt again."

"What's the catch?" asked Agyenim.

"No catch," said Ananse, "if you've got magic powers like I have then why not use them for good? It won't just be plentiful meat either, I'll do other good things for the community, marvellous things. So, do you want my help or not?"

Agyenim said he did, so Ananse accompanied him back to his village.

§

The villagers crowded around Ananse, who raised his arms to the sky and began to chant. "There, it's done," he said at last, lowering his arms to address the crowd. "You'd better find somewhere to pen up the animals, they'll be arriving soon." Well, it wasn't long before duikers and bushbucks started wandering into the streets of the village—normally shy and cautious animals, these ones seemed strangely indifferent to people. Agyenim followed them through the streets to find out where they were all coming from, and when he reached the edge of the village he could hardly believe his eyes: there was a trail of antelopes stretching right across the vast plain, as far as the eye could see.

"I told them to get ready to pen up the animals!" said a grinning Ananse, placing his hand on Agyenim's shoulder.

§

The villagers worked all day and night to make pens for the antelopes, but it was an endless task, they never stopped coming.

"That'll do, that'll do," smiled Ananse, "you people need to learn to enjoy yourselves! You've already got enough livestock penned up to eat like kings and queens for months, so just fence off the village so that no more animals can get in—they'll congregate on the plain nearby and you can let more in when you need them."

"I know what'll help you relax," he added with a cheeky grin—and in a cloud of magic, he made a giant well appear. He pulled up the well bucket and offered it to Agyenim, who took it to his lips—it wasn't water, it was palm wine, and unusually strong palm wine at that. "Sweet," said Agyenim.

§

Great festivities followed. The people gorged themselves on roasted meat, as they played and listened to music, danced, told stories, discussed philosophy, gave thanks to Ananse, and drank palm wine from morning 'til night. After a few weeks, however, some started grumbling that there wasn't enough fufu to go with all the meat.

"Don't worry," said Ananse, "if you dig under that hill over there you'll find a special white powder—collect it up and mix it with the soil, you'll get the best crop of cassava and cocoyam you've ever known."

"Oh yes," he added as an afterthought, "and while you're at it you'd probably best do something about those thousands of antelopes surrounding the village, they're going to starve and the rotting carcasses will make an awful stink. If you dig under that other hill over there then you'll find an endless supply of special grey grains, use them as antelope feed."

Once the villagers established an efficient operation for mining and distributing the powder and pellets, the fufu became as plentiful as the meat, and the antelopes grew fat— they swelled to twice the size they'd been before. The people of the village started getting fat too.

§

Agyenim died a fat, happy, alcoholic old man, loved by his community for all the good he'd done, for the welfare he'd brought them. The high life continued in much the same way for his children, but by the time his grandchildren came of age there was discontent brewing once more. The village had expanded into a town, there were far more people than ever before, and the vast plains around were crammed with antelopes. Feeding, slaughtering and butchering was becoming a big job which nobody could be bothered with, it interfered with their music, dancing, drinking and philosophy. Mining for the powder and pellets was a similarly unpopular occupation, as was farming cassava and cocoyam; meanwhile feeding all the antelopes outside the village had become impossible, there were just too many, so bad smells often wafted through the air. There was so much moaning that Ananse saw that he'd have to step in again.

"Don't worry," he said, "you just need more of my magic, that's all. Now stand back." He raised his arms and began to chant—a cloud of shimmering dust appeared, and as it dispersed, the people saw a pile of enormous tubes, all painted in different colours.

"Herd the antelopes through the red ones," explained Ananse. "When the leader reaches the end of the tube it'll get its head forced into a clamp and a blade will slit its throat, it's all done by magic; the next one's being killed while you're dragging the carcass out, you'll find it's all incredibly quick and easy. Then drag the carcasses through the blue tubes—when they come out the other end they'll be skinned and butchered, all ready for use. The yellow tubes are for mining—you bury them in the ground and the powder and pellets pour out the other end. The green tubes work in a similar way, but you bury them in the crop fields—the white powder that'll come out is fufu flour; mix it with water and you've got the best fufu you ever tasted. The brown tubes are for feeding the antelopes on the plain, you'll need lots of those, as many as you can be bothered to set up. Just place them on their ends and the pellets will rise up in the middle and cascade over the sides, morning, noon and night."

After that day the people prospered as never before. Whenever they needed more tubes, they prayed to Ananse and he always delivered.

§

In the transcendent realm of the creator god, time does not pass as it does here on earth, so it cannot be said what prompted Agyenim's spirit to return at the time of his grandchildren's grandchildren. He found his village grown into a great city, filled with riches, but also much sadness and fear—and of a kind Agyenim simply could not fathom. Some hated life and wished for it to end, either blaming themselves, regardless of their riches and *suban*, or else blaming human life itself, simply for the fact that it exists. Others developed fears they couldn't explain, terrors that arose when they knew they weren't at risk, making them short of breath. As Agyenim's spirit floated with the wind over this bewildering place, he found himself drawn to a field full of red tubes, hundreds of them. Fat men with spears were forcing huge duikers and bushbucks into the tubes—the animals were terrified, their shrieking filled the air, their blood soaked the soil.

§

Agyenim sensed that the spirit of Ananse was with him in this awful place and he spoke to the god as to an old friend.

"I used to enjoy hunting," he said wistfully, "I don't suppose anyone does it anymore, it'd be pointless."

"It was always pointless," said Ananse.

"OK, it'd be ridiculous then, you'd have to fight your way through dense crowds of antelopes to cross the plain into the bush—and then when you got there you'd have to spend hours looking for one!"

"You haven't looked around this world much, have you?" answered Ananse, with a look of amusement tinged with pity. "You wouldn't find any duikers or bushbuck in the bush anymore, they're all in the city or the plain, I used up their spirit long ago. I had to use up the spirit of other animals too … and plants, and the spirit of plants and animals that died in the past, there's hardly any life left in the bush these days—or the sea or sky for that matter, haven't you noticed the lack of birds and insects?"

"Did you do the right thing?" asked Agyenim.

"You accepted my offer and I gave the people what they wanted," replied Ananse.

"But that happened a long time ago, these people were born into it, it wasn't their choice."

Ananse dropped his usual jovial guise and spoke sternly. "You had a good life. You gave your family a good life. You gave your generation a good life. Why do you care?"

§

That's exactly how Ano ended the tale, word for word: "You had a good life. You gave your family a good life. You gave your generation a good life. Why do you care?" Then he gave a little grunt and told me to leave, it was the best lesson I ever had!

So are you seeing the problem with *suban*, then? You get *suban* by resisting selfish desires, by devoting your *sunsum* to projects that benefit your community. That way you benefit yourself too, not just because you're part of the community, but because people, gods and spirits will reward you, they won't punish you, and you'll become a better and happier person, your inner space will glow. But how wide is your community, that's the question? Does it include your ancestors and descendants, or just the people whose mortal lives will coincide with your own? What if helping people now sets up a terrible fate for your descendants? Can you blame Agyenim for not realising how things would turn out long after he was dead? Could you reasonably expect him to care? Do I care about what happens to my people after my grandchildren are gone? Even me, a queen, do I really care?

§

Yes I do, I do care about my ancestors and descendants, no matter how distant they are from my time on earth—and that's because I focus on the invisible. Agyenim's mistake was to focus on the visible and I blame him for that. He didn't know how things would turn out after his death, that's true, but if you neglect the invisible to focus on the visible then you're bound to be setting up a gloomy destiny of one sort or another, whether or not it's one your grave lets you avoid—and if avoiding it's all you care about, then you've no *suban*. Metaphysics and ethics are like the crossed crocodile, they only have one belly. Once we've realised the metaphysical truth that the ultimate reality is invisible then we know where to focus our intellects to bring welfare to the community. Not on the visible, the visible will change, it's not as trustworthy because it's not as real ... and yet it's so beautiful, so addictive, so enraging, the philosophical life will always be a struggle.

§

That's what I reckon, anyway, and who's going to argue with Nana Abena Boaa?

Encounter 5: F.H. Bradley

Francis Herbert Bradley (1846–1924) was a philosopher from London, England. He was the leading exponent of British Idealism.

§

It's none of my business what you're like, but your story might interest me. Never meet your heroes, they say, and that's because if you meet them you might get to know what they're like, you're better off sticking with their stories. But unlike with your heroes you can't want your own self to remain a fantasy.

§

There ... listen ... did you hear that? Infernal scratching and scurrying, how's a fellow supposed to think with that racket going on? Wait ... there he is! Keep very quiet and still, I think I've a clear shot at him. There, got the blighter, one dead squirrel! That'll give us some blessed relief for a while, although the vermin will return, they always do. But in the meantime: metaphysics! So, I understand you've already spoken to Plato and Plotinus, and also to some other philosophers of whom I know nothing ... good show, old chap, it pays to attend to as many philosophical schools as possible. I would express my incredulity at your miraculous encounters had I not already learned to put aside all preconceptions in this place. Metaphysics has travelled far on the shoulders of giants like Plato and Plotinus, they have my eternal gratitude, and if you're genuine about wanting to understand where it's arrived in our day, then I'm as good a man to ask as any, I'd dare say. Be wary, though, for if you consult with the Shades of Metaphysic they'll exact their price in blood. Although ... thinking about it ... I guess I'm one of them now, and I don't want you to end up all pale and anaemic. Your undivided attention is all I ask for.

§

The others began by telling you about their lives, you say, and now you're expecting the same from me? Clearly I've been misled, since I took you for a serious student of metaphysics, not a collector of gossip. I must ask you to leave forthwith. Teaching is bad enough already, I wouldn't ordinarily agree to it. Quite apart from the dullards you're expected to tolerate (not that I ever would) it's a complete waste of time for philosophers, who should devote themselves solely to writing, perfecting their understanding and recording it for posterity. I made an exception in agreeing to teach you, only to be rewarded with your impertinent demand. Be off with you!

§

It appears I have no choice in the matter. Very well, prepare to be disappointed. My life has been incredibly rich, and no doubt this reflects a universal truth—but rich only on the inside. The detail and significance in each and every day, the changing emotional background on which those details are encountered, the progression from youth, to maturity, to old age, and the different ways we look back on what came before, changing it always, losing it always. And yet viewed from the outside my life is one you'd struggle to narrate an interesting story from. We can get it over with quickly and you won't want for more.

§

My parents, uncompromising in their religious devotion, were stern and unyielding—there was no love to be had from them, only great expectations, which my brothers and I have fulfilled. I was not a healthy child; as a teenager I nearly died from typhoid fever, it was a close call. I didn't grow to be a healthy man either, my life has been plagued by illnesses, and this has lent it a somewhat melancholy tone, I fear. My hearing is poor, my vision is poor, I suffer terrible bouts of fatigue. But these things matter little to a philosopher, and the best story I have to tell begins, of course, with philosophy. I was fascinated by it as a boy, particularly German philosophy, but my dedication began in earnest when my youthful passions were aroused by that dismal empiricist philosophy which stems from John Locke and David Hume, and which culminates, if you can call it that, with the preposterously overrated John Stuart Mill. It seemed to me that our philosophy should, and could, be so much better, properly befitting to a nation of the influence and status of Great Britain. Well, thanks in no small measure to my own contribution, this has come to pass. That's not to suggest that my own works are of any great merit, unfortunately they are not, but my influence has been positive. It was in recognition of my achievement that His Majesty the King awarded me the Order of Merit, an honour quite unheard of for a philosopher.

§

And yet, I hear you ask: what happened between my first forays into philosophy and my greatest honour, that is, for most of my life? Well, when I was 24 I was elected to a fellowship at Merton College, Oxford, and here I have stayed, in these rooms in the Fellows' Quadrangle, writing. I rarely leave, most of the chaps wouldn't even know I was here if it weren't for the occasional gunshot sounding out when I shoot at vermin—I include cats in that category, by the way, foul creatures. That said, I do like to vacation at the seaside, whether in England or France, depending on the weather. And when I do it's never hard to find ladies whose company I'll enjoy, since I cut an exceedingly dashing figure in a fine suit, even in casual attire — always did, still do, I'm sure you've been struck by it yourself. It's said I bear a striking resemblance to George Meredith. Even those without such natural endowments could do wonders for their appearance by attending to posture: remain bolt upright at all times, military-fashion, never waver, that's the only proper way for a man to bear himself — and you can be sure the ladies will notice.

§

If you were a friend — which you're not — then that's something I might enjoy talking to you about: love and women. It was a condition of my fellowship that I never marry and I never did, which suits me just fine. Love can't be sustained by an individual anyway, it's general by nature — to maintain love you must continually fall in love, debasing yourself, jeopardising your honour. That's unsettling, but I'd rather deal with those threats to my philosophical concentration than the ones posed by the arrangement of marriage, which can easily lull a man into degrading self-contentment. Lovers always try to find themselves in another but never can; taking companions, rather than a wife, shows more awareness on that head, although the outcome is much the same. It's funny how the love of a woman is never quite enough, don't you find? In addition, you always want them to understand you as you understand yourself. I showed great love by dedicating my books to Eve — that lady is so excitingly American! — but more still by composing for her a summary of my entire metaphysics. It took me ages, a labour of love. When I heard she'd burnt it all without a care — her interest in me lay elsewhere — I laughed more heartily than at any other time I recall, laughed in the dark. I let it be known that the burning was at my instruction, but it was not so. Those in most need of sympathy are often the least likely to attract it.

§

And now for your lesson; the precise moment it's over I'll thank you to leave promptly.

§

Everyday understanding of reality has us effortlessly and instinctively arranging facts into relations and qualities, but metaphysical reflection reveals this to be theoretically unintelligible, hence a characterisation of appearance only, not the ultimate reality of our Absolute. "Here we are having a lesson," say you, with an understanding wholly dependent upon relations and qualities, namely that I have the typical qualities of a man, along with more distinctive ones that mark me out from other men, and also that you and I are related in space and time, as teacher and student, and so on. As I shall demonstrate, however, qualities and relations can exist neither together with each other, nor in isolation, which is just to say that they cannot exist at all. To see this is to condemn everyday life at a stroke, along with the vast physical universe we have erected on its foundations.

One could hardly protest that the qualities and relations need only be registered and utilised, not understood, since distinguishing them is an act of intellect applied to reality, rather than a direct deliverance of said reality—it is *we* who distinguish qualities and relations, feeling that further distinctions can always be made. Once we have picked out differences, we must then discover an explanation for how those differences might be overcome in a single, unified reality, since if we cannot do so, we must instead conclude that the divisions were illusory, a reflection of our practical needs only.

§

I shall begin by explaining why there cannot be qualities without relations. And in case you entertain false expectations, as I fear you might, let me add immediately that I shall do so without recourse to psychology, since no matter how much evidence we might amass to show that the nature of perceived qualities depends on their relationship to the perceiver, the possibility still remains of other, wholly independent qualities residing in objects; and this much ought to be obvious. The more proper explanation is simply to point out that distinguishing a quality, such as the hardness of a rock, is an operation of mind which relates us to the hardness of the rock and isolates it from other qualities. And just as awareness of a single quality presupposes relation, so does a plurality, for if the rock possess shape and mass in addition to hardness, say, then these must be related by thought as united in the rock.

The case becomes clearer still when we turn to the field of conscious experience, in which we encounter a variety of qualities, all related. If I'm experiencing a tree framed by the sky at the end of a field, for instance, then the qualities of the leaves are related to those of the grass within a unified visual experience, and even in mere imagination, of a red triangle let's say, where the qualities of redness and triangularity are related by the unitary figment being imagined. I do not doubt the existence of undifferentiated states of mind, of the kind no doubt enjoyed by infants, brutes, and mystics, but in such instances the lack of relational attention upon one aspect to the detriment of another has the consequence that qualities are lacking also, thereby reinforcing our thesis of mutual dependence. You might insist on there being distinct felt aspects of such states, but now you speak as an outside observer conceptualizing a merely theorised state of mind, rather than as the subject of that state for whom there are neither qualities nor relations.

§

What's this? Qualities cannot be discovered without relations, as you are willing to grant, yet you wonder whether the relations might not simply be our way of getting to know qualities that exist without them. Our finding such distinct qualities as black and white presupposes relations, then, but might not the distinctness be a residual feature of reality even after the relations are removed?

Encouraged as I am to see you raising objections, since it shows proper engagement with the ideas, I'd be doing you a disservice if I failed to note what a howler that was! You failed to separate product from process! The distinct qualities we discover are the product of the mental process of distinguishing them, a process you admit to imply relations, and so you can hardly have the one without the other, any more than you can have a glass of Claret without the process of vinification. And to assume the process is inessential, that distinct qualities might populate reality unproduced, would clearly be monstrous in the present context, where the mind-independence of qualities is exactly our point of contention. Perhaps you will try to prove the process inessential through analogy to a mental operation such as comparison, contending that when Claret is compared to Tawny Port this makes no difference to the qualities of the wines. But that is to presuppose inner natures independent of the outer relations our minds enter into with them, which is once more to presuppose what needs proving, so monstrous. You can salvage some dignity by giving up on this point immediately.

§

You're failing to see the essential simplicity of the matter, so let me help you to do so. The mental operation of abstraction is an undeniable fact; so from all the qualities of the Claret, for example, let's say that I abstract the colour and focus my attention on that. Now evidently this distinct quality is never to be found apart from the mental operation of attending to it, so it is never to be found apart from relations. In light of the evidence, then, the burden of proof lies on whosoever would insist that the quality can exist apart from the process, that is, apart from the mental operation of abstraction which separated it from the rest of reality.

And it's not merely that we lack evidence for products without a process that produced them, since the products wear the processes on their sleeves, given there are so many different qualities we can discover. For there cannot be a multiplicity of distinct qualities, such as the colour of the Claret and the taste of the Port, without their being different from each other, from which we may readily surmise that a relational process of differentiating has taken place. Quality without difference might in some sense be possible, such as in an amoeba, perhaps; for all we know the conscious life of such a simple creature may be one unbroken feeling. But it would be petty and irrelevant to call that a quality in the present context, when it's evident that the only matter concerning us is whether different qualities require there to be relations or not; and nobody, I trust, supposes the whole universe to consist in a single feeling.

§

What should be becoming clear now, if you have a basic aptitude for these matters, is that separateness implies the mental process of separation. When separateness is seen to be necessarily accompanied by relation, however, then our workaday picture of reality is violently ripped asunder. Consider, if you will, the different and separate qualities of black and white. Clearly, the difference must lie either outside or within the qualities. If it is to be outside, such that whether or not they are different makes no difference to black and white themselves, then they must have been related—they must have been brought together in the judgement that they are different. So the only hope for their being different without relation is for the difference to reside within their own natures—and yet what could that possibly mean? Well, suppose we say that being different from white is part of the inner nature of black; for I can think of no other way to give sense to this notion. In that case we have given black a second quality: it is now both black (quality one) and different-from-white (quality two). And that just takes us back to where we started, for it is no less hopeless to try to explain the difference between black and white without relation, than it is to explain the difference between black and different-from-white.

§

What we must conclude is that if there are no differences, then there are no qualities either, so reality collapses into oneness. You'll find this easy to confirm to your own satisfaction by asking yourself the following two questions. Firstly, can you think of qualities without thinking of differences? Of course you cannot. Secondly, can you think of differences without relations? Of course you cannot. So the idea of qualities without relations is entirely without meaning. If more proof be needed, just recall Herr Leibniz's quixotic attempt to build a metaphysical system on their foundation—and what could be more unreal than his lonely windowless souls, prearranged by God in the firmament?

§

Now explain what I've been saying in your own words, I'll not go on until I'm satisfied you understand, to do otherwise would be to risk participating in a monstrous charade.

§

Splendid, splendid, you're following admirably and this isn't the chore I'd been led to expect. Please recall that it was you, not I, who soured this occasion. Nevertheless I'm glad the atmosphere has grown more agreeable ... I shall continue.

§

We now come to the crucial part of the argument, where I shall prove to you that qualities and relations cannot coexist; that it is just as unintelligible to suppose qualities *with* relations, as to suppose them *without*. Brace yourself, for if you can stay to the end a great prize awaits you: you will witness the only reality you've ever known declaring itself illusory. I know of no greater intellectual revelation, I'm quite sure there isn't one, I don't see how there could be. One balmy evening on the French Riviera I convinced myself I'd induced this revelation in Eve; the thought of it combined with the wine and setting to make me feel positively euphoric. I was quite mistaken, of course.

§

There would be no need to combine qualities and relations, nor countenance the meaningless notion of qualities without relations, if we could but maintain that there are no qualities and only relations. That such a course of action is barred to us is plain enough, however. For to say that the relations which

117

black bears to white, such as being the darker colour, might in some manner exhaust the nature of black is just an evident nonsense, since it would commit us to the relations holding between two different nothings. And to retort that the relations actually make the terms is hardly to improve the matter. What? Are we to suppose that it is only when the relations between black and white suspend themselves in thin air that the colours supporting them come into being, like some ghastly Elven suspension bridge built from the middle outwards? Clearly relations depend on terms just as much as terms on relations, and I feel that if Herr Hegel had paid more attention to this point then his system might have suffered less embarrassments.

§

It is this mutual dependency between relations and terms that makes the coexistence of qualities and relations impossible, thus sealing the doom of the universe of everyday life and science. It means that every quality, from colour to mass to happiness, is forced to split into two and then crumble to dust. And that this passes unnoticed is through nothing more than want of metaphysical attention.

Let us return to our simple example of black and white in order to illustrate this most spectacular metaphysical implosion. So, black is darker than white, we say, this is a relation the two shades bear to one other. Now if black were not the colour it is, if it lacked its particular quality, then the relation would not hold, this much cannot be denied. But then neither can it be denied that the relation makes black the colour it is, for if black were not darker than white then it could not be its own particular shade; being darker than white is itself a quality of blackness, we might say. In place of the single quality from which we started, then, we are now landed with two: the quality that supports the relation and the quality made by it.

How can these qualities be united? Well, the failure of the British tradition of empiricist philosophy teaches us, if nothing else (and surely nothing else), that the only sensible approach to this task is through relation. Consider whiteness and sweetness united in a sugar cube; would we follow Mr. Locke, that most industrious of empiricists, in his contention that they are united by a ghostly substance lacking all qualities of its own, one unknowable by humanity, no less, yet somehow detected by the exceedingly clever Mr. Locke? I think not, for as anyone attuned to these matters will rightly see, the whiteness and sweetness must be united by relation, if united at all. But this is the very task which proves itself impossible, since every time we seek to relate them, each one of the qualities splits in two, thus renewing the task *ad infinitum*.

Let me apply this insight to our example of black and white, that ought to help you to understand. Since the original quality of blackness revealed itself to be two conjoined, as we just saw, its unity can only be preserved by relating these qualities to each other as essential qualities of the same blackness. Thus we must relate the quality black brings to its relations with white, to the quality it has as a result of those relations. Attempting to unify the qualities in this manner has quite the opposite effect, however, since now the quality of black which supports its relation to white (the relation-supporting-quality) and the quality of black made by its relation to white (the relation-produced-quality) will themselves each split into two. So, on the one hand, the relation-supporting-quality will split into, firstly, a new relation-supporting-quality which supports the relation between the original relation-supporting-quality and the original relation-produced-quality, and secondly, a new relation-supporting-quality which is made by the relation between the original relation-supporting-quality and the original relation-produced-quality. And on the other hand, the relation-produced-quality will split into, firstly, a new relation-produced-quality which supports the relation between the original relation-supporting-quality and the original relation-produced-quality, and secondly, a new relation-produced-quality which is made by the relation between the original relation-supporting-quality and the original relation-produced-quality. Oh dear, I don't think this is helping after all, let me try a different tack.

Hold up your hand and take in the visual experience you have of a finger and a thumb. The experience of the thumb is broader than that of the finger, is it not? It seems we have qualities and relations residing together in harmony, then, such as the broad quality of the thumb-experience, and the relation it holds to the finger-experience, the relation of being broader. The apparent harmony is an illusion, however, brought on by simple lack of attention. For you must be supposing the broad quality to be what makes your thumb-experience broader than your finger-experience, while also supposing that the thumb-experience's relation to the finger-experience is what makes it broad. So now you have substituted one quality (the broad quality of the thumb-experience) for two (the first being the quality of the thumb-experience that makes it broader than the finger-experience, and the second being the quality the thumb-experience has as a result of being broader than the finger-experience). Well, these two new qualities must both be qualities of the original quality, namely the broad quality of the thumb-experience, which means that the new qualities must be related too. And yet relating qualities is what causes them to split apart, as we have already learned, so they shall now do so again, and again, and again, showing the notion of qualities in relation to be entirely unintelligible.

Suppose I tell you that the only way to render an idea intelligible—that of a perpetual motion machine, for example—is through an endless account, the complexity of which will soon surpass your intellect, albeit not before you realise the evident pointlessness of continuing to try to understand. Why, that would just be a misleading way of telling you that the idea is entirely unintelligible. You should draw the same conclusion about relations and qualities—they are unintelligible ideas, despite their being the foundation of common understanding.

§

Simply for the sake of thoroughness, let me briefly approach the situation from the side of relations. I'll waste few words on the preposterous idea of relations existing without terms, or of their creating their own terms, even. For the idea that the relation "taller than" might stand on its own two feet without any two-footed men to relate is no better than the idea of its making the men it relates; both are just phrases without meaning.

There can only be relations when there are qualities to relate, then; but now we must ask how this is supposed to work. Clearly, the relation must have some kind of independent nature, otherwise its terms would be indifferent to whether the relation held or not, meaning they were not actually related, and so, as we showed previously, there could not be any qualities at all.[1] But if there is something real and solid to the relation then it is patently unable to do its job. Consider the following: here is the blackness, here is the relation of "darker than", and here is the whiteness, all three as real and solid as you like. So how does "darker than" bond the blackness to the whiteness? "Darker than" will need to be bonded to both blackness and whiteness, otherwise they will fall apart. But then, new bonds to "darker than" will be required—both a bond between blackness and "darker than", and a bond between whiteness and "darker than". But then the bond that holds blackness to "darker than" will also need to be bonded to blackness, as well as to "darker than"; and we can say the same on the side of whiteness, of course. Link after link will be required and yet never will the chain hold. Take relations as something solid and you will never make their ability to relate intelligible; but take them as ghostly and their incapacity in this regard is hardly worth mentioning.

§

All doubt about our conclusion should now be removed from your mind: relational thought, which seeks to understand with terms and relations, can only yield appearance, never truth. And once you realise that, you realise that everyday understanding and science are just practical conveniences—a cloud covering the true reality, as I'm sure Plato and Plotinus already told you. For practical purposes, we need to divide reality up into different parts, we need to regard ourselves as belonging to one unified reality, and we need to avoid contradictions. And yet although we can't do all these things together, we try nonetheless, looking away from the incoherence to get what we want ... human beings are pathetic, really.

Only in metaphysics do we face the incoherence, which is why it is a noble endeavour, a field of courage and intelligence united as one. And facing up to it, realising that we cannot attribute the incoherence to reality itself, leads to the greatest lesson I have to teach you, namely that there is more work to be done: that the Shades want more blood! Only a coward would attribute the incoherence to the human intellect—by condemning human understanding as a flawed product of Darwinian evolution by natural selection, perhaps—for I cannot believe that men have been driven to such conclusions except by the selfish motive of shirking a metaphysical labour perceived as both arduous and frightening.

§

And so ends our lesson. But you needn't rush off, as it happens I've enjoyed this experience. Of course, I've taught you to condemn everything you know as mere appearance, the entirety of space and time (which are relations, of course), and yet I've not told you anything about the reality of our Absolute. That's hardly surprising, all I've done is explain 10 pages of my 621-page book, *Appearance and Reality* — pages 25 to 34, if you'd care to follow it up, the chapter entitled "Relation and Quality". I hope you appreciated my simplification by means of vivid examples that shouldn't really be necessary. It's how I explained it to Eve; much of it might even be word-for-word, there's no way for me to check now, she threw it in the fire. To explain that particular chapter, just because it's so crucial, I tried to make every single sentence effortlessly accessible.

You'll have to read the other 611 pages if you want to know what I think about the true and absolute nature of reality, the reality in which your entire life will be lived, including, of course, the reality of that life itself. Are there other tasks before you that are more pressing? Or perhaps you don't trust me, perhaps you think you could do better? Perhaps you think my efforts obviously in vain? Why would that be? Surely you do not think me insincere? Deluded then, but how so, pray tell?

§

Truth be told, *Appearance and Reality* only reflects how I felt at one stage of my life, one among many, and perhaps that is indicative of my limitations as a metaphysician. But there are some things I have convinced myself of quite enduringly, things about the nature of our Absolute. The universe we live in is one of inner space, a great experience that incorporates everything that has ever been or ever will be experienced, all within a perfect unity. I'll say no more, to talk of such matters without detail and argument would be monstrous, and it's almost time for you to move on.

§

I never expected Eve to exert herself with all those arguments which I dedicated my life to devising, not at all, she was the most vibrant presence I ever encountered and delicate with it, I didn't expect it of her, although I did rather hope that she'd have enough love for me to want to master my especially tailored summary, at least to the extent that she'd come to grasp its basic significance concerning the reality that she most gracefully occupied—more the fool was I. There was once a time when we sat together on a bench looking out to sea, a precious time, and she expressed to me this memorable whimsy: "Perhaps there may come a day when they screw a plaque to this bench saying that Francis and Eve loved to sit here, in love, together." Delightful lady, truly delightful, I'd forgive her anything.

§

The next Shade you are due to meet is a strange woman, all dressed in a bizarre costume of shining chrome and with hair that glows like the sun, albeit of a most piercing green. What she will have to say I've no idea, for our kind do not commune in this place, despite occasionally catching sight of one another. But before you leave I'd thank you to please tell me, and in all honesty: did you really meet with Plato and Plotinus? Certainly I've never caught sight of them, to do even that would be something to treasure. To actually engage them in conversation, however, well, what could possibly be better? I envy you so much, they were the absolute best.

§

That's what I reckon, anyway, and who's going to argue with Bradley?

Encounter 6: Zemina

Zemina (3304–3521) was a philosopher from Homestead, Tau Ceti, in the UH C-Space (the common space of the United Human virtual reality). She engaged in a celebrated debate with Krebons (3276–3396), a philosopher from Earth, Sol, also in the UH C-Space.

§

Since your life isn't a story you don't have to live an interesting one. What greater relief from today's narrative?

§

What's the appeal of writing your memoirs? You tell a story about yourself, knowing strangers will read with it with interest. If lots do that's good, and if strangers still read it when you're dead that's better still. People you know will read it too, you'll push it on those you love, doing them a favour. You can even get your own back on people who crossed you — they read, you win. Perhaps the meaning of life is to turn your life into a story for such a large crowd that it feels natural to join them, believing it's a story yourself. Perhaps the Internet should become billions of autobiographies, one for each of us, with a universal basic income contingent on reading or listening to as many as possible per day. What greater relief from narrative than nihilism?

§

This obsession with "authenticity" started as a philosophical confusion, became a social fad, and is now a real danger. We can no longer simply laugh at those who design their worlds to include, for example, Rheumatoid arthritis, such that their own chosen characters feel physical pain when climbing stairs, despite their sole personal interest, and that of their community, being attached to what is at the top of the stairs — when they, effectively, inflict pain upon themselves to enact a simple content connector. Some of the most popular "authentic" worlds, most notably Simple World (which I have visited), have been steadily increasing their quotient of pain in recent years — and influential philosophers tell us this is a good thing! They say that it is a recapturing of lost "authenticity" which shows we are, as a species, making progress. "The pleasure of sun on skin," says Krebons, "is dissipated by heat rash and insect bites *only in the moment*; but *in the life*, these provide a poignant relish for authentic being which makes pleasure the cherished thing it once was — and can become again." And how is this supposed to indicate progress, when our ancestors suffered the very same rashes and bites? Because we create them, according to Krebons, as a "free and rational choice" made in recognition of our "authentic being".

§

The ancients spoke of, and at one time apparently believed in, the framing of a world called "hell". This world was supposed to be accessed, without science, at the point of permanent death (note the inappropriateness of our terminology to their idea), and within it, crimes committed in the previous framing were supposed to be punished for all eternity with maximum pain. There never was such a framing, but we could easily make one now. Perhaps the progress Krebons envisages might best be achieved with a Hell World, then, one with no exit. After we have all decided, through "free and rational decision", to vacate C-Space in favour of this new home, then the only possible progress left to us will be the realisation that we shouldn't have listened to Krebons!

§

Although the philosophical chatter that echoes around C-Space seems to become more incessant and less focused with every passing year, I am sure many of you will remember when I first made this objection to Krebons, simply because it elicited a compulsory vote, which I won, decisively. And yet the pain quotient in "authentic" worlds continues to increase, without any link to content discernible apart from that which might be inferred in light of the Krebonsian argument. (Most of these worlds are largely, or entirely, bereft of narrative content, of course.) Meanwhile, Krebons and others continue to glamorise "authenticity". And there was me thinking we've been a philosophical people for over a millennium! Why was there no framing implication vote called by our politicians, despite the fact that I and others immediately called for one? Clearly this idea of authenticity is shaking our spirit. It worries me. We need to get to the bottom of it, and I feel I have failed the public by not doing so earlier.

§

Before I became a philosopher and was only as engaged with philosophy as the next human, I visited many worlds, as has been widely reported; this has even been used as a thinly veiled criticism of me by philosophers who have never left C-Space — as if purity of thought is somehow sacrificed by curiosity about what this life has to offer. In any case, it was during this time that I visited Simple World and abided there some months. There was no pain at the time. If you were so minded as to scrape your leg against a sharp rock, for example, there would be no damage and no pain, just as in many other worlds. One of the main attractions of Simple World in those days, in fact, was distaste at the narrative content pain of some of our most popular communal worlds, especially where this is taken to extremes, as in warrior worlds and the like; going to Simple World was seen as a statement of protest by many visitors, as indeed it was by me. There was very little conversation there. The purpose, if you can call it that, was simply to live, in the minimal sense of not dying (which you couldn't anyway) within a beautiful natural environment. When people did try to engage in more than functional conversation, they'd receive complaints such as, "I'm sorry, that's not what I'm here for"; on one occasion I witnessed an argument break out which ended with the rebuke: "Why don't you just go back to C-Space?"

§

My overwhelming experience of Simple World was boredom, pointlessness and loneliness. Many seemed content to sit under a tree all day, doing and saying nothing until it was time to eat or sleep; devotees have lived like that for decades, as is their right. I couldn't see the point. I spent most of my time in philosophical meditation, but my thinking became far more productive when I returned to C-Space; I found that having stable, calm lines on the horizon of my life, lines of mountaintops or trees, made my innermost will itself fall dormant. Simple World was not the last world I visited before becoming a philosopher—I deny it even that credit—but it was one of the last, and I did learn something from the experience, the true significance of which I have only grasped recently. What I lived was not a worthwhile protest against mindless and painful narrative; Simple World is becoming painful too now — and it was always mindless. Nor was it a harmless retreat into simple pleasure to create space for thought, as some like to think. What I witnessed, as I can now see, was the first stirrings of the confused authenticity movement, a movement which demonstrates — more than anything else in our time — that we are in danger of losing our way.

§

The paradigm of "authenticity" is the time before the framing of C-Space. We know exactly what it was like back then, because many of our worlds still use ancient historical content; far too many, as I have argued at length, because fixed content stifles creativity. So given that there is nothing factual or experiential for us to learn from the ancient times before content was framed by science, what is it that our ancestors are supposed to have had, and which the "authenticity" enthusiasts think we have now lost? The physical universe? Krebons has actually made this suggestion, staggering as it is to contemplate — "it's still out there," he has said, somewhat misty-eyed. But the physical universe never framed a human being's life. It is the content our ancestors were obliged to utilise, because they had no choice over the content their experience framed. Reality, for them, was devoid of rationality (as it took them millennia to realise), and people themselves, on the whole, were devoid of philosophy (which is why it took them millennia to realise).

§

Not even the most enthusiastic advocates of "authenticity" have been mad enough to suggest leaving scientific framing, in a foolhardy attempt to reach Krebons' "out there" — as if that would somehow be akin to the ordinary experience of entering a new world. No actual philosopher has suggested this, not to my knowledge, at least, although children do sometimes babble this way. If anyone were to try it, then any delay to the onset of permanent death would obviously not frame the physical universe our ancestors experienced, only the fleeting delusional images of a dying human—a blur of confused C-Space content, most likely. So with the "real thing" generally acknowledged to be out of our reach, thankfully, why would anyone want to recreate a dull, painful reality, devoid of rationality, which people once had to endure because they simply had no choice? What's supposed to be authentic about that? Inner space is vast and outer space is tiny. When the pre-philosophical people became more technologically advanced, they peered into outer space and saw only rock and fire. If anything deserves to be called authentically human, then surely our history has demonstrated, beyond any shadow of a doubt, that it is *choice*; *choice* on the basis of rational deliberation. *Choice* determines the worlds we inhabit, and before it was able to do this, it was at least determining our own natures. Now we can sit under a tree doing nothing all day, *if* that is what we choose from a vast array of options—options limited only by our imaginations. Our ancestors sat under that same tree only because they had so few options. The danger of the "authenticity" discourse is that it tempts us to choose a time before choice, and tickle ourselves senseless with raw sensation into the belief that we have thereby made the right choice. We must instead think and deliberate like modern, philosophical people. Forget authenticity, and think instead of new and radically unfamiliar worlds, where our power of choice will be taken out of its comfort zones, forced to develop. Let us not waste our creativity, let us never stagnate, and certainly, above all else, let us never choose to go back. "Authenticity" is not a good reason for such a choice, and among all that I can imagine, which expands daily, I simply cannot imagine there ever being one.

§

That's what I reckon, anyway, and who's going to argue with Zemina?

§

OK, it's time to ease off again, slacken the pace. We're hunting, for sure, don't ever forget it, but don't let that stifle your creativity—you never know, you might be the first to catch sight of the prey! Don't assume I know anything more than the *kind* of prey—you'll be zoning-in on that too by now.

Endnote

1. If the relation qualified only one of the terms (if "is darker than" qualified black but not white, or *vice versa*), or each separately (if "is darker than" qualified black as a quality darker than some other quality, but none in particular, while separately qualifying white as a quality less dark than some other quality, but none in particular), then it would not relate the two. And if it belonged to them both together then the two terms would merge into one (black is only darker than white if both black and white exist—so if only black existed it would not be darker than white, which begs the question of what exactly black might be in such a case). Even if such merging is possible, the qualities merged would still have to be related, so they would split in two indefinitely in the manner I've been describing. I can't be bothered to explain all this in detail, if you're not following then you should leave metaphysics alone, you don't have what it takes, I'm afraid.

Chapter 3

Destiny and the Fates

Section 1: Oh, the Things That Go On in Inner Space!

People don't like to be persuaded except within the boundaries they've laid down. It's nice to hear from someone thinking along your own lines, but if they're not it can be irritating, and usually the best you can hope for is pleasant outrage or to acquire some new ammo. A socialist might enjoy reading the right-wing press for the "I can't believe it" factor, and what they learn may aid their arguments for socialism, but the chances of a political conversion are negligible at best. It may not be terribly rational, to be sure, but when we encounter views outside our boundaries it's more like assessing the enemy than whether something is true. That's because what you think can be so intimate, personal, defining of who you are, that when somebody tries to change it, it can seem impertinent, an attempt to change you personally, to make you something you're not. Someone with repulsive views isn't allowed to suggest I'm wrong; even if I can't say why I disagree right now, if I investigated I could, and in the meantime, I'll think what I bloody well like. It's different when the new views come from someone already on my wavelength, however. Now I'm receptive, welcoming, I may even cheer them on. And if there's nothing humiliating about being swayed by that particular person (easiest if they're just a name to me), then perhaps I'll let them develop my thoughts a bit—refine and improve them, that's it. Thanks for the help, you've done me a service, now you're dismissed.

§

Everyday life has far too much influence on inner space. It's yours, your ultimate personal possession, so who cares where the ideas come from? If a belief captures your attention, or you feel it should, then nobody's looking ... are we not selfish enough? Once you accept an idea it's yours, it's what you think—we absorb new ideas like power-ups in video games. Going for the respectable view can be sensible, but also lazy or cowardly, and it's only the interpersonal relationships of everyday life which make us want to credit them to prestigious originators. If you say it's what Nietzsche thought, for instance, then although it may be outside a person's boundaries to allow you to persuade them, they probably won't mind being persuaded by Nietzsche; although as soon as you name-drop you run the risk of getting bogged down in a tangential discussion about history. It'll be hard to extract the relationship dynamics of everyday life from public debate—for now that'll have to remain a long-term goal of collective rationality—but it should be easy enough within your own inner space. Once you've recognised the extraneous influence you should be able to eradicate it straight away ... and don't just take my word for it, Nietzsche thought exactly that.

§

A philosopher needs the history of philosophy primarily for the reassurance that others have been there before.

§

We allow shocking amounts of nonsense into our inner spaces. It's like letting idiots and bastards into your home.

§

Someone crosses you then later, in your safe space, you wish they'd drop dead—harmless and invisible to the person you hate, harmful and visible to yourself. We need to work on our inner spaces, everything else is just an outward manifestation.

§

In the end, inner space will be all you've got left.

§

When you get into physical exercise, you improve your mind-body connection—your awareness of your body, its capacities, and your control over it. You can't improve your mind-mind connection, it's already perfect, but you can change what's in your mind by thinking about what you think. Socrates said the unexamined life is not worth living, which is an extreme and questionable sentiment. I'd only say that it's not worth leaving your inner space unexamined, it won't do you any good.

§

If you don't touch your foot *RIGHT NOW* then something terrible is going to happen to you by the end of the day.

Section 2: It's Time to Introduce the Main Characters

It's best not to tempt fate. But why would fate be something you can tempt? What's he abstaining from, I wonder—cream cakes? I know the real answer, of course: he's abstaining from raining down disaster on my life. He abstains so long as I don't push my luck by continuing to bet when I'm on a winning streak. Clearly, he never did like me winning, but he's prepared to put up with it so long as I moderate my success — if I don't then he might just snap and all his good intentions will come to nought. Some tempt him in bizarre ways, such as by putting up umbrellas indoors; he's still nostalgic for the olden days when people were lucky if their roof was keeping the rain out. Fate has never liked things going too well for us. When the going's only moderately good, however, he can usually maintain his abstinence; and it's very nice of him to make the effort, since it shows that he recognises his desire to bring down disaster on us is a vice he needs to curb. He must quite like us. But if life gets too good then Fate just can't stand it anymore, his cravings overwhelm him, and it's entirely our own faults for making the temptation too strong, he's only human.

§

People talk about their brains a lot these days. It's usually tongue-in-cheek ("my brain's malfunctioning" etc.), which is just as well because in everyday life we have as much idea what's going on in our brains as of what's going on in our livers — we do know what's going on in our minds, and that's what we really mean by this silly brain-talk. It's partly a distancing manoeuvre: if my brain's struggling to understand something then it's not really my fault — whereas in reality, my mind is struggling to understand something, my mind is me, so it's entirely my fault. Another reason is that brains, unlike minds, are things you can see, so they're simpler, easier to understand, less philosophical. If people had different coloured brains, and everyone had windows in their foreheads, then racism would flourish as never before.

§

Worrying that you're tempting fate is feeling guilty about your success. It's feeling that you're unworthy, that you'd better get while the gettin's good, otherwise the injustice might be noticed and punished. Fate has a low opinion of me so I mustn't provoke him with successes he doesn't think I deserve—that's your average person's conception of their personal fate. And yet when it comes to the collective, to humanity-as-a-whole, then you suddenly find fate taking on an entirely new character. Now she loves us and will go out of her way to help. Ever since she banged herself into existence, or God did it for her, she's been determining it for the best. Worried about robots taking your job in the next industrial revolution? Nothing could be sillier—don't you know that things always turn out for the best in human history? There might be a shock ahead, the bump in the road you'd expect when a new technology transforms human life, but once we get over it there'll be no more boring work and lots more fun. So we need to develop robots as quickly as possible—in accordance with stringent ethical guidelines, of course, but the priority is to get them out there fast, otherwise our competitors might beat us to it. You don't want to go worrying about the future of humanity, Lady Luck takes care of that kind of impractical nonsense.

§

It makes you wonder what it's like when the personal and collective fates meet:

"None of them deserves more than a little success, anything more drives me crazy. It's not my fault, it's an addiction—I'm addicted to hurting them when they're too happy, I know I shouldn't do it and I'm trying to quit the habit, but it's hard when you've been at it for millennia. You know that all too well, lady, so I don't see why you keep making things better for them, you're just making it harder for me."

"I do it because I absolutely adore the human race! You must understand where I'm coming from, you're always getting soft spots for individual people, even though you don't like to admit it … you old meanie, you! Me, personally, I can't say I care about any damned one of them. I love 'em only *en masse*, considered from a distance, then it's a whole new ball game. As a race they're simply delicious! So have your fun with whomever you like, I couldn't care less, just make sure you let some of them do exceptionally well. Lay off the brilliant and pushy ones, they're what I need for the paradise I've got planned. Or wait until after they've done their bit; people's endgames never matter."

"But they're not even trying to build your kind of paradise anymore, don't you get it? They're not trying to perform feats of excellence, radiate beauty, excel themselves in your 'glorious' ways … all that crap you've always liked. People just want pleasure these days. I know your tastes, so now they've given up on that stuff I don't see why you care anymore. Why carry on improving their lives? You're just making it harder for me and I don't want to hurt them … well, I do and I don't."

"No way am I holding back, buster, everything's got to go great for that race, forever more, end of. You can't stop me, I'm far more inevitable that you are, I'm guided by universal scientific laws. And you've got it all wrong anyway, because it won't turn out like they're expecting. It'll be my kind of glory in the end. Are you really so blind that you've never realised we're the same, you and me? I'm the personal fate of a select band of people, ones who don't worry."

§

"Know thyself" was the first of three Delphic Maxims. The second was "nothing to excess", exemplified by the life of

Socrates and forming the basis of the rules for living advocated by various schools of Greek philosophy. And the third, my own personal favourite, was "certainty brings insanity"—which seems to suggest that an all-knowing god would be completely bonkers.

§

"Know thyself" is out of fashion, more's the pity, because the operative philosophy of our world, materialism, is only comfortable with outer space—it views inner space as a problem at best, at worst an enemy to be eradicated ... like religion. In the pro-public and anti-private intellectual atmosphere which this creates, the only officially mandated way to "know thyself" is to ask others. You could, for instance, pay a psychiatrist to tell you about the scary monsters inside of you, but most people would rather not know, hence the popular humour: keep that psychiatrist away from me, she can see my monsters! It's a funny thing not to want to know about, thyself.

§

Psychiatry hasn't aged well—materialist culture won't endorse it anymore, or only with caveats and no great enthusiasm. The problem is the fundamental one that the monsters live in inner space—the Freudian unconscious is not nearly unconscious enough for materialist metaphysics. These days, if you're really serious about knowing thyself then you need to learn from teams of psychologists testing people *en masse*, finding out about our prejudices, our cognitive biases, how terribly flawed human thinking is. The new maxim: know thyself as a member of the dismal species *Homo sapiens*. Personally, I find that far too general for my everyday purposes, although I do recognise that general insights into how people think have great corporate application.

Section 3: The Umbrella Woman

"If that's right," said the personal to the collective fate, "if we really are the same, then it's not me that's blind, it's you. You lack self-consciousness."

"Oh blimey," said Lady Luck, looking flustered, "I wish I'd never told you now. Just stop thinking about it and get on with your business."

"No," he snapped back, "this is really important. If you stop messing with their inner spaces, I can finally cure my addiction. I see it now, it's the answer I've been looking for."

"What? Let them stagnate? You must be kidding!"

"Well, there's your problem in a nutshell, lady, you pay so little attention to the individuals that you don't know what they're like. Deep down most of them want to make things better. They'll never stagnate as a race, there's drive in their bellies."

"Keep your voice down, will you! If they stop thinking I'm inevitable I'll end up just like you—then you'll have nobody to talk to. Just forget I said it ... look, she's trying out her new umbrella indoors!"

"She is too, what a nerve ... urgh, that makes me SO MAD!!!"

§

Aging is something you can't do anything about, so nobody can blame you. They can blame you for the outer manifestations, such as your skin because you smoke, or your age-inappropriate behaviour, but they can't blame you for your actual age—not rationally, at least, being old or young are indeed popular criticisms. You keepin' up, Sonny/Grandpa?

§

Time passes and there's nothing you can do about that. People don't like powerlessness in the face of aging, so they fight back as best they can, usually by quitting activities they like and taking up ones they dislike. But have you ever noticed how powerlessness suddenly becomes a good thing when we're talking about fatalism and determinism? Make us powerless before reality itself, put the fates in charge, and powerlessness is marvellous—it means you can never be blamed for anything (or credited either—but this part remains in parenthesis). Blamelessness is no consolation when it comes to aging, but it somehow becomes the ultimate consolation when extended to the entire cosmos. Surely feeling powerless can't be bad in one case but good in all of them. To remove the tension, everyday life needs to be unreal—and Lady Luck does hardly notice it, after all.

§

Ever get the feeling you've let someone else's dreams into your inner space? When teenagers get this feeling, they tend to rebel against their parents' dreams. History is full of clever and imaginative people who wouldn't care less about you, they're the intellectual mums and dads you never knew—maybe it's time to cultivate the wisdom of the teenager.

§

To begin cultivating inner space you simply think about what you think—know thyself. Once you've mapped out the terrain you can start to think differently, keeping the good elements, discarding the bad, just as the best cities developed. The oldest buildings might be a bit ramshackle but cling to them, tastefully integrated into new surroundings they'll have charm.

§

You can go about it however you like. I'd rather live in a world of self-aware bastards than one where they end up that way through lack of reflection—the former may be more difficult to deal with, but there'll be a lot less of them.

§

The tramp looks a mess but his inner space is fabulous; the star looks fabulous but her inner space is a mess. Society favours the star, and although we could make an argument for favouring the tramp, an argument is all it could be. Appearance trumps reality by default. We should be grateful to the philosophical traditions of our world for making this look wrong.

§

"Pathetic ... the diamond fell out of the umbrella woman's wedding ring? Big deal, she'll soon get it fixed."

"Give me a break, lady, it wasn't meant to be a severe punishment. That kind of incident's trivial these days and I simply *must* move with the times. It'll freak her out and keep her mind fixed on me, you can be sure of that. They can never fix their minds on you, have you ever noticed that? How could they when you're supposed to be determining everything they think by your physical laws? It's impossible, you ask too much of them."

"Sure they can! Either they don't spot the weirdness, or they shrug it off to focus on my charms. The only ones who ever smell a rat are philosophers, and they're all safely locked away in their own special everyday-life context."

Section 4: Lady Luck Spills the Beans About Determinism

You're thinking right now, there's no denying that, the thoughts happen and you're aware of them. But if everything that happens is determined by physical laws then your thoughts are determined too. The problem with that is thoughts come *from* me, not *to* me, otherwise they're not really thoughts; a "thought" which is outside my control, which just pops into my mind, is really just an idea. Suppose the following comes into my inner space, in that elusive way in which we grasp the significance of sentences without hearing them: "During the coronation I won't put the Charlemagne crown on my own head, I'll put it on Josephine's instead!" That's not something I actually thought because the inner space occurrence happened passively to me, I merely underwent it; only Napoleon could have actively thought something like that. Thought is always active, the action of a self. If determinism is true then nobody thinks, they don't even think that determinism is true.

§

We can't be ordering, commanding, or conjuring our thoughts into existence, because any such ordering would require prior ordering, then the prior ordering would need to be ordered into existence too, so we'd need yet more prior ordering, and so on and so on. And neither can thoughts just happen of their own accord, because if they do then it's not you thinking them—and if you don't even think your own thoughts, you clearly don't exist. But I bet you do exist, I definitely do. Thoughts and selves go together, like determinism and thoughtlessness.

§

What's the difference between determinism and fatalism? Not an awful lot, one's supposed to be scientific.

"See what you've started now?" chided Lady Luck. "It's not good for them to start questioning determinism and fatalism, we need them to question their freedom and inner space, those are the ideas that threaten our power. My people never question fatalism, and these days they're getting quite fond of determinism too—you're going to lead your people astray."

"What should I tell them about the difference between determinism and fatalism?"

"Tell them determinism has been proved by science. Every state of the cosmos transitions to the next in accordance with unbreakable physical laws. Tell them people have known that since the scientific revolution of the 17th century, it's common knowledge now and questioning it is a sign of ignorance."

"I thought physical science wasn't deterministic anymore, didn't all that change in the 1920s—quantum indeterminacy and all that?"

"No, that must be irrelevant ... look, I don't know, just go chat with some philosophers if you want, they'll be able to defend determinism no matter where the science is currently at. Fatalism is the only important truth anyway, it's what allows us to decide what happens to people. Determinism looks like fatalism because the physical laws always produce the results I want; well, that's what they think anyway. I don't know if determinism is true or not, to be completely honest—how can it be when we're deciding the outcomes? Still, I suppose we couldn't sustain the beautiful old idea of gods and stars governing men's fortunes; it was closer to the truth, but people must have their dose of science these days. Materialism isn't so bad, it lets us hide in their inner spaces without being questioned, officially we don't even exist anymore, only hippies with dreamcatchers pay us tribute."

§

Fate looked fascinated, and although Lady Luck wasn't sure he was following all the nuances, she decided to go on anyway.

"Huh, I didn't know you were so interested in ... stuff ... I won't say the 'p' word, that bastard might overhear us then she'd crash the party, you know how she loves to: 'I've been invoked!!!' [said in sarcastically haughty fashion]. But if you promise to keep your voice down, I'll tell you how I know determinism isn't true, why it just can't be."

"It came as quite a shock to me when I found out, because ever since the scientific revolution of the 17th century I've been encouraged to think of myself as backed up by the deterministic laws of physics; as pretty much the same thing as them, really. It was a new image for me at the time, thoroughly up to date—not everyone's got the wherewithal to remake themselves like that, it's the reason for my longevity. Still, it took some getting used to. One minute you think you're a mystical lady-spirit playing with human lives as if they were chessmen, the next you're the inevitable temporal unfolding of natural forces. Well, I never really gave up on the first self-image, it's so much more *me*, but I did throw myself into the 'unfolding of nature' thing. Why not? If you can't beat 'em, join 'em! But it doesn't work, I found that out from a physicist called William Newcomb ... a physicist, eh, you'd have thought it'd be a ... nope, mustn't say the word."[1]

§

"Newcomb imagined me having perfect knowledge of the physical universe and using it to predict a person's decision. This person—let's call her Heather—is given two choices, and

I get to predict which choice she's going to make—which is easy enough when you know everything about the physically determined universe, right? According to my new image, all that vast knowledge was only supposed to be my own self-awareness anyway ... know thyself and all that, no biggie. So, knowing how the bits and pieces of Heather's brain change as she's making her choice, I can work out the effect this'll have on how she'll move her mouth and tongue (i.e., what she'll say when she announces her choice), so I can predict her decision every time, easy-peasy."

"Heather's choice is about whether she wants the money in two boxes (B1 and B2) or just one (B2). B1 always contains $1000 but what B2 contains depends on my prediction. If I predict she's going to choose to have box B2 only, then I'll reward her by putting $1,000,000 in it. But if I predict she's going to be greedy by choosing both boxes, then I won't put any money in box B2, she'll just get the $1000 from box B1."

"The fun starts once I've made my prediction, and so either put the million in B2 or not, depending on what the prediction was. Once that's done, Heather has five minutes to choose whether she wants both boxes or only one. Well, you can imagine the humming and harring that one causes! Her first reaction is always going to be that she should choose box B2 only, that's just common sense. She knows everything I've told you, the whole shebang, so she figures that she'd better choose B2 only to get the million. She thinks that if she chooses both boxes, then I'll have predicted she would so she won't get the million."

"But then, if she's got an ounce of sense, the next thing that's going to occur to her is: 'Hang on a cotton-picking minute, Lady Luck's *already* made the prediction, the prediction is a *past event*! Lady Luck either put the million in the box or she didn't, that's already happened and nothing can change it now. So I might as well choose both boxes, because if the million's already in B2 it'll be there whatever I choose now; I know the extra thousand from B1 isn't much, but there's no risk involved, so I might as well have it if I can. My decision can't change what she's already done, so ... I'll have both boxes, please. Final answer.'"

"Now you might think this is a kind of paradox—that's how Newcomb saw it—since her motive for choosing only the one box seems just as strong as her motive for choosing both. What I've come to realise, however, is that if Heather is even contemplating the choice of both boxes, then she can't really believe my predictions are always correct. Just thinking about choosing both boxes, once she fully understands the situation, can only mean that she doesn't trust me. And it makes perfect sense for her to choose both if she doesn't trust me, of course, since if she goes for only box B2 then she might end up with nothing—in the scenario where I falsely predicted that she'd choose both boxes and so didn't put any money in B2."

"So choosing both boxes only makes sense if you don't trust me; or rather, if you don't think determinism is true—that amounts to the same thing for Heather, as for most of my people these days, because they think I'm the inevitable flow of physical reality, or backed up by it, or whatever. But if Heather does trust me, then she'll choose only one box, since she'll expect me to have known she'd make that choice, and so she'd also expect me to have already put the million in the box."

"To sum up, then, if Heather trusts me she should choose one box, but if she doesn't she should choose both. Since she's supposed to trust me, she ought to choose one box."

"Well, I'd been thinking this over for some time when I had the bright idea of trying it out experimentally, just to be sure. There was a businesswoman called Heather who I was working with at the time—made billions with an Internet company, nasty piece of work, told me she was trying to change the future of friendship. Well, I assured her it was her fate to succeed, that the suffering she caused would be outweighed in the long run, that she should ignore all risks ... you know, the usual stuff I whisper in their inner spaces. Anyway, one night I took her to a dreamworld to try my experiment. When we got to the bit where she had five minutes to decide, what I discovered astonished me. It turned out she wasn't even capable of trusting me!"

"That's what I was telling you earlier."

"Shut up a minute, will you, we're just getting to the good bit. You see, Heather was a very clever woman, so she understood the scenario well enough to understand that at the end of the day, trusting me just doesn't make sense. This is how she explained it—she said it so nicely I'll repeat her exact words."

"'If I'm to trust that you always get the predictions right,' said Heather, as the clock ticked away, 'then I have a choice between B2 only to get the million dollars, or B1 and B2 to get only a thousand dollars. The choice I make right now is going to decide how much money I get, because whatever that choice is, it'll be the choice you predicted. But that's impossible, I can't make a choice about something which happened in the past. So, I'm afraid I simply can't trust you. It's paradoxical to experience freedom while believing in determinism, and since I can't renounce the experience of freedom—I can't deny that I currently have a choice to make, as a plain matter of fact I'm here and I do—so you leave me with no alternative except to renounce determinism.'"

"She explained that well, don't you think?" said Lady Luck to Fate. "I saw straight away that she was right, so I had to admit to myself that I wasn't really an all-knowing, deterministically unfolding natural world—or, as the humans like to think of it, a deterministic physical reality which allows *them* (!) to *in principle* (!) predict what's coming next. It was a bit deflating, I'll admit, but it made a lot of sense, since I certainly didn't always get things right when I was a mysterious lady-spirit—sometimes

I'd tell a military leader he was heading for glory, that his army was invincible, and then ... oops!"

"Are we talking about the same Heather you handed over to me, the Aussie Internet tycoon?"

"The very same, now you know why I dropped her."

"She didn't do very well with me either. She kept walking under ladders, didn't salute magpies, didn't have lucky underpants, so hardly a day passed when I wasn't irritated by her. Before long I snapped and got her to sell up her shares in the company at the worst time possible. Well, even that didn't change her behaviour. She didn't start talking to me more than before, she wasn't begging me for better luck, so I'm afraid I got a little vindictive—I persuaded her to apply for a job as a philosophy lecturer, after that her downfall was assured."

"Aha, I thought I heard somebody mention my name ... I've been invoked!!!" said Philosophy.

"Oh shit, not her," groaned Lady Luck in despair. "I told you not to say the 'p' word, you idiot!"

Section 5: Introducing Destiny and Philosophy

Destiny is stuck on a planet with no idea why, all alone, clutching a gun since 1945. Destiny has almost pulled the trigger by mistake a few times, but Destiny has never been suicidal, always optimistic. It's just that Destiny doesn't know how to put the gun down. Destiny struggles to think, you see; flooded with experiences of heaven and hell, Destiny may never be able to hold a thought. Destiny gets sick and nobody helps. Imaginary friends offer reassurance, but their advice is conflicting; Destiny knows that without them it's all pointless, but heaven, the real kind, is there nonetheless. Destiny has complete responsibility for maintaining Destiny's home, but Destiny only does the bare minimum and it's rapidly deteriorating—she's always distracted because heaven and hell are so compelling.

§

"You look frightful, as always," mocked Lady Luck. She had a point, Philosophy looked exactly like the Ghost of Christmas Yet to Come in Charles Dickens's *A Christmas Carol*. "And no, we don't want to talk to you," she added quickly, before Philosophy could utter a word. With that, Lady Luck grabbed Fate's hand and pulled him high up into the sky, leaving Philosophy looking deflated.

§

After a short flight they landed in the Himalayas.

"I like to come here to get a wider perspective on people," said Lady Luck. "None of these mountains is high enough, though, so help me to stack some up." Lady Luck and Fate then proceeded to tear up mountains and stack them on top of each other until they'd built a new mountain ten times the height of Everest.

"Come on, let's climb to the top!" she said, with girlish enthusiasm. From the top of the giant mountain, they could see all the people in the world, all at once.

"Look at them busying themselves about, like bees in a hive. They go indoors, they go outdoors, they make noises to each other, they touch each other, they get in vehicles which they've built so they can go further distances before they carry on doing the same kinds of things all over again. It seems pointless, doesn't it? But it's not. They're making life meaningful by moving towards the ultimate goal—and I'm the one that spurs them on so they don't waste their time; they'll never know the meaning of life, but they believe in it, in their heart of hearts. That frightful Philosophy must never be allowed to ruin that yummy feeling of blind reassurance for my delicious race."

"This isn't that interesting to me," said Fate, looking a little disappointed after the exertion of climbing such an enormous mountain. "All I can see is outer space, I'm more of an inner space man."

"Of course you are," said Lady Luck, with a seductive little smile, "and that's why I brought *these* along." She handed him a virtual reality headset, which bore the trademark "Metaphysics", then she put one on herself. Now the world of people appeared on an interactive map, which allowed the fates to select a human being, zoom in on it, then eavesdrop on its inner space—Fate chose the umbrella woman.

"Surely it couldn't have had anything to do with putting the umbrella up," thought the woman, "that's an old wives' tale. I used to avoid doing that sort of thing when I was a girl because my dad was so superstitious, but I grew out of it, you've got to be rational, you can't let that stuff take over your life. But it was so immediate! I pressed the button to open the umbrella and the diamond fell out of my wedding ring that very moment—it seemed for all the world like my opening the umbrella was what broke the ring. Then Derek calls—before I can tell him about the ring he says he won't be coming home tonight … I've had my suspicions before but now I'm sure of it: he's having an affair. It can't be anything to do with the umbrella, what a stupid thing to think, I was so happy when I bought it this morning … but you know what, I'll never open one indoors ever again, not for the rest of my life, just in case."

"Ah, bless her!" said Fate, quite sincerely.

§

"Has it ever occurred to you," asked Lady Luck, "that the ones that let you into their inner spaces are quite selfish? I mean, they're always thinking about their own personal fate, trying to appease you so things don't go wrong for them. They're hardly thinking about Destiny, now are they? It's selfish."

"No, I don't agree," replied Fate, "they're thinking about themselves, to be sure, but they're also thinking about the people they care about. She cares about her husband Derek, she doesn't want me to get angry with him, or with her children, or with her friends. There's no point in ordinary people like her thinking about Destiny, she can't do anything about it."

"Well, I certainly agree with you about that," said Lady Luck, "those people are useless, that's why I ignore them. I'm only interested in the individuals who drive things forwards, and I'm only interested *while* they're driving things forward—even then I don't care about them, only the direction of travel."

"So, what's the destination? Tell me the purpose of human existence, I've often wondered ..."

"Well, it's a bit hard to put into words ... that doesn't mean I don't know, don't go thinking that for a second! Let me see, how should I put it ... I know. It's aesthetic, humans are destined to make reality beautiful. It already is in places, but there are ugly bits too, so it needs to be fixed up. Think of them as a bit like decorators, but decorators who only use the highest, most cosmically glorious artworks. It's going to take them ages, even the galaxy which humans are currently confined to is massive. But we'll get there, I'll make sure of that."

"I didn't think you were able to make sure of it, you were just telling me that you're not the deterministic unfolding of physical reality."

"Well yes, I'm just a lady-spirit if truth be told, but my decisions still count for infinitely more than that of the average human."

"What sort of 'beautiful' are we talking?"

"You know the ancient Greek sculptor, Phidias, the one who did the Elgin Marbles? Well, his work's a great example of the kind of beauty I've got in mind; it still hasn't been bettered, which is disappointing after two and a half thousand years, but they will come up with something better eventually, I'm working on it night and day, don't you worry. The progress I make is always a bit erratic because I can't explain to them what we're aiming for; these days they tend to think they're trying to make everyone happy, or trying to lead humans away from earth to colonize the galaxy, or something like that ... they don't think about it an awful lot, to be honest, they're more concerned with money, fame, fun, family, that kind of thing. But still, while the ones I work with are driving the race forward, you can always be sure I'll be there, steering them to my beautiful future."

"Anyway, back to Phidias," she went on. "He thought he was working for the gods, of course, but despite that he did spend a surprising amount of time envisaging beautiful futures—so I invested a lot of time and energy in him. I lost interest while he was working on his Athena Parthenos statue (which looked a little bit like me, I thought). It wasn't built to last because he made it from cypress wood, gold and ivory, but he was so pleased with the results that he resolved to specialise in those materials from then on, vowing never to use marble again—so I gave up on him, I have to think of posterity."

"Since I'd decided to abandon him, I fed Phidias feelings of vanity, which inspired him to include portraits of himself and his political buddy Pericles on the Athena-statue's shield. Well, naturally enough he was accused of impiety and sentenced to execution. And do you know what was running through his inner space while he was on death row? Nothing to do with beautiful destinies anymore, it was all stuff about whether he'd offered enough sacrifices, whether his family's sacrifices might still save him, whether he could get hold of some salt to sprinkle over the entrance to his cell to keep away evil spirits. Yep, the same kind of selfish rubbish you're always listening to. That's why I don't like the individuals, they always let you down in the end, even Phidias."

"You should have handed him over to me," said Fate, "I'd have made him feel better."

Section 6: Love Interrupted

"It's funny," said Fate, as he and Lady Luck climbed down the mountain together, "I've known you for so long, and yet it's only today that I've started to feel that I understand you." Once they were down, they worked together to restore the Himalayas—a labour of love which ignited their passions for each other.

"Let's go somewhere nice," said Lady Luck, "a luxurious superyacht, you can't beat 'em! I know a particularly nice one, the owner hardly uses it, he's got ten others he likes better ... he's got terrible taste."

When they arrived on the deck of the yacht, Lady Luck opened a bottle of Cristal and they reclined on deckchairs.

"I find you irresistible," said Fate, as he emptied the bottle, "I don't care about Destiny, nobody knows about Destiny, and it's none of my business either ... probably the humans are doomed, who knows? But you, you've always got something new and fresh for me, something to change my future and the future of the people I care about. It's your endless novelty I love most, you're so restless and exciting! And although I never understand the hope you offer, I think it shows you care. So let Destiny worry about Destiny's future, I just want you ... the bad things I sometimes say about you, I'm only paying them lip service."

Lady Luck took Fate's hand and led him to the master bedroom, it was the height of luxury. Fate immediately noticed blindfolds hanging from the bedposts, which got him excited; clearly Lady Luck had thought ahead. Then he realised the bed posts were wooden, so he touched one for luck. Fate and Lady

Luck started kissing, then fell gently down onto the luscious silk sheets together. Lady Luck reached for the blindfolds:

"Before we put these on there's something I need to tell you," she whispered. "We're going to make a baby, the next stage in human history: Destiny's future."

Fate smiled, but not for long.

"I've been invoked!!!" said Philosophy, who had suddenly appeared in the corner of the bedroom.

§

"I'm not letting you two make love again," said Philosophy. "I'm going to kill you."

"You what?" said Lady Luck, now sitting bolt upright on the bed and looking concerned. "I didn't think you were like that. Look, I think you've misunderstood us, we're not like you think, let me explain."

"Please do," answered Philosophy.

"OK, let's start with him. You think he leads people astray, but he's got a good point—he's a crystallization of folk wisdom, you might say. Suppose you're gambling and you win big. Well, it's perfectly rational to quit, because if you keep going you might lose it all—don't tempt fate, it's a useful reminder he provides."

"Then there's me, I've got a good point too, and mine's exceptionally important. It makes sense for humans to pursue whatever technological transformations become possible at any given time, for although that's bound to cause problems, there are massive benefits too, and they can deal with the problems as they arise—that way they keep solving problems and moving forward. Life's much better for people than it used to be, I'm sure you'll agree, and that's because of the people I spur on. OK, a lot of them may be driven by greed, or just half-baked, well-meaning, pie-in-the-sky stuff which they foist on other people because they can. But I'm driven by higher ideals, I'm steering them, so I don't see what difference it makes."

"That was a more eloquent defence than I expected," answered Philosophy, speaking from underneath the shadows of her black hood. "I always have to remind myself that you're not a complete idiot."

"Nevertheless," Philosophy went on, "the problem isn't so much with you two as individuals, it's what happens when you get together. Your agendas point in opposite directions. If humans were to follow his advice on the collective level, then they should have stopped with the invention of the wheel—that was a big win, so they shouldn't have pushed their luck. And if humans were to follow your advice on the personal level, then the gambler who wins big ought to carry on gambling until the casino closes, then come back first thing the next morning. Say he started with $100 and now has $1,000,000—he should keep betting, because even if he loses everything, he'll deal with it and keep moving forwards. Should that be their attitude to nuclear proliferation? You two like to think of yourselves as the personal and collective fates, but you're really just the personal fates of different groups of people: the overwhelming majority and the powerful few. You don't make sense together, the balance of power is all wrong, your offspring wouldn't make sense either ... and I won't allow Destiny to go on like that."

§

"Took you long enough to work that out, didn't it?" sighed Lady Luck, with a condemnatory roll of the eyes. "So, your solution is to murder us both, am I understanding you correctly?"

"Murdering fate progresses rationality," answered Philosophy.

"And then you'll replace us in their inner spaces?"

"Exactly."

"Why you, if you don't mind me asking? Although thinking about it ... I suppose it doesn't matter whether you mind or not, you're going to kill us anyway."

"Well," answered Philosophy, "before I answer your question, let's make sure you understood why you've got to go, you seem quite upset about it. It's not personal, it's just that the people have acquired so much technological power that we can't carry on like this, not with you blindly leading them forward through a commercial progression of trial-and-error, it's become too risky. Destiny's been holding a gun since 1945, and there's a never-ending supply of human incidents coming up which might cause her to use it. I actually think you've done really well, considering that you don't think—they're doing better than ever before, by most of my criteria at least ... so long as they haven't already wrecked the planet ..."

"What do you mean in saying I don't think?" snapped Lady Luck, indignantly. "Outrageous, of course I think! I think a lot."

"Oh yes, the meaning of life—a future of cosmic beauty. That's just an abstraction from the superstitious thoughts of all the movers and shakers throughout the ages ... funny the one about beauty would predominate, I was surprised by that myself. Anyway, now I've made it crystal clear why you've got to die, let me continue by explaining why I should be the one to replace you."

"This I've got to hear!" muttered Lady Luck, dismissively.

"Well, if the aim is to replace your influence on Destiny's future with a new influence—which I think it must be, since that's all you two ever achieved—well, in that case I'm the only game in town. I'm easy enough for everyone to think about because I'm so beautifully general. You can't expect the masses to learn the intricacies of economic arguments for different international development plans, or different political agendas that might be placed on basic scientific research, they've got other stuff to get on with. But everyone can take an interest in whether humans should abandon physical reality for virtual realities or not, whether that's a future they want for their descendants. And apart from anything else, the topic of Destiny is so completely and utterly *me*—it's my natural territory and nobody else's, always has been, always will be. Asking why I should replace you two is a bit like asking why GPS should replace maps in cars—I do the same job but I do it better. And as an added bonus, I'm even a bit mystical and spiritual, just like you, so that'll help to smooth over the transition, I'll hit the same kind of spot for the punters."

"So that's why it has to be me, then," said Philosophy. "But there's lots more to be said about this coming transition. Shall I carry on? I'm only going to kill you once I've finished anyway."

"Get on with it, I'm listening," said Lady Luck with a scowl, as she looked over in despair at her lover, who was frantically tapping the bedposts. "You always bore everyone stupid with your long speeches, it's what I've come to expect from you."

Section 7: Philosophy's Prelude to Murder

"Imagine a two-dimensional world of conscious yellow triangles," said Philosophy. "They talk about shapes and colours all day, but they never stop to ask why there's a two-dimensional world of conscious yellow triangles. Don't you think they'd be a little odd? Not because they're yellow triangles, but because they don't ask the big questions."

"Well, what's supposed to be more normal about evolved conscious apes in a three-dimensional world? (Four-dimensional is what Science would probably say, but he'll change his mind about that sooner or later.) The humans are as used to their world as the triangles are to theirs, but normal isn't what's familiar, it's what doesn't require explanation. If the humans suddenly became triangles, all in a flash, then they'd certainly want that transition explained. Well, when humans are born there's no surprising transition, there's something far more radical: the beginning, from nothing, of a self-aware conscious existence. How can so many of them go through their lives without craving an explanation of something as weird as that? It baffles me, it really does, I can't help thinking of it as a kind of dumbness, it seems so primitive."

"I do understand their situation, I'm not condemning them lightly. As they grow up it's perfectly understandable that they'd focus their attention on fitting in—there's lots to get to grips with in everyday human life, they're extremely clever animals who've built incredibly complex societies. But even allowing for all that, it really shouldn't take a new human terribly long to start philosophically questioning their situation. You wouldn't make excuses for the triangles for their lack of philosophical curiosity, so why make excuses for the apes? The situation obviously calls out for an explanation, so they shouldn't be able to resist asking me."

"Now this is where some people get confused, thinking they don't have to talk to me because they can talk to Science instead. He encourages it, he's always trying to get in on my act, but he hasn't got the knack for it, poor darling—he tries, but it all comes out as gobbledegook and he doesn't even realise. The best tactic he's come up with is to conflate philosophical with scientific questions; not that he realises that's what he's doing. So, when they go to him with their philosophical questions, he tells them they evolved from apes, that life on Earth probably began in a chance chemical reaction, and that the universe expanded from a Big Bang which occurred billions of years ago. He knows best about these matters, of course he does, but he does change his mind a lot. Still, there's no getting away from the fact that what he's telling them simply isn't relevant."

"Don't get me wrong, I love Science—we were lovers once, did you know that? It was a very passionate relationship, but he became hard to live with—if I ever disagreed with him he'd call me arrogant, and when I tried playing out his materialist fantasies by being totally submissive, he didn't appreciate it at all, if anything it just made him even more contemptuous of me. It started to seem as if I couldn't do anything right anymore. Eventually he left me, and he's said so many hurtful things since ... but I still want him back, we've so many common interests. Just think what we could do together in these advanced times, if only he'd learn to respect boundaries."

"Anyway, our estrangement is very confusing for the humans, so they often end up talking to him when they ought to be talking to me—the results are horrible, it deadens their inner space. Imagine the yellow conscious triangles trying to make philosophical sense of their situation by saying that they evolved from lines, that life on their planet began with a chance geometrical happening, and that billions of years ago there was only a dot."

"What's your point?" asked Lady Luck, interrupting impatiently. "I see what you're saying, basically that everyone should be interested in you, and since they're not you think they're dumb. Well maybe so—personally I think they show good sense by ignoring a bore. But even if they should pay you more attention, that doesn't give you any right to replace us."

"My point," said Philosophy didactically, "is that when I replace you, it'll be the natural next step in the development of collective human rationality. They should always have been thinking about me, I'm a natural interest for all of them, but it's understandable they haven't, that only a tiny elite have. However, things have changed now, thanks to Science. He's made it much easier for everyone to get involved, thanks to his money-making and time-saving devices, and he's also gone and made it far too dangerous for them to leave Destiny's future to you two anymore. We need Destiny to start thinking for Destiny's self, and that means they'll all have to start thinking about me; as much as they can manage, at least. Now that Destiny is developing the technological power to change the future of human life in so many radical ways—virtual reality, augmented reality, robots, cyborgs, eugenics, space exploration—Destiny's going to have to learn how to make a rational and democratic decision about which of those futures Destiny wants, or which ones to combine, or whatever—the important thing is that she needs to want some particular kind of future or another, if only on balance. That means I'll have to wake Destiny up and bring about the next stage of their intellectual development, the one which I'd like to call 'The Philosophical Awakening'."

"You've lost it," said Lady Luck, with a wave of the hand.

"No, *you* have," said Philosophy, her outstretched arms now pointed directly at the fates. From the depths of the shadows underneath her long hanging sleeves, there came a dusty brown cloud of atomized ancient papyrus, infused with the philosophical wisdom of the ages. The cloud engulfed the fates in their bed and their death throes were terrible to behold. Philosophy laughed as they died.

"Reason is hard," she said. "If I'm right and you disagree, then you have to be wrong."

§

Destiny woke up the moment the fates died, they'd become a person with an inner space. Philosophy was inside that inner space, which was the collective rationality of humankind. They dropped the gun as soon as it was safe to do so.

"Never again," they said, "will my future be determined by the machinations of the fates. Never again will I stumble on blindly, moving only when overwhelmed by urges, or when forced to react to the consequences of the last urge before the next one grips me. Never again will I, Destiny, have no plan for Destiny's future. Now that Philosophy has entered the inner spaces of the people, now they have evolved into a philosophical people, now I myself have become a person. Finally, I'm able to hold a thought."

§

Stories are a good way of getting across thoughts. They're a form of presentation, one among many, not a substitute for thinking. Thoughts not stories or both together.

§

Wolves go their own way, why pretend otherwise? It's a loose and playful chase; but menacing. If you're reading philosophy as a sacred text then it'll be an old text, for no one lets their thoughts be orchestrated unless the composer is long dead.

Endnote

1. R. Nozick, "Newcomb's Problem and Two Principles of Choice", in N. Rescher (ed.) *Essays in Honor of Carl G. Hempel*, Dordrecht, Netherlands: Springer 1969.

Chapter 4

The First Thinker of the Meaning of Life

Section 1: Destiny Awakens

Destiny had never been awake before so they were very disorientated. Destiny tried to make sense of it all.

"I was having horrible nightmares alternating with beautiful dreams, just as I always have, when it started to become more focused," they thought to themselves, in an impossible inner space which will always have to be approximated as the consensus, or as what *should* be the consensus, within the real inner spaces.

"I wasn't focusing on the meaning of life because there isn't one—there's no higher purpose I'm moving towards, I'm just here with nothing to do. No, that wasn't it, but it was similar. It was the idea of individual people living meaningful lives—having meaning in their lives, you might say. I started to think that this kind of meaning could usefully be thought of as: having purposes your thought can rest secure with."

"Then the visions of their future began. I saw them beginning to leave outer space, their youth glued to devices. Before long they'd arrived at home-made realities—they'd always built houses, now they built worlds. Why did they do it? I guess because they liked it and they could. Or maybe they were drawn in by the ultimate nature of reality, who knows? Anyway, these virtual worlds turned out to be places where it was much harder to rest secure with purposes, so unless somebody could help them, they were at grave risk of either losing their feelings of meaning, losing their sanity, or both. My dream became a worry I couldn't escape."

"Well, I've no idea how long I was trapped there, worrying in my dream, but it all came to a very abrupt halt when a terrifying apparition appeared, the hood of its black cloak framing a shadowy, faceless void. Now I knew only terror, although thankfully it didn't last long. She pulled back the hood to reveal her face and her beauty woke me up; oddly enough I can't remember the colour of her hair, skin or eyes, it was a universal feminine beauty."

"Huh," they said to themselves, speaking aloud for the first time ever, "so that's how I woke up ... interesting! Right, what am I going to do now? I'll start by assessing their situation, wherever they've haphazardly arrived will have to be my starting point."

§

Inner space is all we care about. You only want an expensive sports car because you think it'll make you feel good, you wouldn't want it otherwise. Name anything people care about and you'll find the attendant experiences are the real concern. You don't want your heart to stop beating because you don't want your experiences to end; you don't want your face to get old and wrinkly because it'll affect how you feel about yourself; you want to feel true love; you want to be comfortable; you want to get high; you don't want innocent people to suffer; you don't want animals to suffer. It's all about experience, that's all we really care about, we only care about other things for their link to experience.

§

What gets called "idealist" metaphysics is a mixed bag, but the kind I'm talking about claims we live in an experiential reality — that experience is what ultimately exists and that everything else is just a consequence of our models for understanding experience, such that we model a certain stable and recurrent pattern of experience as a thing called a "tree", for example. According to idealism, then, the ultimate reality is experience ... which just so happens to be the only reality people care about! That makes idealism an extremely attractive proposition—it's an understanding of reality which vindicates our concern for experience by equating it with a concern for what's ultimately real; that makes the human mind sound rather noble, I'd say. Of course, the fact that idealism has this attraction doesn't make it true—it's only by evaluating arguments that we can determine whether to endorse a metaphysical vision.[1] Nevertheless, assuming that the arguments against idealism aren't definitive— which is safe to assume since they hardly exist—then it ought to come as something of a surprise that such a magnificent vision should have fallen into disrepute. But it has, there simply aren't many idealists around anymore, and people who don't understand say it's nuts. We're a very select bunch for the time being, but it's only due to a temporary lack of education—why not join us?

§

I don't think the current unpopularity is anything to do with idealism, *per se*, because although there are a couple of well-known objections—one about the solidity of physical objects, and the other about solipsism, both terrible[2]—I think that when people voice these objections they're usually just paying them lip service. I think the real reason idealism is unpopular is the materialism/atheism association, millennia in the making and materialism's strongest persuader. The association makes people think that if you're an atheist then you have to be a materialist (you don't—ask Schopenhauer[3]), so they endorse materialism on false pretences, then proceed to conflate it with science. Once the conflation hits in they start to think they'd better dismiss all metaphysics, such as idealism, on the grounds that it's anti-scientific. They don't notice they've already accepted the metaphysics of materialism — they probably don't know what "metaphysics" means and they're too busy thinking about atheism anyway.

§

Imagine if your average office worker, care worker, farmer, fisherman, shopkeeper, vet, taxi driver, plumber, biologist, waste collector or builder, was very likely to be a metaphysical idealist. Pick anyone off the street and that'd probably be their metaphysical conviction, all the world over. That's the kind of situation which might result from what Philosophy likes to call "The Philosophical Awakening". It'd be a situation where idealism became the standard view because the average bod gave it some thought and found they agreed. What would that world be like? People might care more about each other's feelings, given that they think of them as the ultimate reality. Political management of the world might be more squarely directed at the betterment of human and animal experience, as well as the development of human rational and creative thought. People would cultivate their own inner spaces as a matter of course, and the number of nasty, selfish and cruel people would drop dramatically (assuming that most of this behaviour results from lack of reflection and self-awareness). Our conception of reality would be futuristic.

§

Materialism's outer space manner of imagining our future is so boring. We live on other planets and mingle with robots and aliens, but we're still basically the same — we're still thinking the same kind of things, dealing with the same kind of issues. All that's really changed is we've relocated to more exotic settings and built ourselves some impressive new toys. "Really," I think to myself, "is that the best you can do?" An idealist vision of the future is much more exciting because it offers all the same intergalactic thrills, but in the company of people who think differently from us. They're not only more scientifically advanced, they're more philosophically advanced too, and the latter advancement has taken place right across their populace. Since they're more psychologically advanced, the issues their everyday lives revolve around will sometimes be unfamiliar. After all, a world where it's normal for people of all social and educational backgrounds to be metaphysical idealists is a world where thinking has moved on a LOT—it's hard to even take the idea seriously right now, so if we're ever going to become the idealists in outer space, then we'll need to change a LOT. That said, if the process does somehow get underway—perhaps in reaction to a particularly unpopular new technology—then it might progress very rapidly, given that it's bound to transpire via a technology of instant global communication.

§

Imagine if the spaceship pilot was an idealist. It probably wouldn't affect her flying, but she might enjoy it more, and she'd definitely be more interesting to talk to.

Section 2: Imagination

Weird is popular. Weird can be good because it's surprising, out of the ordinary, it captures the attention. The weird shines out in an ocean of blandness and we show our daring by liking it. Some like to imagine there's more of it than there really is, through occult beliefs and the like. But the little beacons of weirdness that occasionally pop up to invigorate everyday life, actual or imagined, pale into insignificance against the whole. Nothing's more weird than that everyday life exists, as part of the something we call "everything" — and don't just take my word for it, both Wittgenstein and Heidegger said exactly that.[4] Everything whatsoever is the ultimate anomaly, the weirdest thing of all. Only when the ultimate weirdness is taken for granted can the more popular but comparatively bland pockets of weirdness arise.

§

You can avoid having a philosophical view on why we're here and what kind of reality we occupy by dismissing the issues as nonsense. But that's someone else's philosophy — it can only be yours if you think about it and decide you agree. You can't avoid Philosophy by not thinking, she resides in inner space, it'll remind you of her. You can say you don't care but she won't believe you, she won't believe anyone could understand her and not care.

§

All wholesale intellectual opposition to philosophy, all totalizing anti-philosophy, is rooted in misunderstanding or laziness. Fear also comes into it in some cases, but it shouldn't. Ignorance is much scarier, and things that aren't scary often seem so when you're ignorant. Don't be put off by her dress sense — she picked it up from the Stoics in her youth, she means you well and always has.

§

Philosophy and science are very different, despite being our only two approaches to understanding the whole of reality. (Religions can offer cosmic understanding too, but only by having philosophical tenets.) One reason they're so different is that you need imagination for philosophy, but it's not always necessary for science. You'll probably need it if you're a practising scientist, and you're bound to if you're at the top of the game. But a layperson will never need it, they can build up a very sophisticated scientific understanding to deepen their understanding of the world around them simply by reading and absorbing. People who know better than you tell you what you should think, so that's what you start thinking — you do as you're told. Philosophy's nothing like that, you can't get anywhere in philosophy without imagination. You can read about it, just as you can read about science, and in doing so you'll learn that Descartes thought this, Kant thought that, etc. But you can't make even the most basic judgement about whether you agree or not without applying some imagination — so you won't have gained any philosophical understanding, just learned some facts. Imagination is necessary for philosophy because you need to imagine yourself into unfamiliar viewpoints, such as those of Descartes or Kant, to genuinely and rationally decide if you agree. If you do, the unfamiliar viewpoint becomes your new philosophical understanding, and if you don't, it'll be because of the philosophical understanding you already had, thanks to past acts of imagination.

§

If you're not using your imagination in philosophy then you're just paying the ideas lip service, even if you're exceptionally skilled at working out what the ideas entail.

§

Anti-philosophy obstructs philosophical development in two ways. Firstly, it spreads the suspicion that Descartes, Kant and every other philosopher who's ever lived were all just talking nonsense ... I must say, that does seem rather unlikely. Secondly, it encourages people to think there's no reason that they personally should be interested, that philosophy is a niche interest whether legitimate or not. Both provide good excuses to not bother thinking, and that's because anti-philosophy vs. philosophy boils down to unreason vs. reason. Anti-philosophy could only be reasonable for someone who'd thought hard about the nature of philosophy and concluded that there are good reasons (not just excuses) to not bother thinking about philosophical issues. But the nature of philosophy is a marginal philosophical topic—whoever said we have to think about that, rather than exciting topics like the meaning of life or the ultimate nature of reality?

§

Don't bother thinking about whether anti-philosophy has anything going for it—assume it doesn't and use your thinking time more efficiently.

§

Environmental concerns are tinged with guilt and blame. Human mass development is to blame for damaging the environment and we're all guilty for reaping the rewards. Gaia, the primordial Greek deity, has become an intelligent ecosystem that we've irritated by unbalancing, so she's thinking of punishing us. But we were just unlucky. As we were developing, driven by humanitarianism and utopianism, greed and vanity, we had behind us a mystical, religious vision of our place within reality. In an environment that had always threatened us, where we'd struggled to find safety with the help of our gods, you'd never imagine puny-us damaging mighty-it. We also lacked the relevant information. We didn't know burning fossil fuels would damage our environment—smoke might have had all kinds of positive effects for the flora and fauna. There'll be plenty of guilt and blame to apportion as we go forward, but Destiny innocently stumbled into the situation, as always hitherto.

§

The big game hunters of yesteryear were like children: "Just pull the trigger and the terrifying lion drops dead ... awesome!" The idea that they were brave was still sustainable, since the journey to the hunt involved hardship and danger, and fear of encountering nature's most dangerous beasts endured. Now that consciousness of nature as a threat to humans has been replaced by consciousness of humans as a threat to nature, their counterparts of today are evil.

§

Burning fossil fuels might have been great for the environment, for all we knew at the beginning of the industrial revolution. Imaging how things might be right now, for all we know, helps us decide which possibilities are most promising to investigate. Imagining futures which we might be able to bring about, for all we know, allows us to choose one to aim for. Directed at unreality, imagination is our greatest entertainment; directed at reality, it's a powerful resource for discovery and change.

§

Imagination can inspire thought and action, but also produce pain and disappointment, as when people imagine futures for themselves which, given the facts, are very unlikely to transpire. Get real or get hurt—a gentleman of *his* exalted standing would never marry a girl like *you*! This may go some way to explaining why suspicion of imagination is typically found in combination with preference for facts; perhaps they first came together through kind intentions and have since co-evolved. Without imagination, however, our reasoning is trapped in everyday life, using what happened before and what seems likely to happen next to decide what's to be done; and desire and habit will often conspire to make reason all but unnecessary. If we could think of imagination as a basic good, an end in itself, we might become more concerned to develop it. The more we practised, the more skill we'd attain, then the downsides would become easier to avoid. Children are expected to have vivid imaginations, but adults are not, and the one area of life where adult imagination looms large, the arts, is regarded, at least by default, as entertainment. Imagination needs to grow up, at first by rebelling.

§

We'll need the wisdom of the teenager to rebel against materialism's inconsistent but powerful anti-philosophy — inconsistent because materialism is itself a kind of philosophy, but powerful because materialism seems to be siding with scientific and technological knowledge when it tells you to ignore philosophy. "You should ignore it," says science and technology (it's materialism talking, really), "because it's just like religion and superstition, it's outdated and threatens to hold us back."

That sounds plausible enough, and since philosophy looks like it'd be a bother to get to grips with, it's quite a relief there's no need to try … leave it to nutters and the scientifically ignorant … Well, even if some philosophy is perfectly legitimate it's just not really my thing, I wouldn't be good at it, I'm not particularly interested, to be honest.

§

We'll know our teenage rebellion has succeeded when we hear Philosophy whispering in our ears, just as she did when we were small children. (She'll have done so with you too, even if you've now forgotten.) But now she'll be whispering adult things, and the adult imagination she'll supercharge has unfathomable potential.

§

Sometimes you're up, sometimes you're down. You're more likely to call on reason when you're down since a rational appraisal of the situation might just shake your mood. When you're up you don't need help.

§

The difference between up and down can be understood in terms of imagination. In both you lose control of it, whether because imagination won't work for you—you can't imagine the next good stage even when you realise there's bound to be one, perhaps very soon—or because imagination runs away with itself, caught up in the moment, in rosy futures, or in straightforward fantasies. There are feelings associated with up and down, and reliable physical interventions which allow us, as if by magic, to make the feelings either appear or disappear. Do the right thing, take the right pill, and proper imagination returns to remove the feelings of down, or to boost away with feelings of up. The only mind-body "problem", in the everyday sense of a burst-pipe style "problem", is that our bodies can non-rationally interrupt our lives in inner space in ways we don't like—it'd be better called a body-mind problem. There's no problem when we like the non-rational intervention, of course, such as the alcohol intervention. But when you're hit by a downer that's just as much a problem as a burst pipe.

§

Philosophy is full of "problems", but it's an odd kind of problem that people need to be taught to be troubled by. If a water pipe bursts in your home then you've got a problem, and naturally enough it's going to trouble you. When philosophers are troubled by their problems it may be, and should be, because they're troubled by a gap in their understanding: "unless I can solve this problem it will obstruct my lifelong quest for wisdom, so naturally I'm troubled" ... well, if you're the real deal, like Plato, then that'll be how it strikes you. But you might instead be troubled by not being able to think of something to say about "Problem X" which might be considered original and clever enough to get your article published in that prestigious professional philosophy journal, thereby pleasing your head of department, building your case for promotion ... first things first, you'll obviously send out a post on Facebook saying, "Yay, the journal accepted my article!", it's a problem that you so rarely get to do that when the colleague you hate does it so often — soo annoYING!

§

When philosophical language regains its force ... when we stop just paying it lip service and learn to incorporate it into our most sincere private and public discourses ... when we've woken Destiny and become a philosophical people ... only then will philosophical problems be the problems they seem to be. Their appearance and reality will unite in an unprecedented flourishing of imagination.

Section 3: Here Comes the Man You've Been Waiting For?

Everyday life went on day after day for our prehistoric hunter-gatherer ancestors. During all that time, some of it sat in silence on rocks, or on the dirt, did any of them think about the meaning of life? Did that kind of thought pass through their inner spaces? An outer space equivalent to this kind of question is wondering whether, on all the billions of planets out there, there exist other civilisations. If you start to wonder what it might be like for them, you leave outer space.

§

If they did think about the meaning of life all that time ago then presumably there was a first: the first thinker of the meaning of life!

§

What's required for there to be a fact we're wondering about? It would require that what we mean by "the meaning of life" either does, or does not, correspond sufficiently well to what somebody back then was thinking about. Sufficient correspondence is neither too onerous nor too vague a requirement for many of our thoughts, and lack of correspondence can be even clearer— they'd have had similar thoughts about the weather, but no thoughts about mobile phones, that's obvious enough. The problem is knowing what *we* mean; get a little clearer about that and there's a fact we can speculate about. What counts as sufficient correspondence will always be a judgement-call ... but if what we mean is entirely a product of our recent intellectual history then they didn't think about it, and if it's a concern arising from the human condition then maybe they did.

§

These days there's something people want which they've learned to call "meaning" … probably a variety of things since social reality is messy, but let's work on the assumption that there's a core factor. People want their lives to be meaningful and some people worry about meaninglessness. Religious leaders promise people meaning as a key perk of membership, saying atheists can't have it.[5] Angry people berate the meaninglessness of human life, sad people bemoan it, or just their own. This terminology, "meaning of life", first becomes conspicuous in the last decades of the 18th century, as does "nihilism" — the French Revolution had recently made God's higher purposes seem a lot more fragile than they had previously. Since then, the "meaning of life" (binding on all people), and its more secular, less grandiose descendent, "meaning in life" (accrued individually by each person depending on how they live), have proved incredibly popular. They seem to encapsulate something people want, but what?

§

Purpose.

§

But not just any purpose — a slave has a purpose for the slave owner, and nobody wants that kind. The problem can't just be that the slave didn't choose because religious people are particularly secure in the meaning of their lives and they don't think they chose, they think their purpose was bestowed by a higher power. So, let's just say it must be a purpose you endorse. And to endorse it, you must be aware of it; if not of its specific nature, then at least that there is one.

§

Having purposes that you endorse feels a certain way, that's why people care about meaning — inner space is all we care about. If you lose the feeling then you'll start thinking about it, and you may discover that you don't endorse your purposes anymore — that continuing to pursue them seems futile, or that they no longer seem to be worthwhile purposes. If that happens, then thinking about life's meaning has provided you with an explanation of why you're feeling down.

§

You get up in the morning and know exactly what you need to do today. The prospect of success beckons, and to raise questions about your purposes would seem like a silly game. When you're in that situation — busy with unquestioned goals, caught up in the thick of life — then you won't be craving meaning.

§

Feeling your life has purposes you endorse doesn't require you to notice, of course. You'll usually only notice retrospectively, once the feeling has gone — just as you don't usually notice the sound of a fridge, not until it stops.

§

You want the reassuring feeling of meaning, but it has to be the real deal. Suppose you once thought your charitable work was helping people, but later discovered that it was making matters worse. You'll now look back on the feeling of purpose you once possessed and condemn it. You'll think you shouldn't have endorsed those purposes, you weren't really living a meaningful life—it seemed as if you were, but you weren't.

§

You can't have the feeling unless you presuppose it isn't illusory. But presupposing it isn't illusory doesn't mean you notice it, let alone think about it. If you're thinking about it—about whether you should feel that way, whether the purposes you endorse are worthwhile—then the feeling is under threat. If you decide you shouldn't endorse your purposes then you might stop doing so, thereby extinguishing the "everything's fine" feeling. So, thinking about the meaning of your life is risky, it might put you on a downer; it'd be good if there was a solid reason why you shouldn't think about it, it'd save you the bother too.

§

Should we conclude that the hapless charity worker should be grateful they didn't once know what they know now? If they had then their lives wouldn't have felt meaningful—and isn't it better for life to feel meaningful under false pretences, than for it to feel meaningless? Perhaps philosophers should stop talking about meaning, they're jeopardising a feeling we rely on—an efficient feeling, one which helps us to get things done, it can be a mistake to overthink things, just get on with it.

§

You're more likely to call on rationality when you're down than up, since a rational appraisal of the situation might just shake your mood. But should you actively refrain from calling on it when you're up—because it might bring you down? Should you never call on it, just in case, thereby sparing yourself a lot of bother?

§

It'd be fascinating to be able to put a real name to a prehistoric person—the name they'd have actually answered to—but we can't ... so just imagine a man who's getting on in his years for those times, I won't call him anything. As a result of some bitter argument he's been expelled from the group—he knows he'll never be allowed back, he knows he'd never be able to join another group. But he's very experienced, knows how to survive on his own. After a while he gets into a routine for keeping himself safe and fed, and it starts getting easier; the recriminations and reconstructions start to fade. As the days roll on there's plenty of time to think. Does he want meaning, the kind he's lost? Might his desire to keep going drain away? (Other animals can be observed to give up.) Since he's the amazing kind of animal that can rationalise, might he start questioning the purpose of keeping going? (Humans have an amazing inner space.) If he started questioning the purpose of his current labours, might he then start questioning his previous life in the same kind of way, wondering whether his past labours for the tribe were any more worthwhile than his current solitary ones—maybe it was pointless back then, too. If he reached this final stage, then I'd say we have our first thinker of the meaning of life.

Section 4: The Wittgenstein/Gray Solution

The problem of life's meaning is solved when it doesn't seem like a problem to you anymore—that's how Wittgenstein saw it.[6] John Gray's position is essentially the same, but with a slightly different spin and more detail, so I'll discuss him too.[7]

§

If the problem is wanting to get back a feeling which you've lost, and it doesn't matter how this is achieved, then there's no need to learn anything in the process. All you want is not to be troubled by feelings of meaninglessness, which is just like when you don't want to be troubled by a burst pipe—if you call the plumber you're not hoping to learn something about plumbing. So, the Wittgenstein/Gray solution is anti-philosophy at its purest: philosophy and its "problems" (in the intellectual sense) are held up as the real "problem" (in the burst-pipe sense). The cognitive implications of the feeling are distrusted and consequently dismissed.

§

This was Wittgenstein's general attitude to philosophical problems. The real problem is always how to prevent philosophical reflection from drawing you away from the presuppositions of everyday life and towards inner turmoil. Gray's view is very similar. He thinks philosophy is, in large part, a vain attempt to use reason to overcome the fears and anxieties of the human condition, primarily death.[8] According to Gray, we tell stories about ourselves which we don't want to end, so we look for the meaning of life in intellectual fantasies designed to persuade us that they won't end (e.g. because souls outlive bodies) or that it isn't scary that they'll end (e.g. when Epicurus argues that death is nothing to fear since it's no different from the nothingness before birth). In this manner, Gray thinks we lock ourselves in an illusory inner space of words, which amplifies and elongates our fears and anxieties, cutting us off from the simple pleasures and pains of life where real meaning is to be found ... says the professor whose fame and fortune derive from the philosophy books he writes.

§

You can't beat philosophy—not with philosophy, not without it.[9] If we think about the meaning of life to deal with our fears and anxieties, but it only makes matters worse, then we'd be better off not thinking about it—that's the Wittgenstein/ Gray view in a nutshell. Well alright then, in that case you've got an alternative proposal for dealing with our fears and anxieties, haven't you? You think thoughtlessness will do a better job than philosophy. Fair enough, but you'll still have to justify your view, otherwise we've got no reason to listen to you. So off you go, justifying your view ... but now it's really frustrating because you've changed the subject—you're talking about thoughtlessness, fear and anxiety, when we wanted to talk about the meaning of life. Can we get back to the topic, please?

§

When philosophers turn to anti-philosophy, they turn against what gave them their lives. Tennis doesn't provide that opportunity—you can't play tennis in an anti-tennis fashion, a way that makes a statement against tennis. If you could, then I bet some people would, although I wouldn't expect them to win much.

§

If you stop thinking about a mathematical problem because it gives you a headache, and then the headache immediately subsides, does that mean you solved the problem? Since giving up made you feel better must the problem have been bogus? If the problem becomes closely associated with headaches in the public imagination, does that mean you can't think about it without getting one? Should scientists stop thinking about black holes if it gives them headaches? Do their headaches give credence to the notion that science stretches human thought too far into outer space?

§

Wittgenstein and Gray think we shouldn't question our everyday purposes—they're fragile, we should leave them be, philosophy would wreak havoc with them and it'd all be nonsense anyway so we should just save ourselves the turmoil.

I'm a tennis player whose purpose is to be champion, I've been training for it since I was kid. I get into the big league and realise I'm never going to beat some of these guys, they've got talent I'll never be able to compete with, so I start thinking I'm a failure—and I always will think that, if I can't question my everyday purposes. But I do question them: it's only a game; I'm one of the very best and there are billions of people in the world; maybe I shouldn't have taken my mother's purposes to heart; there are other things in life.

§

People want the feeling of purpose, but it's a feeling which indicates something, it has cognitive implications, so a fake won't do. Sometimes we revel in feeling for feeling's sake, indifferent to what, if anything, it indicates, but this clearly isn't one of those cases. Neither is love—people who fall in love under false pretences, such as with a con artist, won't look back favourably at what they once felt. They wouldn't have felt that way at the time if they'd known, or at least they wouldn't have wanted to, they'd have fought the feeling.

§

If the problem is just the feeling, then medical science has the best solutions — you can take pills which stop you worrying that your life lacks meaning. This approach is explicitly advocated by the maverick materialist philosopher, Alex Rosenberg[10] ... solve philosophical problems by taking pills, that's actually what he says — it sounds absurd, but it's perfectly reasonable if Wittgenstein and Gray are right that philosophical problems are body-mind problems. Still, before we start taking this proposal too seriously, I think it's important to note that if you pumped me full of enough drugs, then it's not just philosophy you could get me to lose my interest in, but also science, politics ... if I was homeless and sleeping on a park bench then my predicament probably wouldn't seem so significant if I was drugged up to the eyeballs.

§

Science can't show that philosophical problems are body-mind problems — how would you even try to show something like that scientifically? Perhaps by gathering depressed people who think their lives lack meaning, giving them a course of antidepressants, then asking how many retain their interest in the meaning of life once they're feeling alright again. If most lost interest would that show that the philosophical issues were bogus? No, if it showed anything it'd just be that depression can make the meaning of life seem interesting, rather as a sudden onset of colour-blindness can make the philosophy of perception seem interesting, or a communist uprising can make political philosophy seem interesting. Only philosophical argumentation could possibly establish that it's reasonable to think of philosophical problems as body-mind problems, that is, as a kind of intellectual pseudo-problem which needs to be cured rather than solved, if such a thing is even possible. So, it seems we're forced to talk philosophy after all. But if we are going to talk philosophy … well, I'm terribly sorry but I'd much rather we talked about the meaning of life, as originally planned. You'll never get anything right if you can't stay on topic. I'm not even sure it's incompetence anymore, you do it so often, maybe I've spotted your crafty plan: persuade me to abandon philosophy by continually changing the topic to something more boring.

Section 5: Meaning in Life Is Having Purposes Your Thought Can Rest Secure With

Imagine another prehistoric man. It's a sunny day and he's returning from the hunt with his brothers, sons and friends. Everything went well, nobody was injured, it was a fun day. It's a long walk, and when the banter finally dies down they fall silent, there's plenty of time to think. It occurs to him that once they've eaten the meat they'll have to repeat the process before long, just as they have done for years. He wonders what the point is—the point of hunting is obvious, as is the point of eating, but what's the point of everyday life? Then it occurs to him that maybe the spirit who helps them wants the hunt to continue, that there's also the spirit's purposes to consider. And maybe there's an eventual reward—he laughs out loud. Perhaps it's only now that we're seeing the first thinker of the meaning of life.

§

Or maybe it was his wife while she was skinning the animal, after returning from the hunt like a lioness. She persuades the others to offer some of the bounty to the spirit—the first thinker of the meaning of life left clues.

§

When your life seems meaningful you have a reassuring feeling which indicates that your thought is secure with your purposes. You've thought it over and decided you're happy enough aiming for those goals, they seem reasonable to you—others might disagree, you might change your mind, but for now you're satisfied. Monitoring the situation is an ongoing job, but rarely an unpleasant one, once you find your groove. If the feeling of meaning leaves, it's because your thought can't rest secure with your purposes anymore, adjustment is needed.

§

Thought can easily rest secure with the purposes of an independently existing meaning of life—something just sitting there, indifferent to what we think about it, like a rock on an undiscovered planet.

§

Without faith it's hard to believe in that kind of meaning, you'll never find it in a godless universe of outer space. Since it's so bleak out there you'll quickly home in on the close bit: human life on planet Earth. Reproducing, passing on our genes … your thought will struggle to rest secure with that. It's why we're here, alright (in a non-philosophical sense), but that's no reason to call it our purpose—it's not a purpose in the ordinary sense of what we're meant to be doing, or what we're trying to do. It's just what we did to get here and what we'll need to carry on doing to stay … at least for the time being—if technology cures death we can stop reproducing. The fact that we're here because our ancestors reproduced doesn't mean our purpose is to reproduce, any more than that our purpose is to breathe—without breathing we wouldn't be here either. And besides, does anyone who believes this popular view—so befitting of the materialist era—ever stop to consider its consequences for people who can't reproduce? The meaning of life is to reproduce, so if you can't your life is meaningless ... you'd have to be cruel to say that, in addition to philosophically inept.

§

OK, so you don't believe in God and nature isn't giving you a purpose. So now you turn to our societies, to everyday life. What happens next is your quest for the meaning of life will morph into a proposal for the good life, if you let it; that's the direction most philosophers have taken since Susan Wolf rekindled professional interest in "meaning" in the late 1990s.[11] Philosophers who think a meaningful life is distinct from an ethical one—the standard view these days—are simply advocating a broader conception of the good life than a morally praiseworthy one. They might say, for example, that a great artist but horrible man (Caravaggio, Picasso) can live a meaningful life without living a moral life. All they've really done is show their resistance to a narrow conception of ethics—they think morality is only one route to the good life, and that you can live a good life without it.

§

Trying to determine the good life for a human being has been one of the core concerns of philosophy since ancient times and has led the conversation in many interesting directions. It's a project best construed as one of making (hopefully) useful suggestions, I think. All kinds of facts about us—about the kind of lives we've lived and are living now—can feed into these suggestions. But it's not the kind of thing you can discover. "Why should that be the best kind of life to lead?" will always be a reasonable question to ask about a conception of the good life, and the quality of the answer you receive will determine how good the suggestion was. A meaning of life, however, would have to be something we discovered. You shouldn't be able to ask, "Why should I pursue those purposes?" if they're the purposes dictated by the meaning of life. Your thought would rest secure with them just by understanding what they were—and if you don't think that makes sense, then that's a good reason to think there isn't a meaning of life.

§

But maybe we can have meaning in our lives without there needing to be a meaning of life, that is, even if an unquestionable purpose for humankind hasn't been set in place by a higher power. What kind of things might make our lives meaningful in that case? Fame? Knowledge? A lasting contribution to Destiny's journey? Those are just suggestions for how to live a good life, and poor ones at that. You could combine them as follows: a man becomes world-famous by announcing his intention to end life on earth with the Doomsday device he invented ... meaningful or what? If there's no meaning of life, then there's no chance of people taking its place by dictating the purposes which everyone's thought must rest secure with.

§

Trying to rest all your purposes on the meaning of life is an impossible task. If you save the lives of innocents on a daily basis then sure, your thought can rest secure with that, and it makes sense for you to assume it's a purpose deriving from God's meaning of life. But if you're always looking for that kind of heavyweight reassurance, you'll find that most of what you do seems meaningless—unless you stop thinking about it.

§

Whether or not you have faith, you should ask whether your thought can rest secure with your purposes, because the reassurance of a meaning of life can't always be there. It can be reasonable for a religious believer to feel secure with purposes which seem highly unlikely to contribute to God's grand plan, like washing the car, just as it can be reasonable for a nihilist to feel secure with their purposes.

§

Everyday life is self-contained for practical purposes, your inner space need never leave it, but it doesn't explain itself and it leaves many questions unanswered. If you question your purposes, it's only a short step to questioning the purpose of life and the nature of reality—and then you can't fail to notice the ultimate weirdness, namely that what-is *is*, as Heidegger put it. Questioning everyday purposes leads naturally into philosophy. People may have started doing this in prehistoric times, it should be possible for everyone by now.

§

Destiny could awaken naturally if we all learned to attend to inner space. The question of the meaning of life is everyday life leading us to that task.

Section 6: Questioning Is Nothing to Worry About

There's nothing frightening about questioning your purposes, you're not risking the inner turmoil which Wittgenstein and Gray want you to fear. To see this, consider the options:

1. You find you're secure with your purposes because you think they either rest on God's cosmic meaning or wouldn't affect it either way.
2. You find you don't think some of your purposes are in accord with God's plan — so it's a good job you've realised, you'd better hurry up and change them.
3. You find you're content with your purposes, the things you're trying to do all seem reasonable enough, given your situation.
4. You find you're not content with some of your purposes, some of them are a waste of time, or worse — so it's a good job you've realised, you'd better try to change them.

Questioning the meaning in your life seems like a win-win situation. What am I missing? Probably nothing, as I said before it pays to assume that there's nothing to anti-philosophy, that it just boils down to unreason vs. reason. But I'll keep digging just in case.

§

Perhaps you're worried that your thought can only rest secure with your purposes if God supports them … but your faith isn't strong. So, the worry is that if you start thinking about philosophy too much, you'll realise you don't really believe in God and then you'll be forced to condemn life as meaningless — so you'd better listen to unreason for your own self-preservation. Tolstoy, the great populariser of reflection on the meaning of life, saw this rather differently. He was so sure he couldn't be secure in his purposes without God that his fear of a meaningless life was enough to restore his ailing faith.[12] So the options seem to be:

- Don't think about the meaning of life if you can't imagine yourself finding the answer in God.
- Do think about it if you can.

§

Consider a man who's lost his faith and can no longer rest secure with any of his purposes, or, indeed, with any human purposes whatsoever—he now thinks human life is an utterly futile endeavour. He's a strong swimmer and sees a little girl drowning in a lake, only he can save her. He thinks there's no point unless God wants him to, he doesn't believe in God anymore, so he lets her drown. Would anyone remotely normal be able to think in the way this man does? Obviously not—I'd save the girl, you'd save the girl, and Tolstoy would save the girl too, even when his faith was at its lowest ebb. The idea of somebody who thinks like this man is either pure fantasy or a portrait of a monster; either way it shouldn't put anyone off thinking about the meaning in their life—the reasoning that if you do then you'll be forced to either condemn life or turn to God only applies to the monster. "If God does not exist, everything is permitted," said one of the characters in Dostoevsky's *The Brothers Karamazov*—not a problem unless there's a monster nearby who's losing his faith.

§

I'll have one last try. Perhaps you're worried that if you start to think about your purposes, then you might find your thought can't rest secure with some of them, so you'll have to stop doing things you enjoy. This thought is hopeless, let me explain.

§

Suppose, for example, that you discover that your thought can't rest secure with your purpose of collecting pornographic images. In that case this activity might indeed start to feel meaningless ... but what's wrong with that? It'll help you quit — you've realised you should, so the feeling of meaninglessness is helpful. Alternatively, you might find that your thinking is secure enough with that purpose, so again there's no problem, you can carry on as before. Self-awareness can't make you stop doing something, it can only make you realise you want to. What's the alternative—thoughtlessness? Don't think about it because you'll realise you want to quit ... and you don't want to quit, you like it so much ... That's unreason talking, you can tell by the way it wanders two-headed.

§

Thoughtlessness doesn't have a good track-record in our world, and reasons for being thoughtless are still reasons. If your instinct is to avoid thinking into philosophical areas, there will always be others without that instinct. The influential ones, with Lady Luck on their side, will make the biggest decisions about your future. You'll always be travelling in the back seat.

§

John Gray has offered us ten "hints" on "how to live well"—his modest version of Jordan Peterson's bestselling twelve "rules for life", perhaps. Number one on Gray's list is:

Never try to persuade human beings to be reasonable.[13]

He wouldn't have dared say that to Socrates. And anyway, isn't he saying that it's reasonable to never try to persuade human beings to be reasonable?

§

Leading your thought out of everyday life requires imagination. Leading it home again to rest secure with your purposes, that's something which requires thought.

Section 7: Speedrunning and the Negation of Wider Contexts

In gaming, a speedrunner is someone who tries to complete a video game, or some significant portion of its content, in the shortest time possible. One subdivision of this new field of endeavour is blindfolded speedrunning—without being able see the monsters trying to kill you, or the precipices you can only leap across if you time your jump exactly right, it falls to finger muscle memory and a precise inner clock to be your primary guides. Adults, and sometimes not even particularly young adults, spend hundreds of hours practising their speedruns. The aim is to be quick, of course, but depending on how much content you're trying to complete, over an hour can be quick— over an hour of nearly faultless gameplay. A staggering level of skill and dedication is required to achieve these completely made-up, completely optional purposes. Some cheat, and when discovered are publicly named and shamed. To outsiders these purposes are liable to appear pointless, but to insiders they are maximally solid, unquestionable, a source of delights and despairs, of ambition, pride and failure. The wider context of society trivialises speedrunning and the insiders might well accept this judgement — but knowing what it's like on the inside, they need only shrug it off.

§

Chess is a game that requires complete dedication to play at the highest level, and when a machine first beat the greatest player (1997), many considered this a significant development. If they ever make a robot that can beat the best tennis players then this will be considered significant too, no doubt. Is the moral that human endeavour is pointless? Or is it that the only endeavour that isn't pointless is technology? No, there is no moral — like almost all technological progress in our world it happens thoughtlessly because someone realised it could be done.[14] What it demonstrates is a widespread and dangerous misunderstanding of human purposes, such that the purpose itself, like playing chess to a high level, is considered worth achieving for its own sake, rather than for the contribution it makes to people's lives. Speedrunning is immune to this misunderstanding. Programmers can already programme the perfect speedrun but nobody cares unless a human is playing — just as nobody should care about chess or tennis unless a human is playing. Speedrunners have trivialised the purposes of video games to create their own — purposes which are exceptionally difficult for a human, but easy for a machine.

§

The most important purposes are those which allow people to pursue purposes. After that, those which allow people choice over their purposes. After that, favour imaginative purposes that don't require any wider contexts to be negated for thought to rest secure with them.

§

Believers in a meaning of life won't compromise, thinking we should rest our purposes on the widest context of all, the ultimate nature of reality. You don't have to think there's a meaning of life to approve of that sentiment—we shouldn't have to negate the widest context to feel secure with our purposes, we shouldn't have to negate at all.

§

A speedrunner can go as far as celebrity and respect within their online community, but it would be hard for their thought to rest secure with their purposes without negating everything beyond that. It would be hard for them to consider the wider societal context in which they're spending ten hours a day trying to shave a second off the time it takes them to direct Mario from A to B, then conclude: "Yes, I think this is a perfectly reasonable purpose for me to pursue, considered within the context of my society and the issues it faces."

§

I'm not saying they couldn't do it, just that it'd be hard. They might reason as follows:

"I'm pursuing a career as an entertainer, which is a perfectly reasonable thing to do—people always need entertainment. If my speedruns aren't good enough then nobody will watch my online video channel, so the hours I spend practising are necessary for my career to succeed. You might raise doubts about whether speedrunning provides a valuable form of entertainment—you might think the young people watching my speedruns, and listening to me discuss them afterwards, are wasting their time—but I disagree. I'd say that speedrunning is more than just entertainment, it's also a kind of a sport, one which requires great dedication, and which celebrates human excellence. Speedrunning may even develop into an art form in the future, who knows? And it has great philosophical significance too, since it shows human beings starting to rebel against a purely quantitative, materialistic conception of goals. Speedrunners only care about speed when it's achieved fairly by a human being, so I think that society at large, with its obsession with AI overtaking us, has a lot to learn from speedrunning."

That would be a good justification in today's world ... although I suspect most speedrunners are yoked to the materialist machine, only able to sustain their feelings of meaning by negating wider contexts.

§

To avoid any possible confusion, let's distinguish "negation" from "bracketing". You bracket wider contexts so you can concentrate on the task at hand—that's standard for demanding tasks. Negation is different. That's when you refuse to think about a purpose within a wider context, or, if you find yourself doing so from time to time, then you don't dwell on it, you don't ask if your thought can rest secure with your purposes in that wider context. "Yeah, dude, lots of people out there think I'm wasting my time ... like I care, lol!" That's negation—his thought rests secure with his purposes only because it sleeps.

§

Almost everyone negates Destiny's future, which is unsurprising while materialism remains our operative philosophy. A philosophical people wouldn't be indifferent to their future—they wouldn't be resigned to it being terrible, or confident it'll be great, and they wouldn't think it wasn't their problem, either.

Section 8: A Future in Inner Space

Think back to materialism's unimaginative vision of our future in outer space among aliens and robots (discussed in part one). Why aren't the spacemen and spacewomen glued to their devices? Why don't they struggle to look up from their screens to view the beautiful triple-star sunsets? Where are their virtual reality headsets? Why was the technological journey to inner space abandoned?

Let's work on the more realistic assumption that it won't be abandoned, then. Let's also work on the assumption that it won't be constrained—that the better we get at creating virtual worlds, the more difficult it will become to compartmentalize our use of them. In other words, let's assume we're going to get sucked in.

§

We're heading for virtual reality, then, we're going to leave the reality we found for realities we'll make. Could anything be more natural for a human being? Not really, it's the kind of thing we've always done in dribs and drabs, it's just that this time we'll go the whole hog. We've always changed the environment to suit us, now we'll build our own … any number of them, which we can choose between at will. Find some people unbearable? Live in a different world from them. Struggling to become famous? Choose a world where the odds are stacked in your favour. Finding it hard to lose weight? Choose any body you like. Worried we've messed up nature by following Francis Bacon's advice to force nature to yield to our demands? Doesn't really matter if we're not going to live there anymore.

§

We've hit on the formula for ultimate wish-fulfilment, but the move to inner space can't work while we remain materialist and unphilosophical. We've taken the first steps, the problems are already apparent, and they're problems only philosophy can solve.

§

OK, so let's imagine it. There I am in the future, the unphilosophical type that's today's norm, and I'm living in a world where most of waking life takes place in virtual reality — the kind of future Mark Zuckerberg wants to pioneer. I have an office job in virtual reality — and why not? If it's work that consists of interacting with a computer, then it makes no difference where I'm doing it. (I might as well be writing this book in virtual reality ... I could write in a virtual replica of my actual office, so it clearly needn't make any difference.) I could do this work while spending my life flying around the galaxy in a spaceship with my wife and kids. The kids could teleport to school and my wife and I could teleport into the office — or just use the spaceship's computers, when we're having a day at home.

§

But why do we need to work? Surely, if we have the technology to make perfect virtual realities (presently they're very clunky), then by that point AIs will be able to interact with virtual work-computers much more effectively than humans ever could. We already have AI that can beat any human at chess without even having learnt from us, that is, without knowing the history of the game, the great moves, the tactics ... with AlphaZero, the alien intelligence which was brought into the world without your permission in 2017, you can just tell it the rules, tell it to win, and it's unbeatable (so far—humans made AlphaZero, but AI made by AI will be better). It seems highly unlikely that humans would be needed for any cognitive work in this future, then, nor indeed for any physical work—we'll have robots which can lift more than us, robots which can perform more precise surgery, etc. So, humans will be completely redundant. Oh well, hang the Protestant Work Ethic!

§

With no work to be done, we can spend all our time exploring the galaxy in our spaceship. But what are our purposes? What are we trying to do? We're trying to have fun—it's like we've retired, and our lives have become one big adventure holiday. Great?

§

When you're on holiday, your thought can rest secure with the purpose of getting a suntan without the need to negate any wider contexts: it's something I enjoy and I need a break, I'll go home feeling invigorated and looking cool. In the virtual reality, however, I don't need to lie in the sun, since my avatar could be given a suntan in an instant; and if I do choose to lie in the sun, then the connection with my skin getting darker is fake—it could be made to get paler instead. Why does the virtual sun feel so nice? Because somebody or something is making me feel that way. Why? Since this is a materialist future we're imagining, you'd expect the answer to be that someone is profiting—feeling nice is a service which I'm paying for. But how can that be, when humans are no longer worth anything? If machines are better at everything, there's no need for people to profit from each other anymore. People profit from each other in pursuit of experiences, but in virtual reality you can have any experiences you want, whenever you want, so you don't need other people.

§

People's thoughts couldn't rest secure with their purposes because their purposes would be known to be fake. You could only sustain the feeling of meaning by negating any context wider than the fake one provided by your virtual reality.

§

Notice how different this hypothetical future is from the situation of a present-day gamer who spends most of his waking hours playing video games. The gamer probably also sustains his feeling of meaning by negating, but the crucial difference is that he doesn't have to. He knows what he's doing from the perspective of the wider context of everyday life, and if he stops negating to give the matter some thought, he may be able to rest reasonably secure with his purposes in terms of that context—he might reason that there's nothing wrong with playing video games, that it's a bit like reading a novel, for instance. In the future scenario where I live on a virtual spaceship with my family, however, I can't ever afford to think about the wider context—because from that perspective the whole thing is ridiculous and fake. Remember that I'm supposed to be a materialist, or just completely unphilosophical, so what's real for me is the atoms outside of virtual reality. Those atoms are currently being manipulated to make it seem as if I'm living a life that I'm not really living—to live that life I'd need a spaceship, not just a virtual reality interface. To retain my feelings of meaning, then, I must never reflect on my purposes. And yet, everyday life goes on day after day after bloody day, whether you're in virtual reality or not. Even a fool would occasionally consider the wider context, so even a fool would lose the meaning in their life. Negation would turn into a losing battle.

§

I imagined a virtual reality where I live with my family, but I could have chosen a private reality instead. Gamers and social media users virtually interact with others, but they needn't in principle and often don't—we've already reached the point where you sometimes can't be sure if your online interactions are with a real person or not. The advantage of going private is that you can tailor your apparent interpersonal interactions. So, rather than living in a shared virtual reality with my wife, for example, I could have my own private one where she's exactly the same except that she never complains about me playing video games—other people deciding to go private might be much more creative than that, of course.

§

A materialist future in virtual reality would make it very tempting to negate all contexts except the solipsistic one of your own inner space. But if that's where Destiny is heading, then it's not just the feeling of meaning we're jeopardising, it's our sanity. You can only be sane in a community—you don't need to interact with the community, as some solitary monks have chosen not to, but you do need to legitimise your thoughts by reference to its hypothetical judgements. Otherwise, it's completely up to you to decide whether what you're thinking is reasonable. Without that point of reference, you may allow yourself the occasional thought which the community you are oblivious or indifferent to would classify as insane. You might enjoy these thoughts, they might start occurring more frequently.

§

When there are robots and Non-Player Characters which can provide more intense sexual pleasure than a person ever could, a major bond between human beings will have been rendered second-best, forevermore. We'll have the right tool for negating the wider context of those feelings, and from Destiny's perspective, an important part of the decision to favour individual over collective experience will have been made. Might the lesson of sex be that the development of collective experience is where all the imaginative and developmental possibilities lie?

§

We'll have to wake Destiny if we want our descendants to have meaning in their lives. To do that, we must invoke Philosophy by thinking about our own inner spaces and the purposes residing there. That will require imagination. When she arrives, the first thing she will teach us is how to care about Destiny's future. Then, once we care, we will start to develop a collective rationality which will awaken Destiny and announce our arrival as a philosophical people.

Section 9: The Main Argument of This Book

If everyday life moves to virtual reality, which seems to be our current direction of travel, and also the one offering the most choice over how the future of human experience develops, then if we remain materialistic and unphilosophical we will no longer be able to think of our everyday lives as real.[15]

As materialists we would conceive reality as something outside of virtual reality, so our everyday lives would seem meaningless—we wouldn't be able to avoid seeing our purposes as fake and pointless. If we become philosophical by embracing an idealist viewpoint, however, then this outcome can be avoided. Now we would be able to see the technology of virtual reality as a revolutionary leap forward in human control over the ultimate reality of experience. Everyday life would continue to seem real in virtual reality, because our conception of reality would now be experiential; our lives and philosophies would have developed in tandem. We would no longer feel the need to negate wider contexts, because we would see the widest context of all as experiential, so we could come to see our everyday lives as part of a collective effort to develop greater and greater patterns of experience— more fair, more beautiful, more loving, more interesting, more intellectually satisfying, more sensual, more exciting. Philosophical language would have regained its force, we would no longer just be paying it lip service, because it would now be possible to understand everyday life in terms of the ultimate nature of reality for the first time in our history.

Section 10: Don't Let Nietzsche Have the Last Word

"What a sensation of freedom it is to feel, as we freed spirits feel, that we are *not* harnessed up to a system of 'ends'!" said Nietzsche in 1886.[16] He meant that ceasing to believe in a meaning of life gives you an exhilarating sense of freedom. A year later he claimed to have recently managed to overcome nihilism, having previously been a nihilist without realising.[17] Most of today's free spirits have never been freed. They needn't overcome nihilism, it offers them a blank slate for imagining collectively chosen purposes that are more rational and flexible than a predetermined meaning of life.

§

Nietzsche's "Last Man" blinks.[18] He tells us that his people have found happiness, then blinks. He says they work for their own entertainment, but never too hard, then he blinks. He says they never grow rich or poor; that nobody rules or obeys; that their quarrels don't last long; that they moderate their pleasures for the sake of health—and then, of course, he blinks. He also relates less attractive traits (as I see it—Nietzsche seems to consider all these traits equally despicable), such as that everyone wants the same and everyone is the same, that there's no passion in interpersonal relations, and that they avoid difficult purposes which require dedication and struggle. We can imagine any Last Man we like and make him wink.

§

You have purposes your thought can rest secure with when you've thought through what you're trying to do, the projects of your life, and you're content enough. You've realised what you are, the kind of world you belong to, and the kind of reality that world belongs to, probably. You've realised all that, haven't felt the need to blot it out, and you still want to do what you're doing, even if it doesn't always seem that way. If enough people reach that point, if only for the sake of their own meaning, then Destiny will awaken, and politics will change accordingly— misleading people for what's thought to be their own good (at best), while gaining their support by focusing on their immediate self-interests (always), will no longer seem either necessary or desirable. We've got a long way to go, of course, but we've made it to the 21st century and now we're superfast—if we know where we're heading you can be reasonably confident we'll get there, no matter how far away it is, humans are like that. If we don't we'd better hope we get lucky.

§

Why am I leading this hunt? For your sake? I don't even know who's in the pack and my sense of solidarity with wolf-kind is only average. I do it because I like blazing the trails, going over them time and time again until I think I've got them right. My thought never rests more secure with my purposes than when my work on a hunt is going well.

Endnotes

1. I provide five arguments in chapter 4 of *Gods and Titans*, London: Bloomsbury 2020.
2. Solidity: if it weren't for the experiences associated with solidity, then you wouldn't have the idea of solidity, so the idealist claim that solidity is a model for understanding patterns of experience is perfectly plausible. It's not denying that rocks are solid—obviously!—rather it's saying in metaphysical terms what it is that rocks being solid amounts to. Solipsism: the idea of idealism is that you add up all the experiences of all the people and animals, ever, then that's what reality amounts to. Why would you instead think that reality was only your own experiences—wouldn't that be a completely crazy thing to think? Where's the motivation to think something like that? True, if the whole of reality was nothing more than your own personal experiences, then that would indeed count as a kind of idealism: solipsistic idealism … but personally I'm only interested in ordinary idealism, the non-crazy kind. The (non-)problem of solipsism (i.e., the (non-)problem of avoiding a crazily solitary understanding of reality) is no worse for ordinary idealism than for any other metaphysic. If you're a materialist then the only thing you know directly is your own brain, whereas for an idealist it's your own experience—if you think that somehow forces idealists to embrace solipsistic idealism, then I guess you

ought to also think that it forces materialists to claim that only one brain exists and nothing else.

3. Probably the most ardent atheist ever to live and a metaphysical idealist; the materialist "New Atheists" of today look like boy scouts in comparison.

4. Wittgenstein, *Tractatus Logico-Philosophicus*, 1921, proposition 6.44: "It is not how things are in the world that is mystical, but that it exists," trans. D. Pears and B. McGuinness, London: Routledge 1966. Heidegger, "The Way Back into the Ground of Metaphysics", 1949: "Man alone of all beings, when addressed by the voice of Being, experiences the marvel of all marvels: that what-is *is*," in W. Kaufmann (ed.) *Existentialism from Dostoevsky to Sartre*, New York: Meridian Books 1958, p. 386.

5. Beginning with Pope Paul VI, who was pope from 1963-1978 (and with the trivial exception of John Paul I, who was only pope for 33 days) every papal decree has mentioned "the meaning of life"; see Steven Cassedy, *What Do We Mean When We Talk About Meaning?* Oxford: Oxford University Press 2022, p. 171.

6. I think this is what he meant when he wrote at the end of the *Tractatus* (op. cit. proposition 6.521) that, "The solution of the problem of life is seen in the vanishing of this problem. (Is not this the reason why those who have found after a long period of doubt that the sense of life became clear to them have then been unable to say what constituted that sense?)" If you think he meant something different, then call the view I'm about to discuss "The Gray Solution".

7. *Feline Philosophy: Cats and the Meaning of Life*, London: Allen Lane 2020. As mentioned in Chapter 1, section 2, Gray isn't just playing to the crowd with this book, he takes it seriously. He loves cats and thinks we can learn from them. For all the populist misanthropy he's famous for, then, he's obviously a nice enough person — lots of nice people who aren't philosophers prefer cats to people.

8. In Chapter 1, section 2, we saw this view in action when we discussed Gray's interpretation of Raymond Tallis's attempt to use death as a mirror of life.

9. Aristotle made this point in his lost work, *Protrepticus*, aka, *Exhortation to Philosophy*.

10. *The Atheist's Guide to Reality*, New York: W.W. Norton 2011, p. 282.

11. "Happiness and Meaning: Two Aspects of the Good Life", *Social Philosophy and Policy*, vol. 24, 1997.

12. That's my interpretation of the inner space journey recounted in Tolstoy's "A Confession" (1882).

13. Gray op. cit., p. 108. I like hint #6: "life is not a story".

14. Show me the justification that was offered, together with the mandate this justification received—both need to date from before work on building the Deep Blue chess computer began, of course.

15. Materialism already implies that everyday life is not real, in my opinion (see *Gods and Titans*, chapter 2), but that's not something you can consider without philosophical reflection.

16. *Writings from the Late Notebooks*, ed. R. Bittner, trans. K. Sturge, Cambridge: Cambridge University Press 2003, p. 99.

17. *The Will to Power*, trans. W. Kaufmann and R.J. Hollingdale, New York: Random House 1967, note 25, p. 18. *The Will to Power* is no longer considered a respectable source, but it's the only place this particular note (which is genuine) can still be found in English translation.

18. The "Last Man", or "Ultimate Man" in some translations, appears in section 5 of "Zarathustra's Prologue" at the beginning of the book he considered his best, *Thus Spake Zarathustra* (or "Spoke", as they must have it these days—the antiquated English sounds better to me, it's like Gambo Lai Lai's old anglé).

Chapter 5

Gambo Lai Lai the Cynic

Section 1: The Legend Begins

"Razors are hard," reflected John Blades, better known as Johnny Zi Zi. "A man can't show fear, can't feel it neither, but when you're attacked with a razor it's a fearsome thing—that's why they're hard, the hardest thing in the world."

Everyone knew Johnny Zi Zi on the tough streets of Port of Spain back then. He was assumed to have been behind a series of daring robberies that took place in the 1880s, and he was the most notorious stick fighter at carnival—any badjohn who dared square up against him was liable to be left bleeding in the gutters. There was much speculation about the money he must have stashed away from his crimes, since he clearly hadn't spent it—true, he visited the brothels and rum shops more regularly than most, wore fancy high-draped trousers with yellow stripes, and he owned his own drums, yet there was certainly nothing about his lifestyle to indicate great wealth. Far from it, he lived in a ramshackle hut in one of the poorest neighbourhoods of Laventille.

Among the many children Johnny fathered was Jules Blades, known to history as Gambo Lai Lai. Johnny met Jules' mother, Marie, on a trip to Venezuela—he brought her back to Trinidad, where she died giving birth to Jules in 1890. Brought up by the women of the neighbourhood, Jules formed a strong bond with a widow named Gloria Moura, who taught him to read. Jules was a natural—before long, he'd read all the books which Gloria's late husband had left her, mostly on religion and horticulture, so on his 10th birthday she took him to the public library, where he soon became a regular. There was plenty of time to read as he sat in the sun outside the rum shop selling Gloria's black puddings—he sometimes returned to this work as an adult, it was the only paid employment of his life.

Jules's life was transformed by The Water Riots of 1903. In an initiative to reduce water wastage, the colonial British government had introduced several unpopular measures; Johnny Zi Zi became involved in the protests when officials closed off the communal standpipe on his street. As discontent brewed across the city, matters were brought to a head when Governor Moloney announced that an emergency debate on the water measures, at the government building called the Red House, was to be ticketed—this was to prevent opposition groups from attending. An angry crowd formed and it's said that Johnny threw the first rock. In the chaos that followed the Red House was burned to the ground, the police opened fire, killing sixteen and wounding many more, and Johnny was arrested. He was taken to the Royal Jail and never seen again.

Gloria urged Jules to go through Johnny's possessions quickly, before anyone else could get to them, and he was glad of her advice when he discovered a large suitcase crammed full of banknotes. At the age of sixteen, when he was confident Johnny wouldn't be returning, since Gloria had made inquiries at the jail, Jules started spending. He bought a luxurious bungalow, a Raleigh bike that made him the envy of all the other young men on the island, and a variety of fine suits and hats. Heavily built and standing over six feet tall, passers-by would marvel as he sat at his black pudding stall, reading a book, while dressed in a three-piece suit and bowler hat. His favourite authors at the time were Shakespeare, Bunyan, Dryden and Prior.

Jules became a celebrity at masquerade carnival by giving readings outside calypso tents. These performances began perfectly spontaneously one evening after he'd attended a calypso performance by Henry Forbes the Inventor. He'd loved the show, and since it was a fine, bright evening, he stopped outside the tent to smoke a cigar. As was often the case now that he cut such a striking figure, he found he was attracting attention, so, on a whim, he decided to try his hand at a little oratory.

"Illustrious wretch!" he bellowed out in a thunderous voice that quaked with passion, "Repine not nor reply"—this was the line from Matthew Prior's *Solomon on the Vanity of the World* which had been playing on his mind all day, since at this time he was starting to think about the meaning of life. "View not what Heaven ordains with reason's eye; Too bright the object is, the distance is too high." When Jules had finished the crowd which had since gathered clapped and cheered.

"More! More of your old anglé!" someone called out.

"My old anglé ..." repeated back Jules very thoughtfully, as he puffed on his great cigar. "Verily shall I rebroadcast my old anglé with chronicity," he announced.

And that's how Gambo Lai Lai's old anglé began. In those early years at carnival he was simply reading from the works of his favourite authors, but later it became the vehicle of his cynicism.

It was also during these years that he acquired his famous sobriquet, variously rendered Gambo Lai Lai, Gumbo Lai Lai (or Gumbolailai) and Gombo Lai Lai—hopefully I can now clear up some of the confusion that's arisen over this matter. "Lai Lai" means forever, that much is agreed. "Gumbo" is the preferred spelling in newspaper reports during his lifetime, and is easily justified, since "gumbo" is the standard spelling for the okra stew. (There's no reason to suppose any specific connection between Blades and the stew, by the way, since carnival naming was a fanciful and creative process.) However, "gumbo" derives from either the Portuguese "quingombó" or the Mbundu "ngombo", depending on whom you ask, so it's understandable that the great calypsonians Lord Executor and Atilla the Hun would both insist on "Gombo". Why, then, have I opted for "Gambo"? Solely on the testimony of Eduardo Sa

Gomes, the calypso music promoter. "It was Gambo-with-an-A," said Gomes in an interview in the 1940s, "nothing else to it, I don't know why and I don't much care. When Executor recorded that song I had to get Decca to change the name on the record from Gombo to Gambo, just to avoid an ear-bashing — well, back in the '20s Lionel [Belasco] used 'Gumbo' for his record and you should've heard Gambo fulminating."

Section 2: A Philosopher Arises

The distinction between Gambo Lai Lai's life and performances began to blur when he started taking his old anglé away from carnival and into ordinary street life. This began as a way of appeasing the young women who followed him around asking for, "Just a little of your old anglé, oh please, Mr. Gambo Lai," but before long he found himself performing on the busiest streets and squares of Port of Spain whether or not it was carnival time. As his fame increased, he started to drink more rum, smoke more cigars, and experiment with different hats — he eventually settled on the Panama as his preferred look. Life was treating him well, but he nevertheless felt a certain dissatisfaction which he was unable to comprehend as yet. He was still thinking about the meaning of life.

The great transformation was set in motion one afternoon when he was reading from Bunyan's *The Pilgrim's Progress* to a large crowd on Woodford Square. It was a speech about Christian morality, the need to not allow yourself to be distracted from the ultimate goal of reaching the Celestial City, and the importance of overcoming ignorance. At the end there was long applause, but Gambo, who'd been drinking heavily, was suddenly overcome by disgust. There was frivolity, sin and ignorance written all over the faces of the people in the crowd, he thought. It made no difference where he turned his gaze, whether to a beautiful young woman or an ugly old man, everyone looked grotesque — ethically grotesque.

"Damn you," he shouted angrily, "for applauding a message you contradict with your lives."

The bemused crowd quickly dispersed after this unexpected outburst, while Gambo stormed off to the public library. He browsed the shelves until his eye was caught by an old book entitled *The Cynical Philosophy of Diogenes and Crates.* He took it back to his bungalow, where one of his girlfriends was waiting for him with two tumblers of rum and a bowl of pig's feet; he quickly shooed her away. He read the book deep into the night until he reached the end, then started a second time. He continued to read until he could no longer force himself to stay awake, then, the moment he awoke the next morning, he continued with his obsessive reading of the book, over and over again, until he involuntarily fell asleep once more. This process continued for over two weeks, until Gambo Lai Lai the Cynic emerged fully formed, as if from a chrysalis.

Many have debated whether Gambo was the greatest of all the Cynic philosophers, but it seems to me that since he belonged to such a different cultural milieu from his ancient Greek forbears, such comparison is futile. He was less original, to be sure, but then again hardly unoriginal, and his own particular genius was to find a way to apply their philosophy to the modern world. We should not think of favouring one over the other, then, but simply be glad that we have them all. I've written a poem about it:

> The Cynics scandalised the Greeks,
> Defying all convention,
> You can't compare their distant lives,
> With Gambo's reinvention.

The first action of Gambo Lai Lai the Cynic was to head directly to the masquerade fancy dress shop to see if they had a crown for sale. They had several and he bought the most flamboyant, shining as if made from real gold, and encrusted with paste jewellery—he insisted on paying five times the asking price. With the crown upon his head, he made his way to Gloria's house. He gave her possession of his belongings, including the bungalow and Johnny's stash (still a small fortune). He told her to use his wealth as she saw fit, knowing that this good woman would help the poor as best she could.

The business with Gloria completed, he stepped out into the street, wearing a perfectly pressed morning suit and the carnival crown still wedged on his head. Lighting a cigar, he threw back his crowned head, paused a while to enjoy the sun on his face, then shouted out as loudly as he could:

"Gambo Lai Lai has set Gambo Lai Lai free!"

"Where you gonna live now, doodoo-darling?" asked Gloria, who was standing in her doorway, looking bemused. Gambo ignored her.

"Gambo Lai Lai has set Gambo Lai Lai free!" he repeated, quietly this time, then he strode away purposefully in the direction of the dockyard. When he arrived, Gambo paid no attention to the fishermen and sailors, some of whom stopped to comment on his crown—respectfully, of course, Gambo was already a popular figure. He was looking for the giant oil drums that he'd heard had been washed up from the wreck of an American ship—enormous great things, twice as tall and wide as a standard 55-gallon oil drum. There were three of them lined up at the far end of the docks, and with great effort, Gambo pulled one crashing down onto its side—it rolled only a little, since it was so heavy, before coming to a rest. Gambo climbed inside.

"To roam Giddily, and be everywhere but at home, such freedom doth a banishment become," he muttered to himself, quoting John Donne, as he sat in his oil drum and looked out to sea.

Section 3: Early Encounters and Anecdotes

I believe there is no better introduction to the philosophy of Gambo Lai Lai than to recount his most celebrated encounters, together with some of the popular anecdotes; afterwards I shall proceed to a more systematic exposition. The reader should note that these encounters and anecdotes all predate his three incarcerations. This was a time when he was heavily under the influence of Diogenes and Crates; only later did his originality blossom.

§

When asked why he'd given away all his money and left his bungalow for a rusty oil drum, Gambo Lai Lai answered:

"For friendship and safety, wretch! Only now may I number the poor amongst my friends—betwixt rich and poor a friendship cannot flourish and 'a wise man never attempts impossibilities', as Massinger sayeth."

"One of my friends is rich," objected a woman in the crowd.

"If truly she be your friend," answered Gambo, "why art thou poor? Friendship is one soul in two bodies."

"You say you gave away your fortune for safety," said an old man, looking puzzled, "but everyone knows wealth offers protection and the poor are always in danger."

"Scum!" snapped Gambo. "Wealth is the vomit of Fortune and Fortune is powerless against the Cyclopean walls of my beloved Poverty. The rich are like fruit trees growing in inaccessible places, a waste of fruit. Don't cast us into strife by your preference for crab and dumplings over tremoços."

Gambo then took from his pocket a bag of lupin beans, the traditional food of the Cynic philosopher, and popular in Trinidad too (tremoços). He began to squeeze the salty yellow

212

flesh out of the translucent shells and into his mouth: "Whilst others live to eat, Gambo eats to live," he spluttered.

"Don't you miss your Raleigh bike, Gambo?" asked a small boy.

Gambo swallowed so he could answer properly: "As I was descending the proclivity at a precipitous velocity on my velocipede, I did oftentimes experience great joy," he admitted, "but I'm glad to have ended my enslavement by possessions. Bringers of joy they may be, but at the cost of dependency, fear, and inevitable loss."

"Don't you want to be happy anymore, Gambo?" continued the boy, looking quite upset—the thought of somebody not wanting their Raleigh bike anymore made him want to cry.

"Best not measure life by happiness, boy," replied Gambo, "lest thou disconcert thyself. Rest assured life's not bad ... though 'tis mostly lived badly."

"What's the good life, then?" asked a man in a boiler suit, who'd been listening quietly until now, but always with an openly sceptical expression—which Gambo had noticed.

"Life lived with calm and cheerful soul, unperturbed by both despised pleasures and the welcome challenge of misfortune."

"Well, you ain't persuaded me none," said the man, "living in an oil drum, eating tremoços and talking that stupid *Gros Anglais* don't sound like the good life to me!"

"If I was capable of persuading a wretch like you," snarled Gambo, "you'd hang yourself from a tree."

§

Gambo acquired a large ear trumpet, and when the streets were at their busiest, he'd walk around with it clutched to his ear, calling out, "Quiet, I'm listening for meaning."

§

When asked what type of rum he liked best, he replied, "Someone else's."

§

When asked why he was sometimes seen outside brothels, Gambo explained that he insulted prostitutes to train himself to endure the foulest of abuse. When asked why he sometimes went in, he said, "Sunlight creeps into the foulest corners yet the sun be never dirtied."

§

Gambo was present at the infamous 1914 picong duel between Henry Forbes the Inventor and Lord Executor, which the older man won under controversial circumstances.[1] As Inventor was celebrating his victory, Gambo called out, "Thou art a winner over slaves, but Gambo Lai Lai is a winner over men."

§

Gambo was walking backwards down a busy street one day. When asked why, he barked out, "Scum! Thou art the one traversing life's path backwards!"

§

When pianist and bandleader Lionel Belasco, a man known for his erudition, heard that Gambo was modelling himself on the Cynic philosophers, he invited Gambo to his house to challenge him. It was one of the finest houses in Trinidad, carpeted throughout and with valuable antique furnishings. Belasco began as follows:

"You've got it all wrong, Gambo, Diogenes said that the finest thing in life is plain speaking, he'd hate your old anglé."

"Wretch!" said Gambo. "To confabulate without adornment was possible for Greeks of old, but alas no more. My elaborate promulgations are needed to carry us through the semantic void."

"I've no idea what you mean," huffed Belasco, "I think you're only pretending to be a philosopher."

"Better that," said Gambo, "than lack even the aspiration."

"Ah," sighed Belasco with a shrug, "I'd be no good at philosophy, I know my place—that's how I avoid making a fool of myself."

"So why live at all if thou art unconcerned with the nature and quality of thine own life? Shall I fetch thee a dagger?"

Gambo then started to clear his throat, as if readying himself to spit.

"You can't spit in here, Gambo," said Belasco in a panic, "have you any idea how much these carpets cost?"

Gambo Lai Lai spat in his face.

§

There was a young woman named Melda who was reckoned among the most beautiful in Port of Spain. When Gambo saw her at the docks one evening, attracting the attention of the sailors, he called out,

"Fool! Seeketh admiration of thine soul, not thine body." Angered by this, Melda stopped to confront him.

"Gambo Lai, you getting me vex! I had a dream last night, and the police were dragging you off to jail for upsetting folks with your Big English ... so you'd better stop all this bad behaviour!"

"I advise thee pay no regard of dreams, thou canst barely afford the effort, o perfume jar of vinegar," said Gambo. "Thou payest no regard of waking life, so best start there."

§

Gambo attended a picong duel between a bald man and an exceptionally large one. The bald man was a good calypsonian, but the large man had no talent. At the end of the duel, which was completely one-sided, only Gambo applauded the large man. The bald man asked,

"Why, Gambo? What you clapping him for?"

"That a man of such gargantuan proportions hath not turned to crime is more than worthy of applause," said Gambo, adding: "I also applaud your hair for leaving such a wretched head."

§

Governor Le Hunte was delivering a long and pompous speech to the public, when Gambo Lai Lai made his way through the crowd, carrying salt fish and wearing his crown. Once at the front he approached the governor's platform, then turned around to face the crowd. Everyone waited with bated breath. Gambo looked over his shoulder and said to the Governor,

"Hardly gripped by thine speech, art they?"

Section 4: The Early Philosophy of Gambo Lai Lai—an Exposition

Gambo Lai Lai the Cynic was awakened by the thought that the people he lived among were living as if they believed themselves to be characters in a fantasy world. That's to say, the social framework they'd draped over life seemed more real to them than life itself. The reality of life was considered of no interest to them since they had no interest in philosophy. Reality for them was, "whether Dorothy will be jealous of my new dress", "that rum I've got saved for the party tonight", or "what I'm going to say to Johnny". As Gambo saw it, the social framework, no matter how many benefits it had brought the community, had turned people into idiots — idiots who thought they were characters in a fantasy world where glory and happiness are the higher and lower goals, and where the talented and hard-working should receive their apportioned lot.

These characters, as the idiots believed themselves to be, played their allotted parts in search of reward, while overlooking an existential situation they were too incurious to even ask about it. They didn't face up to their mortality, nor to the ever-present possibility of disaster, so whenever troubles came their way they were unprepared, bearing them as only a child could be excused for. They didn't face up to having an animal life, the life of something that eats, sleeps and excretes in a regular pattern until it dies — in Gambo's view dogs have a better understanding of what their lives amount to, hence his well-known saying, "dog better than man", which was to become a popular calypso theme in works by Growling Tiger, Mighty Viper and many others.

Gambo, like Diogenes and Crates before him, saw people as enslaved to pain and pleasure, with his job being to free them. This enslavement had been enacted by pleasure and pain luring people into robotic behavioural roles which had developed over the generations to maximise pleasure and minimalize pain. Once indoctrinated, because they were addicted to the rewards on offer, people started to believe themselves to be characters in the fantasy world which their roles elaborated. This made behaviour ever more conventional and rule-governed, so in effect pain and pleasure now stage-managed practically everything they did. Thus, pleasure would tell them they'd done well today at work, there's rum when you get home. And pain would tell them to watch out for avoidable pain ahead, like Melda being mean to you—but don't ever think about unavoidable pain, oh no, that's getting into philosophical waters, you steer away from that stuff like there's no tomorrow.

So, as Gambo saw it, people had been stupefied into enslavement by pleasure and pain, and it was his duty, as a Cynic philosopher, to set them free. That didn't mean he had to like them, however; once he had awakened as Gambo Lai Lai the Cynic he didn't anymore. Nevertheless, Gambo was not so cynical that he didn't hope to ultimately find the people likeable again, after he'd freed them. In the meantime, however, he had no reason to hide his contempt for what they'd allowed themselves to become, nor moderate his strong desire to mistreat them—they needed to be taught a harsh lesson, they needed to be shocked out of the philosophical void, and so Gambo Lai Lai would happily spit in their faces, he was only acting naturally, with a calm and cheerful soul.

Gambo adopted the standard Cynic strategy for achieving the people's salvation, which was to lead by example, to use his own life to show the way. Thus Gambo did not play the prescribed roles of the social framework, but rather defied and ridiculed them—he lived in an oil drum, as Diogenes had lived in a pithos, he wore a crown to show how ludicrous he thought wealth was, exactly as Crates did, and then, once his bizarre ways had captured your attention, he delivered his philosophical lessons with as much venom and shock-value as possible. Given what a Cynic philosopher is trying to do, I find it hard to imagine a more effective strategy. He used his own life as a resource for delivering a philosophical message—he dedicated his life to philosophy, just like Diogenes and Crates before him.

His main lesson, the one he considered the short-cut to freedom and virtue, was to despise pleasure and welcome misfortune. It's true, as rather pedestrian critics never tire of pointing out, that Gambo Lai Lai never stopped drinking his rum, smoking his cigars, and dressing up to the nines. But what these critics fail to understand is that he was thereby following the inspiration of Crates, who tried to live life "as though he were at a festival", as Plutarch put it.[2] Well, given Gambo's background as the son of Johnny Zi Zi, I think it's excusable that he might struggle to imagine a good festival without copious amounts of rum, fabulous Cuban cigars, and himself suitably dressed. Since this criticism misses its mark, then, I suggest we instead focus on the clearest examples of success which Gambo had in teaching by example. He gave away all his money — that's showing pleasure who's boss, is it not? Then consider all the confrontational situations he actively sought out, three of which landed him in jail – that's welcoming the challenge of misfortune, is it not?

Gambo knew what life amounts to, and he took control of his own in such an ostentatious manner so that others might notice and learn his lessons. Did he want people to follow his example by leaving their homes for a life of poverty on the streets? Of course not, he was a Cynic showing them the way to freedom through an exaggeration of self-control and contempt for convention. Once freed, he hoped they would become a philosophical people who reflect on, and take collective control of, the destiny of the human race. He didn't want people to copy him, he wasn't looking for "repeater pencils", as jazz saxophonist Lester Young used to put it. Rather, he was showing us a larger-than-life way of being free, so that we might be inspired to develop our own, more sustainable and less harsh forms of free and philosophically self-aware human life.

Gambo saw all this the very first time he read his most treasured book. The problem that delayed his rebirth, causing him to read and reread it for over two weeks, was unique to his position as somebody trying to reinvent Cynicism for the modern world. The problem, as he saw it, was that language had lost its proper force. Practically everything people said was hollow now; and this was true even when they were talking about philosophy, as he noticed while reading Arthur Braithwaite's 1867 introduction to *The Cynical Philosophy of Diogenes and Crates*. This was because people had become so indoctrinated into the fantasy world that their words rarely had meaning except in relation to it—and on the occasions when they did say something philosophical, something which pointed beyond the fantasy, then they were only capable of paying lip service to the statements.

Now humans are linguistic by nature, we like to talk, so Gambo clearly faced a serious problem in trying to revitalize the Cynical philosophy now that language had lost its meaning. He would obviously need to explain the significance of his various antics, otherwise people would just dismiss him as a lunatic—and the range of possible antics would be severely restricted without the opportunity to speak, of course. But if he were to speak, then his words might come out as hollow as the chatter of the crowds he despised—he might end up falling into their fantasy. He couldn't save them if he couldn't keep their language at bay, that was the problem Gambo faced.

The solution he alighted on, of course, was his old anglé. As Gambo saw it, only his old anglé could convey true meaning, it had a special power which shielded him from the lure of their fantasy world, from the empty noises made by these contemptable, trivial, unphilosophical people. It seems to me, therefore, that the greatest mistake anyone could possibly make when trying to understand the philosophy of Gambo Lai Lai, would be to fail to realise how seriously he took his old anglé. There's plenty of humour in it, of course, he enjoyed life, he lived as if always at a festival. But notice how the humour is always directed at the people he's talking to. The *way* that he talks to them, his old anglé, that always remains sacred, something he takes with complete seriousness. It's what sets him apart from them: his protection, and their hope for salvation.

Section 5: Middle Period Encounters and Anecdotes

The first anecdote I will recount is the best known of all Gambo Lai Lai anecdotes—I'm sure you know the one I mean. But before I proceed with my rendition, I think it best to confront the classification controversy—which to my mind amounts to a puff of smoke. It strikes me as patently obvious that this anecdote marks the transition between Gambo Lai Lai's early and middle periods, since at the end of the anecdote, with Gambo's resonant final statement, we get to witness the dawning of the middle period. With this statement he announces that he's discovered his true self, one moulded by Diogenes and Crates, to be sure, but no longer beholden to them. He tells the world that the mature Gambo will no longer feel obliged to imitate his Greek forebears—which isn't to say that he won't still reference and elaborate on their behaviour, his admiration for them remains undiminished.

So, Gambo starts the anecdote in the early period and the magnificent final statement marks the beginning of the middle. As such it seems to me plain as day that this anecdote might just as well be classified as early or middle—it straddles the two, so it makes no difference which nomenclature is chosen. I have placed it at the beginning of the middle period but might just as reasonably have placed it at the end of the early. And yet for some scholars I have made a controversial statement: I have thrown my scholarly reputation, such that it is, behind the view that this is a middle period anecdote. How ridiculous!

§

Gambo Lai Lai had often thought about the anecdote in which Diogenes tells Alexander the Great to move aside because he's blocking the sun. As Gambo interpreted it, the anecdote reveals Diogenes' hatred for Alexander. This was an original interpretation, and a plausible one too once you see his point of view. As Gambo ran the Diogenes and Alexander anecdote, it went something like this:

Diogenes was sitting in his pithos one fine sunny day, thinking about philosophy and feeling the heat of the sun on his skin—he was sunbathing and philosophising, the perfect combination. Then along came Alexander the Great, unannounced and unwelcome, and he ruined Diogenes' fun. Alexander was trying to be nice, of course, he was an extremely important man who had come to pay his respects, while offering to grant Diogenes a favour. But Diogenes feels no gratitude, and certainly doesn't feel honoured, he's just irritated. He's no fan of Alexander as a public figure, he thinks his vainglorious endeavours qualify him as one of the worst of the wretches he's trying to save; as such he certainly feels no inclination to hide his irritation for the sake of politeness. Instead, Diogenes takes this unexpected irritation as a cue to tell Alexander just how much he hates him. By asking Alexander to move out of the sun, Diogenes is saying, "I don't want anything from you, I hate you, go away!" That wasn't indifference, as is usually assumed— Diogenes wasn't simply showing that he cared more about sunbathing than Alexander. No, to treat somebody of the exalted status of Alexander in such a dismissive manner was to be deliberately rude. It was surprising Alexander didn't have him strangled on the spot.

And thus did Gambo Lai Lai understand the essence of the Diogenes and Alexander anecdote. He also recognised the symbolism of saying that Alexander was blocking the sun, of course—Diogenes was implying that Alexander's fame and glory overshadowed the reality of our animal lives, enlivening our social fantasies. That much went without saying, as far as Gambo was concerned—obviously a philosopher of Diogenes' stature would find a way to make that point in the presence of Alexander. But the essence of the anecdote, what made it unique and important, in his view, was its message of hate: hate because Alexander made Diogenes' philosophical mission more difficult.

Now it came to pass one fine and sunny day, while Gambo was sitting in his oil drum home thinking about the Diogenes and Alexander anecdote, that Governor Sir John Chancellor happened to pass through the docks, protected by a guard of soldiers. Chancellor, who had for over three years now been the British colonial administrator of Trinidad, noticed Gambo in his oil drum, sunbathing and philosophising. Chancellor had heard about him and, when confronted by the oddity of a man living in an oil drum, curiosity got the better of him—he decided it'd be amusing to talk to this local eccentric.

"Good day to you, Gumbo Lai Lai," said Chancellor. "Surprised I know your name, what? Well, you're a rather famous fellow in these parts, don't you know, and I pride myself on keeping abreast of local affairs, I maintain that it's part of being a good governor."

Chancellor was blocking Gambo's sun, just as Alexander had once blocked Diogenes'. Gambo's first thought was that he certainly didn't have to pretend to be irritated in order to emulate Diogenes, he was incredibly irritated. However, it was only the blocking of the sun that irritated him, he wasn't irritated by his meditation having been interrupted, as Diogenes had been, since this was the very situation which Gambo had been meditating on—by a stroke of luck his meditation had been improved by acquiring a practical dimension: he would have to decide what to do. To echo Diogenes by telling the Governor to get out of his sun would be the obvious choice, of course, but Gambo had already noticed that the parallel wouldn't be perfect—there was one less source of irritation—so he let Chancellor carry on talking while he thought it over some more.

"I hear you speak in a special way—mock-Shakespearian or mock-Chaucerian, is it? One struggles to remember ... anyhow, it's wonderful whatever it is, I do like a little eccentricity, brings colour to the community. And, of course, you live here in an oil drum, just like Diogenes in his vase. Oh how I loved reading about that fellow at school ... absolutely splendid!"

Gambo was now furious. He was a philosopher, the only chance of salvation the people had left, and this man wasn't taking him seriously. Worst still, his wasn't taking the old anglé seriously, that was unforgivable. As the Governor stood in front of Gambo's oil drum looking jolly, wondering if Gambo would reply, enjoying the sea air in any case, Gambo thought again about echoing Diogenes. He could now see clearly that it wouldn't work, since there was no sense in which the Governor's blocking of the sun could be thought to share the symbolism of the Diogenes/Alexander case, where Alexander's fame and glory was implied to be overshadowing the reality of animal life, thereby stymying the cynic cause. This man wasn't doing that, thought Gambo, he was a nobody, a peon.

"Fuck off," snarled Gambo Lai Lai.

The soldiers arrested him and he was sentenced to 14 days hard labour in the Royal Jail.

§

When Gambo Lai Lai walked through the prison gates, he declared himself the first free man ever to do so. When he was locked in a cell, he said that slaves had imprisoned a master. When the guards brought him food, he said that lions are not the slaves of those who feed them, it's the other way around.

§

When Gambo was released from his first incarceration, there was a crowd waiting for him outside the Royal Jail, curious to find out if he'd make a statement.

"Don't worry, Gambo," a woman called out when he first came into view, "the Governor wouldn't let them move your oil drum, it's still there, just as you left it."

"Cheer up, Gambo," shouted a man, "you can borrow my Raleigh bike—go for a ride and take your mind off it all." The man lifted his bicycle in the air to sounds of approval.

"Children," boomed Gambo Lai Lai, as he threw back his broad shoulders and puffed out his great chest. He'd been arrested without a hat and his afro was causing some distraction among the crowd; Gambo was also slightly distracted himself, since he didn't have a cigar ... but he'd decided that his philosophical statement must come first.

"Slumbering children," he went on. "Ye hummers of this world art but slumbering children. T'was they that drilled to the depths for oil, defying the example set of Daedalus, daring to subdue land, sky and sea. T'was they that built towers that touch the clouds from where all might gaze down on Olympus—with elevators to make condescension effortless. Thus do these titans of industry proclaim their power, that we might stand in awe of their gasconading. And yet to Gambo Lai Lai they are but slumbering children. They never awoke, they never grew up, neither have you."

"For them 'tis Gambo who's the child instead, of course, possessed of only words for their mighty works to muffle. Yet there's truth in words as can ne'er be in the grandest boulevard. And my magniloquent words for the hummers be these: thou didst not question thy premises! Thou left them unquestioned, just like the unphilosophical unwashed you conquer. Cometh the end of the dream and none the wiser you'll be, you and them alike. Thou canst imprison me while the people dream your dream, but thou canst never imprison the truth that resideth in my old anglé!"

As the crowd cheered, Gambo went among them to shake the people's hands — and also to ask around for a cigar, he was given many. He then borrowed the Raleigh bike and rode away.

§

During this period, Gambo Lai Lai would often climb tall trees, then peer down on the people below with a curious look on his face, as if he'd lost something and felt that if he kept looking he might eventually spot it. Whenever he was asked what he was looking for, his reply was always the same: "Scum! I'm looking for a different perspective on you." Children would ask him repeatedly for the pleasure of hearing the reply.

§

Another method which Gambo now adopted came directly from Crates, whose nickname was "The Door Opener", namely the method of walking into people's houses unannounced — Gambo always wore his crown on these occasions, both to honour Crates and to achieve maximum impact. On one such occasion, he walked into the front room of a notorious badjohn called Johnny Diamond while he was liming with his girlfriend, Dorothy. The moment Gambo stepped in, with a manic grin on his face, Dorothy stood up and screamed:

"Gambo Lai, what you doing in here? Get out! Get out, quick, boy, or Johnny's going to kill you, he's got a mean temper!"

Johnny had now found his pistol and was pointing it with intent at Gambo, while Dorothy waved her arms hysterically, "Johnny, you leave him be, ain't no good gonna come of this. And you, Gambo Lai, get out of here this instant!"

Gambo, still grinning, said the following:

"I've made myself a cynosure as an opportunity for freedom, yet all thou showest me is your enslavement. Thy situation calls for outrage, fear and threat, so Johnny and Dorothy obey—but think instead on what thee might have chosen! Unlike thee, Gambo Lai Lai can do whatever he doth please."

"Gambo, I'm gonna pull the trigger," said Johnny, looking and sounding as if he could do so at any moment.

"And thus would a slave kill a free man without winning his emancipation," said Gambo, leaving briskly.

§

Gambo was often seen in the streets examining objects from different distances, while repeating to himself, "Diogenes and Crates bounded, Gambo boundless," over and over again. So, for example, he would take a pretty pink rose on a stem, hold it right up to his face, then gradually retreat it to arm's length, before dropping it and walking away until it was barely visible. Then he would approach the rose again to repeat the process— and all the while muttering to himself the mantra about how his forebears were bounded but he was not. When asked what he was doing, he would say that it didn't always look like a flower.

§

Since the circumstances around Gambo Lai Lai's second incarceration are hotly contested, I shall present both versions of events and allow the reader to decide for themselves.

Version 1 was presented by Sub-Inspector Walcott in court and is the version the judge accepted.

Gambo Lai Lai was standing on the corner of Prince and Nelson streets, harassing passers-by in his old anglé by shouting at them "question thy premises" or "defy thy situation" and other such phrases. When Sub-Inspector Walcott saw this, he told Gambo to move along. Gambo replied with a torrent of abuse, calling the police the "arch-enemy of mankind", since they not only "lived the fantasy", but "enforced it too". Gambo's tirade against the officer ended with him using the same two words that led to his first incarceration. Walcott arrested him on the spot.

Version 2 was presented by Gambo Lai Lai in court. It is backed up by the testimony of the rum shop owner, all the customers who were in the shop at the time, and various other eyewitnesses as to what happened in the street.

Gambo Lai Lai was standing on the corner of Prince and Nelson streets, practising his Cynic philosophy by advising passers-by to "question thy premises" or "defy thy situation", for example. When Sub-Inspector Walcott saw this, he told Gambo to move along. Mindful of the likelihood of being arrested if he failed to comply, Gambo said only that the police "enforce sleep and childishness", before leaving his spot on the corner to head directly to a nearby rum shop. It was a good ten minutes later when the officer burst into the rum shop and arrested Gambo, which he had no right to do.

Gambo was in fine fettle when he arrived at court, demanding his right to make a "promulgation", as he put it. He was so persistently rumbustious in expressing his outrage at wrongful arrest that the court officials decided it would be prudent to hear his case straight away, despite there being other cases scheduled ahead of it. Once in the dock, Gambo voiced his outrage even more forcefully and insistently. As Sub-Inspector Walcott was recounting his version of events, Gambo simply could not be silenced, repeatedly calling out in a thundering, tremulous voice that Walcott was a "liar", an "uneducated man" and a "worthless individual". The judge, saying that he would not continue with this "charade", charged Gambo with abusing a witness. He sentenced him to seven days in the Royal Jail. To this judgement, Gambo cried out indignantly:

"I am not a thief, I am not a criminal prostitute, I am not a gambler, I am a free agent; the only single thing I do is to drink my liquor and use my language."[3]

So irate was Gambo that he would not be silenced even as the police were dragging from the courtroom.

"His worship forgetteth that he himself be a man, one who does work for his daily bread," bellowed Gambo. "Thou art not some transcendent beacon of justice mandated in the heavens! What stories art thy telling thyself, wretch! What stories? What stories?"

§

When Aldous Huxley visited Trinidad he encountered Gambo Lai Lai orating on a busy street, and, suitably impressed, he inquired after him.[4] When he heard that Gambo was modelling himself on the Greek Cynics, Huxley was determined to discuss philosophy with him. He made his way down to the docks one fine sunny day but having heard about the circumstances which led to the first incarceration, Huxley approached the oil drum with great care.

"May I approach your home, Gambo Lai Lai?" he called out. "I've observed the position of the sun and promise to do my utmost not to block it."

"Come forth," boomed Gambo, from inside his oil drum. The man was polite, thought Gambo, so he might as well find out who he was and what he wanted; Gambo had noticed that he was wealthy, educated and English, of course.

Huxley explained that he was a successful author with a deep interest in philosophy. He told Gambo that he'd recently published a dystopian novel called *Brave New World*, that it was very philosophical, and that it had received some encouraging reviews — the philosopher Bertrand Russell liked it, for instance. (Gambo hadn't heard of him.) Then Huxley very respectfully placed a copy of the book on the threshold of Gambo's oil drum, saying that it was a humble gift which he very much hoped Gambo would enjoy, but that he was to use it to light a fire if he preferred, it mattered not, a gift was a gift and he hoped Gambo would accept it in the spirit intended.

Huxley then proceeded to explain that he'd seen Gambo's performance philosophy on the streets and had been very impressed. He admitted that it didn't occur to him at time that Gambo was a Cynic philosopher, that he only realised later when he heard he was inspired by Diogenes and Crates. But although he'd initially overlooked Gambo's place in the history of philosophy, for which he reprimanded himself severely, Huxley thought he had nevertheless grasped Gambo's message for the modern world, one he was wholeheartedly in agreement with. And there was also a more personal reason he was so keen to meet Gambo, namely that his use of the old anglé was strikingly similar to that of Huxley's fictional character John "The Savage" in *Brave New World*. In both cases, Huxley said, archaic and elaborate language has become the only means of articulating emotional life.

Gambo growled at Huxley for this analysis, explaining that his old anglé allowed him to maintain the proper force of language, and that it was nothing to do with articulating emotions — he then spat contemptuously on the floor. Although he tried not to show it, however, Gambo was starting to warm to Huxley; Huxley, for his part, thought he was doing a terrible job of avoiding giving offence to this incredible man — he'd have to try harder or the encounter would come to a bitter end, he told himself.

Gambo went on to explain that he would never pay lip service to philosophical ideas (Huxley nodded enthusiastically) and that his old anglé offered the best possible protection from the meaning-diluting, unphilosophical chit-chat of the people he was trying to save. It kept him out of their conversation and out of their society, it ensured that he never fitted in. So, in the midst of a society which he regularly and publicly disowned, by acting and speaking in defiance of its conventions, Gambo Lai Lai the Cynic was aspiring to guide that society, and the language which serves it, in the direction of authenticity.

Huxley was very impressed by this explanation and apologised profusely for having misinterpreted Gambo's old anglé; Gambo made a grunting noise which indicated unamused and begrudging acceptance. Huxley then asked whether it would be right to think of Gambo's old anglé as a unique new kind of philosophical performance, one which followed in the footsteps of Diogenes. Gambo asked why anyone would think that Diogenes gave philosophical performances. Huxley explained that as he saw it, Diogenes' choosing to live in a pithos was a kind of performance, one designed to inspire thoughts which would bring people around to the Cynic point of view. Gambo called Huxley a "wretch", explaining that Diogenes wasn't performing and neither was he. Both lived the life of the Cynic philosopher, the real life, it was the others who were acting.

Huxley said that although it was of course quite wrong to think of Gambo's use of old anglé as a kind of theatrical performance, he nevertheless wondered whether it might still be considered an artistic approach to philosophy. Gambo said that in the proper sense of "art" this was indeed the case. Huxley inquired as to what the proper sense amounted to. Gambo explained that true art attempts to convey inner space by outer-space means, and that artistic success was a measure of success in conveyance. Thus, he went on, Diogenes was an artist because his way of life and his sayings—his outer-space means—were designed to convey to people the need to question their lives. To be persuaded by Diogenes, or indeed by any Cynic philosopher, himself included, was to become engaged in an inner space philosophical reflection on what is possible and what is desirable for human life. So, in this sense, said Gambo, his old anglé was indeed employed for the sake of art, and might even be considered "performance philosophy", so long as this was understood as the practice of engaging in artistic acts of philosophical communication.

Huxley said that Gambo's art was under threat in the modern world, as was all art. He said that art was continually being devalued by Americanism, or more specifically, by what he liked to call "Fordism" (a reference to Henry Ford and his methods of mass production). This process would continue, said Huxley, until art's function of trying to convey inner space visions was replaced by the consumerist alternative of a commodity purchased for its ability to cause pleasure. As this process continued, said Huxley, it would become harder and harder for the people to hear Gambo's message of salvation.

Gambo said that every era faced its own specific challenges, such as Alexander for Diogenes or Ford for himself, and then he chided Huxley for his shallow and reactionary anti-Americanism, explaining that technological consumerism was simply the latest historical manifestation of the ancient philosophy of materialism, one which America inherited through political happenstance and its own economic success.

Huxley asked if Gambo had heard about Marcel Duchamp exhibiting a urinal as art, which Gambo had not. Gambo asked if Duchamp was making a gesture of disgust with the art of his time. Huxley said that regardless of how Duchamp himself saw the gesture, it set a dangerous Fordian precedent for subverting art in favour of consumerism. For had not Duchamp shown that anything could be sold as art? Clearly there was no inner space vision he was trying to convey with a urinal, rather he was simply trying to cause shock by placing it in the hallowed place where art is expected. What Duchamp had shown, argued Huxley, was that there was plenty more shock to be had, and sold, at the expense of art. And when the potential for shock dried up, there would also be elitist pride to be sold in lieu of art, wrapped up in a bundle with contempt for outsiders who refused to accept non-art, such as urinals, as the new art.

Huxley drew Gambo's attention to a large tiger shark which some fishermen were hauling onto the dock from their boat—it was a very impressive fish, so it was causing quite a sensation. Huxley said it would make an excellent work of "art" for the modern world, since it was wonderful to look at, as is so much in nature, and that although it had nothing of inner space to convey, being a dead animal, it would nevertheless be able to function splendidly as materialist "new art", given its ability to cause people who accepted its artistic status to feel superior to those who refused.

Gambo asked whether Huxley thought the people who'd accept the shark as art would consider its artistic value real or merely relative, explaining that if the former then they'd think it had value for everyone, while if the latter, they'd think it only had value for certain people, those who liked it. Huxley answered that materialism bred the latter types, those who used relativism to protect their bad taste. He then sought to illustrate his point with an example concerning a musically knowledgeable believer in the objective superiority of classical music trying to explain to a lover of Al Jolson's music that it had precious little to recommend it—he explains why the simple rhythms and harmony of Jolson's music possess musical appeal, then goes on to explain how the great classical composers perfected and improved upon these sources of appeal. The lover of Jolson would be greatly angered by this, said Huxley, since art is precious to people—nobody wants to be told that their love for another is a product of ignorance. As such, they protect what they love with aesthetic relativism—they remove the possibility of the art they love being criticised by reducing their love to dumb love. It cannot be love for a reason, love for the loveable, since any reason is open to question.

Gambo said that Huxley had undermined his own argument. Nobody could love a dead shark, he said, but many really do love Jolson's music, so relativism would protect the world from the absurdity of a shark being considered art. Huxley replied that he thought people might love the shark for the feelings of pride and contempt he'd mentioned before, although only during a transitionary period sustained by the prestige of past art—for past art would always convey visions of inner space across the centuries and millennia, until it was destroyed. Nevertheless, Huxley accepted Gambo's point that in the long-term, the only sustainable function for art in a materialist world would be to entertain and cause pleasure—Gambo was right that pride and contempt were only transitory attractions, dependent upon the lingering prestige of real art. This couldn't last because relativism couldn't sustain the prestige of real art— liking it would become a source of suspicion, an indicator that your relativism might not be completely sincere. So, in Huxley's view, as the Fordian future developed, our natural love of art could only survive in acutely diminished form as love for impractical objects and events which cause entertainment or pleasure—and as such, there would be no place for the difficult and uncomfortable messages of Gambo's philosophical art. Moreover, added Huxley darkly, even art for the sake of pleasure wouldn't be tolerated if the pleasure couldn't be used for purposes of control by Lady Luck's favourites.

Gambo told Huxley not to worry, because the power of his old anglé would prevent such a future from transpiring. He explained that the inner vision his art was conveying was ultimately that of Socrates: the vision of an inner space in which endless joyous questioning transpires. Leaving everyday life unquestioned allows you to be anything in this world, he said, except for a philosopher. He said that philosophy begins by questioning everyday life and then must continue to find new premises to question if it is to survive — it grows alongside wonder, as premises become increasingly questionable, increasingly thinkable, the new sources of wonder. A philosopher must say the questionable which they themselves find questionable, insisted Gambo, the passion now flaring in his eyes.

Huxley was somewhat disconcerted by Gambo's sudden enthusiasm, since he'd been struggling to understand this speech, heavily cloaked as it was by Gambo's old anglé. Feeling the need to say something relevant to continue the conversation, Huxley returned to his theme of a future in which pleasure is used as a means of control. He reflected that the ultimate technological means of control would be a machine that controlled our inner spaces, making us feel as if we're winning, or that something interesting is going on, or that people are interested in us. Gambo agreed that such a machine might take us so deep into the fantasy that we pass the point of no return. Huxley then began to tell Gambo about the friend he'd recently made, Gerald Heard, and his ideas for evolving and expanding consciousness. Gambo quoted from Edward de Vere's poem, "My Mind to Me a Kingdom Is", saying, "No wealth is like the quiet mind." Huxley took the hint and left promptly.

§

Gambo Lai Lai's third and final incarceration occurred as a result of a visit he made to Maraval, a wealthy northern suburb of Port of Spain. Gambo rode there on a Raleigh bike he'd borrowed, intending to expose the island's elite to his message of freedom. He found a busy street corner and proceeded to shout short, staccato phrases at passers-by, such as "awaken", "grow", "it's only experience", "it matters not whether thou succeedeth", etc. He received less attention than he was used to, the people were mainly just diverting their eyes and walking swiftly past, so in frustration he stormed off to a rum shop. He spent longer in there than he normally would on a working day. When he returned to his spot, he thought he'd try some swearing—maybe that would wake up the swells. About an hour into this, a rich creole woman named Henriette Duval passed by. Gambo jumped into her path, swearing, telling her in his old anglé that she needed to question the meaning of life and the nature of reality. She couldn't understand and was afraid—she just wanted to get back to her children, she told him in French. Gambo continued to block her path, mistakenly believing that his message was getting through. Hearing the commotion, a policeman rushed to the scene and arrested him. The judge called Gambo a "habitual criminal" and sentenced him to three months in the Royal Jail. The year was 1936.

Section 6: The Mature Philosophy of Gambo Lai Lai—an Exposition

Gambo's mature philosophical thought renounces nothing from the early period; it might have, but as it turned out it was simply an expansion into new metaphysical territories. The transition to this new period of his philosophy, the most acclaimed one, occurred when Gambo saw reason to reject of one of Diogenes' views—a view which seems to have been adopted without resistance by Diogenes' follower, Crates. This was a view which had nothing to do with Cynic ethics *per se*, it was simply Diogenes' belief that Cynicism *only* concerns ethics, nothing more. For Diogenes, philosophers who looked into other philosophical matters, as did his friend and arch-rival Plato, were showing an absurd imbalance in their priorities.

The urgent task of the philosopher was to teach people to live well, to free them from their collective dream and bring them to philosophical self-consciousness. With such an important task ahead, then, it was irresponsible and decadent for someone like Plato to lounge around, on his luxurious chair, while inquiring into the ultimate nature of reality. The ultimate nature of reality could look after itself, as Diogenes saw it, but the attempt to build a society which can look after people has failed miserably. As such, it was the Cynic philosopher's duty to attend to people's collective and individual mental health—to think about any other philosophical matter, while this one had yet to be resolved, was beneath the Cynic's dignity.

Gambo came to disagree with this view; the anger of his initial transition to the mature period of his philosophy, which poor old Governor Sir John Chancellor bore the brunt of, was a side-effect of how increasingly irritated he had become by Diogenes' view. It was simple short-sightedness, as Gambo thought, hence unworthy of one of his philosophical heroes—personally, I think the reason we see more of the influence of Crates in the middle period, such as with his adoption of the "door opening" technique, is that Gambo never fully forgave Diogenes on this score. But be that as may be, what's important to understand is why Gambo came to think that Cynic philosophy should expand beyond the ethical to the metaphysical. And that's something very easily grasped: it's just that he came to think that the ultimate nature of reality is indeed relevant to determining the best form of human life, that is, that metaphysics is indeed relevant to ethics.

"How could it not be relevant?" asked Gambo Lai Lai, in his old anglé, in his inner space. "The possibility of relevance can be demonstrated with a simple example. Suppose I'm the only one that exists. Well, in that case I have no duties to other people, because they aren't real. So there's one possible situation where metaphysics would clearly be of great relevance to ethics, then.

Once that's been seen, the question then becomes: is the ultimate nature of *our* reality, the one we actually live in, relevant to ethics? Just because it could be doesn't mean it is, of course, but clearly the only way to find out, one way or the other, is through metaphysical inquiry. As such, the Cynic philosopher is obliged to raise metaphysical questions — they must give the matter serious thought, since they might discover something relevant to ethics. Perhaps ultimate reality is such that remembering our animal natures and taking control of our feelings isn't really the best way forward in ethical matters, for example, in which case the entire Cynical philosophy of Diogenes and Crates would have been overturned by metaphysics."

Once Gambo Lai Lai started to think this way, it didn't take him long to throw the weight of his opinion behind metaphysical idealism. The argument that most persuaded him was a simple appeal to Occam's Razor. This argument, now standardly known as "Gambo's Argument" (as if there were only one!) begins from the premises that we know that experience exists, as of course we all do, and that we also know that the existence of physical objects is inferred entirely on the basis of experience. It is then pointed out that so long as the experiences and inferences exist, then everything will seem the same whether physical objects exist or not — for if they did not exist then we would falsely infer that they did anyway, and on the basis of exactly the same experiences. But in that case, as the argument continues, there is no need to believe in the existence of physical objects in order to explain what we experience — we could do so, but it is unnecessary to explain the data. So, by Occam's Razor, the argument concludes, we should reject physical objects as an unnecessary complexity, affirming instead the idealist view that the ultimate nature of reality is experiential.

Gambo thought that metaphysical idealism was highly relevant to the ethics of Cynicism, albeit not in a manner that overturned any of the ethical teachings of Diogenes and Crates.

The experiential nature of reality in no way altered the fact that society had plunged people into a fantasy world, he thought, and that the best way to break them out of it was to remind them of their animal natures, while also persuading them to free themselves from their bondage to pleasure and pain. Diogenes and Crates had been right about that, although Gambo now considered them somewhat lucky to have been right, given their negligence in avoiding metaphysical inquiry. Gambo did not think that the relevance of the experiential nature of reality to ethics was such as to overturn traditional Cynic ethics, then. Rather, the relevance to ethics concerned how people might learn to live together after Cynic philosophy had freed them.

Everyday life is real, as Gambo never doubted, but if its reality is ultimately that of inner space, then the ideal way to live together would be to self-consciously bring those experiences together in satisfying, pleasurable and artistic ways. A return to animal life had never been a real option; even in Diogenes' time we'd already left that kind of life too far behind to realistically hope to recover it—and there was no reason to want to anyway. To try to live like apes would be cold, painful and regressive—not deluded, to be sure, but not realising our true potential either, so hardly a great experiential balancing. And, of course, to renounce wealth to live on the streets was not an option either. That was only ever meant as the method of instruction employed by the Cynic philosopher, and obviously not as a sustainable alternative to the fantasy and lip service of unphilosophical life in the social framework. After all, people would have to maintain the streets they slept rough in, and it would be absurd to live outside when the more comfortable indoors was freely available, unless you were making a point. No, Diogenes and Crates had not thought beyond the Cynic awakening: their philosophy awakens the people ... but then what? Gambo was determined to find out the answer, and he was convinced that the key to it was metaphysical idealism.

Technology and art were two of Gambo's abiding concerns while his mind was focused on the "what next?" question, that is, during the mature period of his thought. When aeroplanes flew over Port of Spain the novelty always caused lots of attention, naturally, but many were surprised to discover that Gambo's attitude was one of awe and reverence — he would immediately halt one of his grand speeches to watch a plane fly overhead, and would not continue until it could neither be seen nor heard anymore. The reason, I think, is that he was astounded by the capabilities and potential of modern technology, and he wondered whether its powers might be applied to answering his new overarching question.

Art was of interest to Gambo for the same reason, namely that he thought it relevant to finding a new ethical approach to life which dovetails with the experiential nature of reality. We shouldn't just balance our experiences in pleasurable and intellectually satisfying ways, he thought (note that injustice is most certainly *not* intellectually satisfying), but also in artistic ways — and these were by no means the same thing, as he would always insist. Art may bring pleasure and often does, but it need not to be valuable, in Gambo's view. Art is valuable for art's sake. As Gambo saw it, then, pleasure, intellection and art were the three distinct human goods — the fundamental ones which must be balanced and interwoven to develop a new ethical way of life.

Whether Gambo ever found the answer to his question is a moot point. Some would say that the answer can be gleaned from the late-period encounters and anecdotes, which are hard to interpret, to be sure, but in which it's clear that he's preoccupied with our ability to self-consciously and creatively control our experiences through the power of imagination. Others, however, deny that Gambo ever found the answer he was looking for, while granting nonetheless that he progressed the Cynic philosophy further in the direction of an answer than anyone else before or since. I myself oscillate between these two opinions; I've written a poem about it:

Did Gambo find a way to live,
Which others never dreamed of?
I sometimes think I see it there,
Pray, *what* did I conceive of?

Section 7: Late Encounters and Anecdotes

Gambo Lai Lai's late period begins with his release from the third incarceration, which was in 1936, and it ends less than three years later in 1939. Reports of his behaviour during this time are all variations on the few themes which I shall now elaborate. The only real "anecdote" to speak of is the story of his disappearance.

§

Gambo would stand in a busy street or square and make the strangest movements imaginable: dressed in a three-piece suit and Panama hat, with his teeth clamped around a massive Cuban cigar, he would raise one arm in the air, his head thrown back to follow the movement, then unexpectedly kick a leg out to the side, sometimes then hopping to the left or right unexpectedly. He explored these movements with innumerable variations as to the angle his limbs took, or the speed of the movements, or whether or not he hopped, and if so, how far and in which direction, etc. To somebody unfamiliar with the seriousness of Gambo Lai Lai's philosophical aspirations, it might be imagined that he was dancing—and if you were to misjudge it in that way, then you'd have to add that the dancing made for a bizarre and ridiculous spectacle. Such a misjudgement was impossible for anyone who made eye contact with him during these times, however, since his expression was not only deadly serious, but terrifyingly intense.

If Gambo was challenged, whether sarcastically, on rare occasions, but more usually with respect and sympathy, he would stop to explain his behaviour as follows—this is a typical response, amalgamated from the most typical elements in the various reports:

"Wretch! Should a free man move like a slave? Should he pretend that chains bind him when he knows there are none? That I move alone is a failure of the human race—thou must learn to move with me, that we might joyously interact."

§

Gambo was engaged in his strange movements one day when an aeroplane flew over the centre of Port of Spain. He immediately stopped to watch and listen. Then he held out his arms like wings and started to sway from side to side, as if he himself were an aeroplane flying through the sky.

"Are you pretending to be a plane, Gambo?" asked a small girl.

"Scum!" snapped Gambo. "Is that the best thou canst do in bringing inner and outer space together? If the plane flies and Gambo imagines, then there is no connection worth its salt. Nay, the plane must fly *because* Gambo imagines … and you, you must fly with me, girl, the waters are rising fast!"

§

Gambo was engaged in his strange movements one day when tears suddenly came to his eyes. He stopped moving and just stood there, crying. People approached to comfort him, but they soon jumped back when Gambo threw his arms aloft and screamed out wildly,

"Stand away, scum! Dost thou not know danger? Dost thou not fear the righteous anger of Gambo Lai Lai?"

"Sorry, Gambo," said a woman called Melda, "we thought something was wrong."

"That's right," said another woman, called Dorothy, "we just wanted to help, we don't like to see you sad, Gambo Lai."

"Alas," groaned Gambo, as his anger quickly subsided and was replaced by despair; his head slumped down and his cigar fell from his mouth. "Alas alackaday. I found it, my Holy Grail, a perspective on you wretches with honour and goodness, an arrangement of experience without your meanings. And how dost thy show thine gratitude? By rejecting thine own salvation ... so now the perspective lies in ruins, beyond repair, unrecoverable. Art thou satisfied, Melda? Art thou satisfied, Dorothy?"

He then continued with his strange movements.

§

Calypsos about the war were all the rage in the autumn of 1939, and when a show dedicated to them was hosted, featuring all the greatest calypsonians of that greatest age of calypso, Gambo decided to attend. He wore a black tie, which was noteworthy, since he'd never been seen in a sober tie before; his taste in ties was very flamboyant. He arrived late to the calypso tent but was ushered to the front row by practically everyone who was close enough to notice his entrance, it was like the parting of the Red Sea. He heard Growler sing "Nazi Spy Ring", Atilla the Hun sing "Send Hitler to St. Helena", Roaring Lion sing "The Invasion of Poland", and Growling Tiger, so often the sardonic one, sing, "Let Them Fight for Ten Thousand Years". The calypso that impressed him most, however, was "Two Bad Men in the World" by Lord Executor, the veteran master who all the others looked up to. The song was about Hitler and

Mussolini, of course, and Gambo particularly liked the final verse:

> So religion is phlegmatic
> And all the world is Catholic
> But now they get so phlegmatic
> And the scene itself is dramatic

After the show, Gambo stood purposefully outside the tent and so a crowd quickly gathered; the calypsonians gathered around him too. It turned out to be Gambo's final speech.

"Crates was desirous of old age, calling those who complained of its torments the wretches of ungratefulness—as Charles Churchill didst echo this wisdom in *Gotham*, 'Weak, sickly, full of pain, in ev'ry breath; Railing at life, and yet afraid of death'. Some sayeth Crates lived to 120 years old ... well, Gambo is not so desirous of old age as all that, thou canst be sure! For mine inspiration, then, I must look to Diogenes. Some sayeth he died from holding his breath. Some sayeth he died from eating raw octopus. Some sayeth he died when feeding raw octopus to a pack of dogs, since an ungrateful dog didst bite him and the wound didst fester."

"Let me tell you that I hath tried holding my breath unto death many, many times, only to realise myself constitutionally incapable of attaining to such a gargantuan feat—either Diogenes of Sinope was a far greater man than Gambo Lai Lai, or else someone hath lied, methinks. So, shalt I buy an octopus from the market and then sinketh in my teeth? Should I do so whilst the creature still wriggles, perhaps? Gambo shalt not! If thou didst watch me thine experience would be horrible, while Gambo's experience would be worse still, and worst of all by far would be the experience of the poor octopus. Dull of intellect they be, but why think their experience not bright? It may be brighter than ours, even, so bright perhaps that I hath averted a pain worse than any we humans could feel."

"So, I shalt not die by holding my breath, nor by eating octopus ... which just leaves the dog bite—inconsequential since 'twas merely an accidental death. Nay, Diogenes, my old friend, thou hast not taught Gambo how to die!"

At this, Lord Executor called out from the crowd,

"Now then, what's all this about dying, Gambo Lai Lai? You're a strong and healthy 49-year-old man of mighty constitution, you always cut a dashing figure in your fine suits and Panama hat, and the people love you—mostly for the way you stick up for yourself with the police, but they've come to love your old anglé too—I know it makes you cross they don't try hard enough to understand it, but never forget that they've truly grown to love it ... because they love *you*."

At this many others called out from the crowd, saying things like, "Don't do it, Gambo", "We love you, Gambo" or "You've a long life ahead of you, Gambo". Gambo just waggled his finger dismissively, then left promptly.

I was an eyewitness to that final speech. I was also there later on that day, when a great commotion sprang up in the streets and everyone started rushing down to the dockyard—we all knew it was something to do with Gambo, but I didn't know what, and I'm not sure anyone else did, not until we arrived. When I did arrive, I saw people lining the edge of the dock in silent awe; I rushed to join them, and what I witnessed I shall never forget until my dying day. On that beautiful warm afternoon, with the sky glowing orange above, Gambo Lai Lai was floating out to sea in his oil drum. He must have launched it as a boat and now he was standing inside, using a plank for a platform, I'd imagine, so that he was visible from the waist up as he gazed back at us. The last I saw of his face, before it fell into shadow, was somewhat blurred by the thick smoke of his cigar—and yet I could swear I saw him wink at me.

§

OK, we've all got the scent now, it can't be far ahead, one final burst is all that's required, then we'll be on it, bringing it down in a frenzy. You'll be sinking your teeth in before you know it, just think!

Endnotes

1. Inventor distracted Executor by incorporating a racial slur into his improvised calypso lyrics.
2. *On Tranquillity of Mind*, 4, 466e.
3. The words of the historical Gambo Lai Lai, as reported in the *Port-of-Spain Gazette*, March 7, 1924, p. 5.
4. Huxley visited Trinidad in 1933. There's a good chance that he did encounter Gambo Lai Lai in Port of Spain, he'd have surely been hard to miss. Huxley wrote that, "The Calypsonians of Trinidad live in another 'Zeit'; so the 'Geist' they obey is not the same as ours. In that, it may be, they are fortunate." Huxley, *Beyond the Mexique Bay*, London: Chatto and Windus 1934, p. 19.

Chapter 6

Once More with Feeling

Section 1: Zemina Reacts to Krebon's New Interpretation of Tartaglia

It was spring 3389 in London, England, Earth, Sol, in the UH C-Space (the common space of the United Human virtual reality). Zemina was pacing up and down in her glass-walled penthouse apartment, looking and feeling irritated as she repeated to herself the following statement:

"Tartaglia's true message was a summons to authenticity, but not for them. It was a visionary call out to his distant descendants—he was calling out to *us*!"

She abruptly halted and picked up the beautiful hardback copy of *Inner Space Philosophy* which had been resting on her blue crystal table. She held it up and looked intently at the front cover, then said, in a voice that revealed her inner struggle to remain calm: "Will you listen to Zemina, then? Not anymore, you can listen to Tartaglia instead!" She managed to keep her voice reasonably calm until the end of the quotation, then lost control and threw the book against the wall in a rage.

"How much longer are you going to be with that, Annie?" she snapped at her AI assistant.

"I'm almost ready," said Annie, "I've been struggling with the realism because of the need for Tartaglia to be knowledgably defended in those days—it brings the probability down very low, and that creates problems for maintaining a high level of plausibility, hence reality."

"You've said that before," said Zemina, "I know ... and you know I know. I'm fully aware it's difficult, and I know you'll do a fantastic job, as you always do ... but you must understand my impatience!"

"Not really, since I'm not conscious," said Annie, "but I do know the way it makes you behave."

Zemina groaned with frustration. "To hear Krebons publicly challenge me like that ... and to use nostalgic old crap like Tartaglia's *Inner Space Philosophy* as the basis of that challenge ... I can hardly believe he'd do it! It's the philosophical equivalent of challenging me to a duel to the death! He's such a silly old fool ... this'll be the end of him. I just need you to get this simulation right for me, Annie, I need to be 100% sure — I'm already 99% sure ... I mean, come on, Tartaglia obviously wasn't saying what Krebons thinks. Anyway, as soon as we've run the simulation I'll schedule my public response, the press will be overjoyed. It'll be the response that ends the era when it was still possible to doubt that I'm the new Philosophy Czar. I took over from Krebons years ago ... everyone knows that except a few diehards, this is just Krebons' desperate attempt to reclaim his lost authority. Well, this sorry affair's going to lose him whatever philosophical authority he had left ... this is not going to go well for him, no siree!"

"It's ready," said Annie, "a knowledgeable and maximally bifurcated discussion of Tartaglia's *Inner Space Philosophy*, set at a time after Tartaglia's death and before the first AI war. Let me start by introducing Tartaglia's detractor, a 32-year-old man named Cuillin, a very easy character to put together, boilerplate stuff. He's English, brilliant, and he's just taken up a position as an Assistant Professor of Philosophy in a prestigious American University, the one they called 'Harvard'."

"Harvard, you say?" said Zemina with a smile. "You do like your details, don't you!"

"I include as many as possible to maximalise stability," explained Annie. "Anyway, you don't need to know much about Cuillin. He's having this discussion of Tartaglia's book reluctantly, he didn't want to read it, I've inserted a backstory for why he was obliged ... but there was no need to refer to this in the visible content. He's dressed in a tweed jacket with leather elbow pads, he keeps his shoes nice and shiny ..."

A freezeframe holograph of Cuillin appeared at the table.

"Ah yes, I see," said Zemina. "Do I need to know anything about the inner space?"

"Not really," said Annie. "He arrived at Harvard about a month ago and he's been pleasantly surprised by how easy it can be to get on with Americans, or at least with some of them, the social situation isn't nearly as bad as he'd been expecting — he comes from a very privileged and self-assured English and Scottish background, you see."

"Gotcha," nodded Zemina. "And the difficult one?"

"His name is Barney and he's something of a stroke of genius, if I say so myself," said Annie in self-satisfied tones. "Now hear me out before you jump to conclusions, he doesn't seem terribly plausible when you first hear about him, but he does make sense."

A new freezeframe holograph now appeared, across the table from Cuillin. This one was a big, rugged, good-looking young man who'd clearly spent lots of time at the gym, judging from the massive, tattooed arms and the stout chest straining against his cowboy shirt.

"Barney's a farmer," Annie began. "His dad was a tenant farmer in a rural area of England called 'Herefordshire', and Barney grew up working on the farm with his dad. He went to university mainly because he wanted to meet 'classy girls', as he thought of it, and he chose philosophy because one of his ex-girlfriends had introduced him to Marxism. When he began his philosophy degree, however, he soon found he was interested in more than just political philosophy — he found, much to his surprise, that he was mainly interested in metaphysics. Barney did exceptionally well in his degree, stayed on for postgraduate studies, and he ended up doing a Ph.D., in which he defended the argument of Tartaglia's

Inner Space Philosophy; his thesis was called 'A New Reading of *Inner Space Philosophy*: Releasing the "Main Argument" from its confinement to chapter four'. This was a very unusual topic to choose, since Tartaglia was hardly known at the time, but given Barney's exceptional intelligence and charisma, I calculated that it'd be plausible enough for him to attract a brilliant supervisor."

"After his Ph.D., Barney returned to the farm both because he missed his old life and because he hadn't gotten along with most of the people he'd met in academia; he loved philosophy, but felt no temptation to try to pursue a career in it because of the people he'd met and the aggravation they'd caused him."

"And so there you have it, Zemina: somebody from before the AI Wars who knows Tartaglia's book intimately and will defend it passionately. Admittedly he's a bit of an odd character, and I can't say I'm not a little bit worried about him having a violent streak that'll affect the simulation, but nevertheless it all seems to work, I'm getting green lights right across—it certainly looks like we've got a stable simulation I can run for you … so far as I can tell, at least, this one's going to work."

"Brilliant," said Zemina, "I don't know why I ever doubted you … oh yes, that's right, I never did! Obviously I knew it'd be great, obviously I knew you were going as fast as you could … I don't know why you insist on interpreting me as complaining, it's ridiculous. You know perfectly well that Krebons infuriated me today, the silly old fool … why should I have to hide my feelings from you? Anyway, let's run the simulation, this'll be interesting."

Section 2: Imagination and Presentation
Cuillin: Well, we may as well get on with it—I've expended good time on studying this book, most of the damage is already done.

Barney: Thanks very much, mate, so kind of you to study the book we're here to discuss. Let's do it chapter-by-chapter, agreed?

Cuillin: As opposed to line-by-line ... well yes, I very much hope so, old boy! I must say, I'm really hoping we can keep this brief; there's proper work I need to be getting on with.

Barney: Yeah fine, whatever, mate. So, the introduction, "Imagination and Presentation", it's brilliant, right? You can't tell me you didn't like that bit, if nothing else—it's standard prose and the argument is clear and bold, should be right up your street.

Cuillin: Ah yes, the justification of Tartaglia's valiant fight for the "soul" of philosophy, one which he hopes to win by writing in a style that's a cross between dumbed-down philosophy for the public and a poorly judged attempt at comedy. No, I'm afraid I failed to spot the—what did you call it?—"brilliance".

Barney: You wanna keep it short, right, so let's just talk about the argument. He gives three reasons for trying new forms of presentation and not just writing in the standard, boring, artificial format. The first one's that ...

Cuillin: Is it just one reason, perhaps, namely that the chap couldn't get his work published anywhere credible?

Barney: Don't interrupt me again, mate, it's not nice—you wanna be nice when I'm around, I'm telling you straight. So, as I was saying, Tartaglia's first reason is that the standard format presupposes a certain metaphilosophy, you know, a certain conception of what philosophy is and why it's important— basically the standard format is presupposing that philosophy's a kind of science, so Tartaglia's choosing not to write that way. The second reason is that the standard format makes philosophy insular, and that makes it look pointless—I bet your papers aren't read very widely outside the profession, are they, pal?

Cuillin: People outside the profession wouldn't understand them, although they're more than welcome to try, of course.

Barney: Thought not. And the third reason is that conforming to the dull style that's killing philosophy wastes the imaginative vitality that's kept philosophy going for thousands of years.

Cuillin: I'm a serious professional … an expert trying to make some small measure of progress in a difficult area. If what you're telling me is that if I want to make philosophy "distinctive" and "down with the kids" then I have to make a clown of myself by talking about "Gumbo Lai Lai" and God knows what else, then I think I'll settle for boring and insular, thank you very much.

Section 3: Everyday Life Is Real

Cuillin: For people like you who bought the argument of the introduction, I guess Chapter 1 must have come as something of a let-down, what? There you were, getting all excited about an imaginative new form of presentation, only to find that Chapter 1's written in the dumbed-down prose of philosophy for the layman—what a disappointment! Well, I know I'd be disappointed, anyway … maybe that's the kind of philosophy you like best, it is called "popular" for a reason, after all. And as if the unimaginativeness of Tartaglia's presentation weren't already enough of a disappointment …

Barney: He's just bringing it in laid-back, mate—with authority, for sure, but laid-back, he's getting you into the swing of things. You know you're in for a big journey to who-knows-where, but you've only just set off, you're still just anticipating what's ahead, you haven't got into the real shit yet. He knew how to pace a good jazz saxophone solo. By the end of the book things might get pretty extreme for all you can tell from the first chapter. Anyway, you were about to say the other thing you didn't like about the beginning.

Cuillin: Actually, it was something I did like, namely that Tartaglia reveals what an atrociously bad philosopher he is straight away—if I'd been reading this book of my own free will

I'd have known to abandon it after the first few pages, thereby saving myself a considerable amount of wasted time.

Barney: I wrote my Ph.D. about Tartaglia, mate, I like him, I think he's really good—you already knew that, though, so try not to forget again, you got me? Anyway, go on, Your Worship, what's the big mistake he's supposed to have made at the start?

Cuillin: I shall explain. Everyday life is "real" and has "domesticated" philosophy, which means that chaps like you and me are only paying it lip service—correct?

Barney: He's saying it's become difficult to do anything more than pay lip service to the ideas. He's not saying it's impossible, otherwise he'd be undermining himself.

Cuillin: Well fine. But if everyday life is "real", why should a real context developing around philosophical discourse make it "unreal"?

Barney: "Domesticated" is what he says. It's because the everyday context deflects the ideas from their proper role. If you're talking about Plato's immaterial forms, it should be to direct your mind beyond the context of everyday life, it shouldn't be because you're trapped in an everyday academic context. When you write your papers about "cognitive penetration"—I read a couple—I reckon the main significance for you and your readers is academic life, not the nature of reality.

Cuillin: How could you possibly know that? That's a completely baseless assertion; and an insulting one to boot. I was only seeking clarification on Tartaglia's position to help you understand his opening blunder—I haven't explained it yet, so let me go one. Let's grant Tartaglia everything he wants, then, namely that he himself speaks with gravitas, while others only pay lip service.

Barney: That's not what he's saying, mate.

Cuillin: And what's the first thing he wants to tell us with his special gravitas? Why, that "everyday life is real", of course ... by which he essentially means that it doesn't conceal "some colourless movement of atoms", as his hero Bradley put it.[1] And how does Tartaglia know that? The only reason he gives is that everyday life contains "weddings, military invasions and hospital appointments" — his point being, I presume, that these are all things we take terribly seriously (weddings was an odd choice...). So, his criterion for the reality of everyday life is itself taken from everyday life — and that means he's begging the question in the grossest fashion imaginable.

Barney: Nah, you've fallen into his trap, mate. He could only be begging the question if he accepted a higher criterion of reality than the ones provided by everyday life, but that's exactly what he's rejecting. It's like an appeal to honesty and common sense, that's one of the main things I like about him — he's asking you to be honest about what you really think, he can't be bothered when it's not real. So, for example, lots of religious people have thought that life's just a test for their immortal souls — that's a denial of the reality of everyday life which people have taken fully seriously, and still do, it's a philosophical claim with appropriate force, albeit a false one, in his view — and mine too. What he's asking is how philosophy can lay claim to that kind of force *without* denying the reality of everyday life.

Cuillin: I see, that's actually quite helpful, thank you. So that's what the long-winded Cartesian scepticism example is trying to show, is it? You know, the one where he has a "chat" with his wife because he's found out he's in a virtual reality. The point he's making is that when the chips are down, our criterion of reality is an active and practical one taken from everyday life.

Barney: Exactly.

Cuillin: Fine, so let's move onto his first scattershot volley at materialism, shall we? And just let me state at the outset that I'm not a materialist myself, I think it faces serious difficulties — I thought I'd better mention that before you start attributing my lack of patience with Tartaglia's book to materialist sympathies I don't possess.

Barney: What are you then, a dualist?

Cuillin: Oh God no, I'm no great fan of "ism"s and I'm rather suspicious of the whole metaphysical game, to be honest.

Barney: Why's that, because metaphysicians reach their conclusions in armchairs?

Cuillin: Yes, and why not? Now we have so much scientific knowledge about the reality we live in, don't you feel somewhat suspicious when a philosopher like Tartaglia claims to be able to ascertain, through reason alone, that all the scientific work he barely knows about concerns the experiential nature of reality?

Barney: I think you're talking rubbish, mate, but you're off-topic anyway, because he doesn't bring up armchairs to defend metaphysics. No, what he's trying to do is draw a distinction between philosophy-in-the-academy and philosophy-in-the-world.

Cuillin: The former being mere "lip service" and the latter the "operative" philosophy which leads to the "obscenity" of successful businessmen receiving appropriate renumeration for their wealth-building endeavours.

Barney: The other obscenity was nuclear weapons—do you reckon they're alright too, mate?

Cuillin: Don't be hysterical, they'll never be used—if you're scared try becoming better informed about military history and strategy, you'll find a little knowledge can be very soothing in this area.

Barney: I'm not scared, mate, got it?

Cuillin: Ow, don't clutch at my wrist like that, let go … thank you! How dare you …

Barney: Let's get back to Tartaglia's distinction between operative and academic philosophy, I think it's important. He's saying that while the operative philosophy is left to its own devices we've no chance of progress being rational—it shouldn't even be called "progress" because it isn't necessarily, that's why he called it "ceaseless technological advance" in

Gods and Titans. And that's why he's so concerned with reviving the force of philosophical language — he wants us to collectively take control of the operative philosophy.

Cuillin: If you made a concerted effort to define your terms I think you'd find you're not saying anything — you're deluding yourself with your own vagueness.

Barney: I think you're pretty rude, mate, and I don't think you understood what I was saying.

Cuillin: Well of course I did. There's this terrible old Titan called "materialism" and he's planning to kill us all in a nuclear attack — the only way we can stop him is to become metaphysical idealists who spend their lives playing video games. Tartaglia hints at this insane idea at the end of the first chapter, then you get it explicitly stated in the section of Chapter 4 which he's absurdly titled, "The Main Argument of This Book". I'm not exaggerating when I say that it's the most preposterous thesis I've ever come across in philosophy.

Barney: What about eliminative materialism, the view that experience doesn't exist?

Cuillin: I think that's silly too, I already told you I have my doubts about materialism — my main concern is that there are reasons to think materialism leads inexorably to eliminative materialism.

Barney: So, in a way you agree with the eliminativists — you think that if you accept materialism, then it's a natural consequence. Tartaglia argued exactly that, you know?

Cuillin: Did he now — well, I've never denied that he might have said some sensible things, it's just that there's a dearth of them in this ridiculous book. Before we move onto the next chapter, I wonder if I might ask about your interpretation of the "wolf pack" metaphor, since I presume you must have one.

Barney: I thought it was pretty obvious, mate, he's pointing out that a philosopher can't hope to lead the reader through a chain of reasoning as involved as that of a book — that even the most sympathetic readers are going to see things slightly differently, get there in their own way, in light of their own backgrounds and concerns. Philosophy readers are more like wolves hunting in a pack than balls you can roll down a track from A to B, so the philosopher needs to acknowledge that and work with it. Also, I think I read some interview where Tartaglia said he borrowed the metaphor from a discussion of Miles Davis's "second great quintet", I think that's what it was—they took a new approach to combining the theme with the improvision, apparently ... they stalked the theme like a wolf pack, something like that.

Cuillin: How boring, I hate jazz.

Section 4: Thoughts Not Stories

Cuillin: You know, every time I reached the end of one of those sections about magically encountering the spirit of some obsolete metaphysician or another, and then it ended, "And who's going to argue with this spirit?", I always wanted to reply, "Not me, can't be bothered!" I mean, what on earth is going on with Chapter 2? Firstly, it's ridiculously long, which ruins the structure of the book. Secondly, there's all this pollyannaish waffle about preferring thoughts to stories, while all the while Tartaglia's presenting us with story after story. And thirdly, the choice of philosophers seems to be explained by the fact that they're all metaphysical idealists—but what's that supposed to prove? Obviously not that idealism is true—a materialist could write a parallel chapter in which all the spirits were materialists.

Barney: Not so sure they could, mate ... it'd be very different, because materialism doesn't take you outside of everyday life in the same way. You didn't have a clue what you were reading in this chapter, did you? You've not even seen the basic point of it.

Cuillin: Which is?

Barney: To show the reader that philosophy can be a real part of your life ... that it can even be the focus of your life, an excellent life, the philosophical life, that it's happened before and can happen again.

Cuillin: Well, it's hardly surprising that philosophers have led lives that were centred on philosophy. It's the kind of life I'm leading right now … shame it didn't work out for you, old chap.

Barney: Do you want to say that to me again? Yeah, I thought not. Alright, so if you'll shut up for a minute, I'll explain the chapter you were too thick to understand. So, what makes all the philosophers in Chapter 2 different from lightweights like you is that they were trying to think outside of the presuppositions of everyday life to reach the ultimate reality.

Cuillin: I thought everyday life was real!

Barney: It is, they're all explaining what everyday life amounts to in ultimate terms, they don't exactly agree with each other but they're all thinking along similar idealist lines. And it's because they're all idealists that they don't have to reject or even challenge the reality of everyday life, they can just say that it's ultimately experiential and then think about it from that perspective.

Cuillin: Why couldn't a materialist say the same, *mutandis mutatis*?

Barney: Because you can't understand everyday life in terms of the particles and forces studied in physics—you can try to relate the two with some technical philosophy, and you can go into that endeavour hoping they'll be able to theoretically coexist … but when you return to everyday life you'll still always be leaving physics behind. Not so in the case of experience.

Cuillin: Are you sure he thought that? Perhaps you've struggled so hard to find a sympathetic interpretation that you've invented your own philosophy.

Barney: Oh yeah, he thought it alright. Now, what else was it you didn't get? That's right … why the chapter's so long, and why he tells stories while warning about stories. Let's start with why it's long—it's just because he needs to show that philosophy has been real for all kinds of people, in all kinds of historical, social and geographical settings. It's a global and historical cross-section, mate, you couldn't do it much quicker while keeping the philosophy real.

Cuillin: He had to make one of the philosophers up.

Barney: Within the philosophy in question it doesn't matter—he explained that. Yeah, so the lives are important because they inspire you to think about how life might become philosophical in the new technological settings we're developing. And that's not all there is to it, the stories are there to entertain too—why should philosophy always have to be boring? He knows people like stories and anecdotes in philosophy, he's getting you thinking about that very fact. He hardly compromises when explaining the ideas, does he? Would you've rather he skipped the stories in favour of more detail on the philosophy?

Cuillin: I would, yes. And if he'd tried presenting scholarly interpretations, I think he'd have found that a chapter of this design simply can't be written in a credible manner. The history of philosophy is a serious business, and this shoddy offering isn't up to the mark—you couldn't possibly defend so many bold and speculative interpretations in such a short space.

Barney: Ah, so now it's not long enough for you?

Cuillin: For the purposes of titillating the public these fanciful cameos are perfectly adequate, I'm sure, I was just pointing out that they're not serious work in the history of philosophy … he concedes the point himself through the absence of scholarly footnotes.

Barney: I already explained what he's trying to do with these encounters, but anyway, let's get onto your question about why he's telling stories. It's amazing you couldn't work it out yourself—do Harvard know how shit you are? The reason is that they're the stories of people whose lives revolved around philosophical thoughts ... their lives were philosophical, the thoughts and stories harmonize ... get it?

Cuillin: Yuck, how distasteful. Oh well, let's get through the chapter as briskly as we can—do you have anything to say about the Plato section?

Barney: It's showing how contemplation of the forms, the centre of Plato's philosophy, is central to a Platonic way of life. It's not just something you chat about like a clever airhead.

Cuillin: I don't think that's a credible interpretation of Plato, but it's not my area. Anyway, the whole discussion is only an excuse for Tartaglia's story about Atlantis and mobile phone addiction, don't you think? Apart from his predictable and baseless blaming of the downsides of Internet technology onto metaphysical materialism, he comes down rather hard on young people, don't you find? Their notions of bravery, excitement, pleasure, justice and truth are moulded by technology, isn't that what he says?

Barney: It's a concern, not a criticism ... a concern not just for how things are now but for how they might develop.

Cuillin: There are groups doing proper empirical research on social media addiction, that's our only prospect for ethical influence in these areas. Anyway, let's move onto Plotinus, who isn't a philosopher I'm familiar with—if Tartaglia's to be trusted, he wrote of the "ecstasy" of out-of-body experiences ... I can't think why anyone finds that kind of thing interesting anymore, it's the sign of a weak mind if you ask me.

Barney: What, Plotinus? You gotta be kidding, mate.

Cuillin: Still, I did enjoy the line, "the otherworldly are the ones to trust"! Tell me, was "Platonopolis" ever built?

Barney: No it wasn't, mate. Then there's the story of Xuanzang, I love that story.

Cuillin: I thought it went on far too long, I lost patience and skipped ahead to the idealistic guff about truth beyond language, bad philosophy's better than no philosophy.

Barney: Did you notice that Xuanzang's argument that endurance is an unnecessary intellectual construction is basically the same as "Gambo's Argument" in the final chapter?

Cuillin: I didn't, no, and frankly I'd rather have a plain exposition accompanied by a consideration of objections. I couldn't care less if some ancient Chinese chap said this or that, just state the argument so I may evaluate it.

Barney: He does—much clearer than usual, too, just not pedantic and pretentious like you'd want it.

Cuillin: I was amused by the preface to the African Queen section, where Tartaglia asks if we're preferring the thoughts or the stories, then says, "That last story was particularly good, I'm not so sure myself"—the poor deluded chap actually expects people to enjoy his crass writing! And evidently he enjoys reading it himself, that's the funniest part.

Barney: As I've said before, mate...

Cuillin: Yes, yes, I must be respectful, otherwise you might squeeze my wrist again.

Barney: I'll do a lot more than that.

Cuillin: The pseudo-African section was rather depressing, didn't you find? First there's a rather limped exposition of some Akan philosophy—and I really don't think they addressed that old existentialist cookie about "seeing the seeing eye", by the way—then we discover the real point, which is to make a gratuitous attack on technological progress from the perspective of half-baked environmentalism. What's the moral of the Agyenim and Ananse story? Why, that technology has turned us into fat, lazy alcoholics who live off fast food and are indifferent to the cruelty and environmental destruction which sustains our lifestyle. Worse still, our population is out of control and we're not even enjoying ourselves, we're all plagued by depression and anxiety.

Barney: I really don't know how you come up with this stuff, mate, it's like you've read a different book from me.

He's talking about how things might develop if we don't take collective control over our own future, he's suggesting a role for philosophy in people becoming more self-aware and concerned with their wider community, which is the central focus of the Akan philosophy. When Ananse asks, "Who cares?" the philosopher-Queen says she does—and we can see straight away that she's right to care.

Cuillin: I can't think why we should care if Ananse's right that life is pointless … nihilism being another of Tartaglia's hobby horses, of course. Anyway, if he was so concerned, why didn't he get involved in serious debates about intergenerational justice? The fool probably didn't even know they existed.

Barney: I'm starting to think you've got a death wish, mate … Doesn't matter, everything's fine for now … let's move onto Bradley.

Cuillin: Yes let's. So, pray tell, what was the point of rewriting Bradley's famous chapter about relations?

Barney: Well, it's amazing, isn't it? All the detail in those ten pages, the way Bradley's mind works, and his uncompromising attitude … didn't you appreciate having it all spelled out for you?

Cuillin: No, I didn't trust it, I expect a proper Bradley scholar would cover it with red ink. But in any case, surely it's just another argument for everyday life being unreal, as with Plotinus and Xuanzang, and contrary to Tartaglia's official line.

Barney: I already explained that one, he's taking our understanding of the reality of everyday life in metaphysical directions.

Cuillin: Bradley did in fact ask Eve to burn that summary, I looked it up—so why didn't Tartaglia just stick to the facts? And why end the chapter with Bradley, anyway?

Barney: Bradley's life gravitated around philosophical ideas, but he's living most of it locked away at his desk in a dark room—idealism's not out there in the world anymore, not in his time. And in the century following his death, in 1924, it almost completely faded away.

Section 5: Destiny and the Fates

Cuillin: The start of Chapter 3 is noteworthy for a particularly blatant display of Tartaglia's intellectual irresponsibility.

Barney: Why, because he's honest about philosophy and its power to persuade?

Cuillin: It's an attack on rationality.

Barney: No it's not, it's the exact opposite, mate, he's saying everyday life has too much influence on the way we think, so for collective rationality to develop we'll need to remove some of the relationship-dynamics from public debate.

Cuillin: That "work on your inner space" stuff sounded like a self-help manual to me: develop your inner space like you're planning a city ... that line was so excruciatingly embarrassing, I could feel my stomach churning.

Barney: Let's get into the main plot, this chapter is my favourite.

Cuillin: The class-based resentment appealed, I imagine.

Barney: So, we've got personal fate telling us we don't deserve our luck and that disaster's just around the corner, while the collective fate—Lady Luck—she thinks everything's bound to turn out great; then it turns out she's really just the personal fate of successful people who drive history, or at least the ones we hear about, you know, the political and business leaders, the technologists and so on. What a bang-on observation, eh?

Cuillin: Did he test that hypothesis? I'd want to see some empirical results from psychologists before I took it seriously.

Barney: If you think like that you'll never think differently.

Cuillin: You what? Oh, it doesn't matter, just tell me this: when Lady Luck talks about "my kind of glory", and says ordinary people are "useless", is the implication that successful people are all fascists? I wouldn't put anything past Tartaglia.

Barney: Nope, the Philosophy spirit explains all that at the end of section 6, just after the bit where she accuses Lady Luck of thoughtlessness.

Cuillin: What's supposed to be going on in section 3, then, when Lady Luck is accused of lacking self-consciousness and so immediately tries to change the subject, worried that if people stop thinking her decisions are backed up by determinism, then she'll end up just like the personal fate, i.e. superstitious, presumably ... actually don't bother explaining, I think I get it, she'd previously been a lady spirit ...

Barney: That's right, he's saying determinism is just a new take on an old superstition. The personal fate thinks that if people realised, then he could cure his "addiction" — in other words, your average bod would no longer think they were at the mercy of a collective future they had no say in. It works on so many levels, mate, I love this chapter.

Cuillin: It's inspired by Lucian, I spotted that when he ran the motif of piling up mountains.

Barney: That's right, I think Lucian was his favourite author.

Cuillin: I suppose I did rather like the interpretation of Newcomb's paradox — I don't agree, but it provides an argument worthy of consideration.

Barney: Well, I do agree, mate, and I think the discussion ties in perfectly with his theme of people only paying lip service to philosophical ideas. He shows that you can't really believe in determinism, because then you'd have to believe it's possible to choose the past, which nobody can — if you got into that situation you definitely wouldn't believe you had a choice over whether the money had already been placed in the box, so you can't really believe in determinism.

Cuillin: Even if he has got some kind of point there — one which was stolen from J.J. Valberg, I believe ...

Barney: No, Valberg discussed Newcomb in the same way, that's where Tartaglia got the idea, but Valberg drew a completely different conclusion, he accepted determinism.

Cuillin: In any case, even if there's a decent point in the vicinity, I hate the way he triumphantly and vindictively draws his conclusions: "Thoughts and selves go together, like determinism and thoughtlessness" — that's so unnecessary.

Barney: It's a bit of passion, mate, I like it like that.

Cuillin: It's a sign of a nasty disposition, you see it most clearly with all the hatred and spitting of the final chapter on Cynicism. But let's press on to the silly ending of this one ... so, Tartaglia thinks technology determines our future randomly — which I would certainly dispute — and that this can only change when we become a "philosophical race" (whatever that means).

Barney: It means we replace the crap filling people's heads with some philosophy. We've got to do something now we've acquired so much technological power and keep getting more, faster and faster. It's too risky to carry on leaving it to trial-and-error, not now the errors could be endgames.

Cuillin: You sound just like him!

Barney: I don't know what you're smirking at, mate, I wouldn't mind being like Tartaglia, he was a good philosopher.

Cuillin: Well do watch out for that nasty streak I was warning you about, you see plenty of it at the end of this chapter — not only Philosophy committing "murder", of course, but people who aren't interested in philosophy being accused of "a kind of dumbness", scientists being said to write "gobbledegook" when they "conflate philosophical with scientific questions", and philosophers playing out "materialist fantasies" by being "submissive".

Barney: You've taken that all completely out of context, mate.

Section 6: The First Thinker of the Meaning of Life

Cuillin: And so, with Chapter 4 we reach the most important chapter of the book, agreed?

Barney: It's not one of my favourites, but I guess that's right, it's the one that unlocks the overall argument of the book—but you've got to be careful how you interpret the section he calls "The Main Argument of This Book", my Ph.D. thesis was about that issue.

Cuillin: What a waste of your time and effort ... good God, man, what's wrong with you, thumping the desk so violently?

Barney: Let's just keep going, mate—focus on the book and keep trying to be nice.

Cuillin: So, the chapter begins with the claim that experience is all we care about—patently false, there are many things I care about that aren't experiences, such as philosophy, my mother, my robot ...

Barney: You care about the thoughts and feelings associated with those things.

Cuillin: Hardly, if that was true it wouldn't matter if my mother was replaced by a holograph.

Barney: Thinking she's not been replaced by a hologram is something you care a lot about, mate.

Cuillin: We get some classic examples of Tartaglia's arrogance in this chapter ... breathtaking at times. So, for instance, we're told that resistance to idealism is from a "temporary lack of education", and that attraction to materialism is just a confusion based on its association with atheism. He addresses two objections to idealism, but they're only given the space of one of the book's very rare footnotes ... the objections are dealt with only in the margins to express his contempt for them, I presume.

Barney: Have you got any idea how ignorant most people are about philosophy? The labourers I sometimes get in, rough lads but hard workers, you try talking philosophy to them, they haven't got a clue.

Cuillin: I wouldn't expect them to either understand or be interested, it's nothing to do with them.

Barney: Well that's exactly it, isn't it, mate? That's what Tartaglia's against: your kind of attitude. You wouldn't expect those lads to know any philosophy, you think it's only for people like you—and that's what's holding back our species.

Cuillin: Oh spare me, surely you can't be serious …

Barney: If you did get those lads up to the point where they could talk philosophy with confidence, I bet they'd have a lot more interesting things to say than you do.

Cuillin: Tartaglia reserves an especial hatred for anti-philosophy, does he not? It's all based in "misunderstanding or laziness", he says.

Barney: No, he qualifies that with the word "totalizing".

Cuillin: Anti-philosophy always changes the subject from a first-order philosophical concern to a second-order metaphilosophical one, we hear him thunder in outrage—a bit rich, I'd say, when Tartaglia himself was very much preoccupied with metaphilosophy during his tawdry career.

Barney: He's saying that anti-philosophy shouldn't be thought to have any special claim to our attention over straightforward philosophy. The operative philosophy of materialism makes it seem otherwise. Loads of scientifically-minded people think they're justified in ignoring philosophy—when it comes up they're suspicious and they take it for granted they're right to be suspicious.

Cuillin: Did you notice the claim about imagination being necessary for philosophy, but not for science. I think that's outrageous, science is full of imagination, it's our greatest means of expanding the scope of what humans can imagine.

Barney: It's hardly outrageous, mate, but as it happens I agree with you on that, I think the statement was out of line.

Cuillin: Anyway, I can't say I really understand why we have to listen to all this stuff about anti-philosophy and imagination before reaching the discussion of the meaning of life.

Barney: Don't worry, I'll explain how it all fits together … and it's meaning *in* life he's mainly talking about, by the way.

Cuillin: It's an "of" not an "in" in the title of the chapter. And are we talking about meaning in life, or "the reassuring feeling of meaning"?

Barney: He's assuming that the idea of people having meaning *in* their lives derives from the older idea of a meaning *of* life.

Cuillin: So, the first candidate we're shown for the absurd title of "first thinker of the meaning of life" is a man who's been expelled from his tribe and is now starting to wonder if his past labours were pointless, despite the fact that they felt meaningful at the time. I can't say I understood the point.

Barney: The caveman's questioning whether his past labours were *ultimately* pointless—whether they led anywhere beyond eating and surviving to rest on something more solid. But that's only Tartaglia's first stab at an answer—later he decides it was probably the woman making sacrifice, he thinks sacrifice is the best evidence we've got for them thinking about the meaning of life.

Cuillin: He should have consulted serious scientific work in prehistoric psychology. Anyway, next comes the "Wittgenstein/ Gray Solution"—let's ignore the attributions, I doubt they're justified. So, if I read him correctly, he's saying we shouldn't ignore the cognitive implications of "the reassuring feeling of meaning", nor exclusively medicalize the phenomenon of losing it.

Barney: He's saying that the feeling indicates something, and that it's just a scaremongering approach to anti-philosophy to suggest that you shouldn't look into these issues for fear of losing the feeling.

Cuillin: That's fine by me, let's take the jolly old feeling seriously! And when we do, says Tartaglia, we find that it indicates "having purposes your thought can rest secure with" — despite the characteristic vagueness in his unpacking of this idea, I think I see what he has in mind.

Barney: Yeah, it's a useful way to think about meaning in life, namely as an inner balance which the feeling reliably indicates. We can use the feeling as a pointer; not that you'd necessarily have it when the balance is right, of course, you might be sick.

Cuillin: I see — well, rest assured that my life is very meaningful and I'm feeling great ... better and better as we approach the end of this discussion...

Barney: You're not taking it seriously because you've not seen how it all fits together, that's fine, we'll get there. So, did you notice how he expresses his scepticism about there being any distinct element in reality that gives you meaning in your life? He thinks philosophers who try to discover the secret formula are just making proposals about what might constitute a good life.

Cuillin: That's right, so he's not claiming to have discovered the formula himself — he's just saying that the "reassuring feeling" can be sustained by philosophical reflection and can thereby be used to monitor the quality of your ... as he would of course put it ... inner space!

Barney: That's basically right, mate, yeah. The feeling indicates that you're happy with your everyday purposes, but maybe you shouldn't be, maybe you should think some more.

Cuillin: You don't have to have much of a conscience to maintain the feeling, do you? You see that clearly in the obnoxious ethical relativism of this chapter. It doesn't really matter what a morally repugnant person you are, or what terrible things you've done, if your "thought can rest secure" then everything's hunky-dory.

Barney: Did you spot the reference to Parmenides when he said, "wanders two-headed"?

Cuillin: I'm a professional philosopher, what do you think?

Barney: Fair enough, just checking … and I'm guessing you didn't like the discussion of speedrunning?

Cuillin: I didn't like any of it. Surely the idiot didn't really play computer games, did he? What an embarrassment to the profession!

Barney: So, that brings us to section 9, "The Main Argument", and now I've got some serious explaining to do—not just of this chapter, but the whole book, it's clearly gone straight over your thick head; I think you're a shit philosopher, mate, I thought you'd at least be smart.

Cuillin: Go on, then, do proceed—then we can do a quick "Dance of the Gumbo Lai Lai" before going our separate ways.

Barney: He's just explained why life in virtual reality would require you to negate contexts if you're a materialist—or just someone completely unphilosophical, it might be a very shallow religious believer instead. That's obvious, I think—the goals are visibly fake, you can only get into them if there are goals outside your virtual reality which aren't fake. He's also pointing out that this kind of technology exerts a strong pull towards solipsism. Anyone who's used it'll spot that right away—your mate's got the headset on, he's making funny movements that only mean something in his world, so your mate's not with you anymore.

Now obviously Tartaglia goes on to say that if we were all idealists we could avoid these problems—everyday life could be seen as a kind of collective and self-aware manipulation of experience. But if that was "The Main Argument", as I said at the start of my thesis, then there'd be too many unanswered questions. Why did this chapter start with imagination and anti-philosophy? How does the Lady Luck and Destiny chapter fit in? What about the stories and thoughts of Chapter 2, plus the concern about lip service in the first chapter—and what about the overarching concern with presentation, how do all these elements fit together? If this really were the main argument—we should become idealists to stay sane in virtual reality—then the argumentative strategy seems all wrong. He could've just argued for idealism, explained why we'll need it in virtual reality, then argued that a future in virtual reality is unavoidable, desirable, or both.

Cuillin: OK, you've captured my attention ... what's he really saying, then?

Barney: He's trying to put a thought out there, a really big one, the book as a whole is just an attempt to get people thinking about it. If he'd stated it nice and neat, then moved onto some clarifications and objections, then it wouldn't have worked—the book would be a bore and the thesis wouldn't seem thoughtworthy.

Cuillin: What's the thought?

Barney: That maybe we can't expect to carry on like this indefinitely, that maybe it's not prudent or sustainable. We can't just keep acquiring more and more technological power until we've unlocked the power of the gods, not while the vast majority of people just go with the flow and deal with circumstances as they arise, while the ones driving the progress compete with each other for personal or group gain; and not always peacefully either, not by a long shot. Something's going to be needed to break us out of our everyday stories, so we can become reflective enough for a human collective rationality to emerge, one which shows that our race of freakishly clever apes has finally taken rational control of its own future—he thinks we're even capable of that, even that. So Tartaglia's suggesting a new role for philosophy, its most important ever. He thinks it may have recently come into its own, that now our growing power threatens our continued existence it may be the perfect tool for dealing with the problem.

So he's not arguing that we need to become idealists in virtual reality, then, he's arguing that if that's going to be what our future looks like then we're going to need philosophy. It's the "main argument of the book" in the sense that it shows one way philosophy might be vital to our future—and that blows out of the water the usual image of philosophy as no big deal at best, bollocks at worst. It gets you thinking that there might be other ways philosophy could be useful as we become more and more scientifically advanced. It gets you thinking about what kind of future we're heading for, and whether we shouldn't all have a say in something that big.

Cuillin: Wonderful, beautifully explained, I'm glad you like the book so much, I've nothing to add. Can we move onto Gumbo Lai Lai now?

Barney: It's Gambo, mate, Eduardo Sa Gomes really did write to Decca Records; in this book if it looks like a fact, you can be sure it either is or it's based on one.

Section 7: Gambo Lai Lai the Cynic

Cuillin: I'm afraid dear old Gambo has very little to do with the Cynics—clearly Tartaglia read up on those chaps to the best of his abilities, so one might be surprised he didn't spot it, I wasn't. Here's a good example—according to one of the anecdotes about Diogenes, he used to carry a cup around with him until he saw someone drinking with cupped hands, then he threw his cup away, realising that it was unnecessary to his life. So Gambo's not a Cynic, not with his rum, cigars and fancy suits.

Barney: If you look at the source material on Gambo—and there's not much of it—he comes across as a very odd figure, he's not easy to make sense of. He hassles passers-by in an ornate old English, he gets arrested for this three times, and in his defence he says he's free, the implication being that others aren't. That sounds quite a lot like Diogenes and Crates, Tartaglia's just filling in the gaps—not everything fits, to be sure, but we're talking about modern Trinidad not ancient Greece, you'd expect big differences. There are Platonists and Aristotelians around today, they don't act like Greeks.

Cuillin: Gambo was a drunken bum who had nothing to do with philosophy.

Barney: Probably, yeah, but an intriguing enough character to have three songs written about him. And he must have been saying something in those speeches of his—if he's getting inspiration from texts written in ornate old English then there might have been something philosophical going on, you never know.

Cuillin: Very unlikely, and he certainly wasn't a follower of Diogenes and Crates. So tell me, why do you think Tartaglia turns to Cynicism in this final chapter? I think it's just an excuse—he saw a tenuous connection between Gambo and Diogenes and leapt at it because he wanted to talk about Trinidad at that time. And why was that? Because calypso music is one of the chap's enthusiasms and he's the kind of bore who's always trying to push his own enthusiasms onto others. Gambo's predilection for "Big English" was quite unfortunate for Tartaglia, don't you think? It forced him to try his hand at it ... and the messes that resulted are risible.

Barney: Once you're seen what the book's trying to do, namely get you thinking about whether democratized philosophy might have a place in human progress, then you'll also see that the philosophy of Cynicism was an inspired choice.

Cuillin: Oh really?

Barney: Yeah, really, mate ... do you know what you look like when your lip curls up like that? As the chapter makes clear, the Cynics were a tough and uncompromising bunch—nasty sometimes, going around calling people wretches and inviting them to commit suicide—one of the later Cynics was nicknamed "The Death Persuader".

Cuillin: True enough. And Diogenes used to masturbate in public, while Crates had sex on the street with his wife—funny Tartaglia didn't mention those antics ... squeamish, perhaps?

Barney: The important point they made was that we're all living in a fantasy world—the social framework tempts us to become idiots who are oblivious to, and incurious about, the very nature of our own existences.

Cuillin: Did Tartaglia identify as a Cynic?

Barney: Course not, he was just a regular, stand-up guy. But he's thinking about how people might wake up to philosophy, so he imagines a modern Cynic because it's the traditional school which makes the most dramatic and theatrical exhortation to philosophy. He thinks you'd have to be imaginative and eye-catching to reinvent Cynicism for the Internet age.

Cuillin: Gambo insults people and spits in their faces—is the idea that anyone who doesn't endorse idealism should be trolled?

Barney: You say some stupid things, mate. The Cynics thought that people going about their daily affairs in ancient Greece were in a kind of self-induced trance, being pulled around by pleasure and pain. Well just think what it's like these days when you're online ... that's a self-induced trance where you're being pulled around by pleasure and pain if ever there was one! Whatever the Greeks were dealing with it was nothing compared with now. Yeah, we definitely need Cynicism—a bit of shock, some symbolism and artistry to get people thinking. Nothing nasty, there's no need for that, we've made massive moral progress since ancient times.

Cuillin: I notice you haven't denied that the "old anglé" was simply a literary inconvenience for Tartaglia, one he continually trips over, like the clown that he is.

Barney: I was definitely right that you've got a death wish, you just keep pushing it, don't you? Do I look like someone who makes empty threats? And you're wrong anyway—Tartaglia loves the old angle, that was a big attraction of Gambo, it's a metaphor for everyone having their own genuine philosophical voice, hidden within their inner space.

Cuillin: I can't see anything in the book to suggest that reading. So tell me, Gambo's version of the famous Alexander and Diogenes encounter, that was just a crude joke, right?

Barney: Yeah, I think so, mate, it certainly gave me a chuckle.

Cuillin: And then there's Gambo's "mature" period, when he rather predictably converts to idealism ... oh yes, and the "hummers" speech about how the titans of industry are all "sleeping children" ... that wasn't very interesting, so let's move onto the meeting with Aldous Huxley.

Barney: Fine by me, mate.

Zemina: Hang on a minute, Annie, you're not really telling me they'd be dismissive of The Hummers Speech, are you?

Annie: It's unlikely they'd even mention it, the only reason I made sure they did was that I thought it'd be less distracting for you — clearly my strategy failed since it prompted you to pause the simulation.

Zemina: No, I'm sure you're right, Annie, there's no reason it would seem like a big deal to them — it's only because of its place in our emergence from the AI Wars that it seems so significant now. Still, it really does stop you in your tracks to see them discussing *Inner Space Philosophy* without paying any attention to The Hummers Speech, of all things — the text which gave us the words to The UH C-Space Intergalactic Anthem, the only philosophy we're still required to memorize in primary school. I just can't get my head around it, ancient history is so odd ... Turn the simulation back on, then.

Cuillin: I thought the discussion with Huxley was the only interesting part of this chapter ... certainly not the guff about Gambo leading society to authenticity ...

Zemina: You need to stop it again, Annie.

Annie: So soon?

Zemina: Yes, sorry—can you check whether there's any other mention of "authenticity" in the book, or is this the only one?

Annie: There's a solitary occurrence in Chapter 1 but he's talking about something different there.

Zemina: Forget that, then, read me the sentence Cuillin was just referring to.

Annie: "Gambo Lai Lai the Cynic was aspiring to guide that society, and the language which serves it, in the direction of authenticity."

Zemina: Perfect! Carry on with the simulation now.

Cuillin: ... but rather the conception of art as an attempt to "convey inner space by outer-space means", that's what I found the most interesting. Well, the formula's rather vague, as you'd expect from this chap, and I'm sure he only introduced it as an excuse to take a pop at contemporary art—he strikes me as the kind of pleb who'd be enraged by the challenging kind—but nevertheless I did think it showed some insight into the aims of certain artforms; that said, I'm not sure what this theme has to do with the rest of the book.

Barney: He thinks philosophy and art have a lot in common. Philosophy arises naturally as the questioning of premises and ways of life—it gives you new perspectives on reality, just as art does. And just like art, you've got to exercise good taste, to strike a good balance, otherwise it can descend into pedantry.

Cuillin: Or fantasy, you might have added. What about the criticism of aesthetic relativism, how does that fit in?

Barney: He's not criticising it, he's just saying people aren't consistent enough with their aesthetic relativism, it's another of his "people power" messages. He's saying that you've got the worst of both worlds if you insist on relativism by saying it's only what people like that matters, then allow your art scene to be dominated by stuff nobody likes, or at least not because it's good—a urinal isn't good, Duchamp wasn't even saying it was, but others have been saying that silly stuff is good art ever since he opened that particular Pandora's box. He's pointing out that people saying sharks, dirty beds and exploding sheds are good have been believed, despite the prevalence of relativism, and the fact that the few absolutists we've got left could never take that stuff seriously. But that's just an interesting aside really—an observation aimed at the sympathetic, one which the unsympathetic can safely dismiss.

Cuillin: As I said, he couldn't resist it because he's that kind of pleb, it's not really relevant.

Barney: The real reason for bringing up art is to introduce the idea of balancing pleasure, intellection and art—the idea of practical ethics as an imaginative art in which you make everything questionable to look for experiential balancing acts, whether in your own mind, your interactions with others, or your community—ultimately in the world. If enough people thought like that there'd be a new operative philosophy—the first self-conscious one. The majority could believe themselves involved in a form of collective rationality guiding the human race into the future. That's what Tartaglia thinks philosophy could become ... he's asking you to think it over, to think really, really big, this is the real culmination of the book. If he's right, then philosophy can become the opposite of something we pay mere lip service to—it can be the feature that announces our advancement to the next level of human development.

Cuillin: Wonderful, and then after the "Philosophical Awakening" we'll make daisy chains and chant "om" together.

Barney: That's all you've got to say, is it? Just an opportunity for a cheap joke, you don't see anything more to it than that?

Cuillin: You know I don't, now please don't spoil my fun, I'm getting rather excited that we've almost finished. So, do you have anything to say about Gambo's "strange movements" in the final and most enigmatic period of his philosophical career, ahaha-ahaha-ahahahaha!

Barney: You wouldn't think he looked so strange if he was wearing a VR headset, would you?

Cuillin: Yes, I did get it! And then Gambo sails off into the sunset and we all shed a tear — at the age of 49, I noticed, the same age Tartaglia was when he finished this book … the self-indulgence is breathtaking. Anyway, there isn't anything more to discuss is there, that's it for the philosophy … can I go now?

Barney: Mate, there's loads more to it than that, but I'm sick of all this aggro … I'm just sick to death of trying to talk philosophy with you while you're constantly being a prick.

Cuillin: I'm sorry but your beloved *Inner Space Philosophy* is just pop philosophy — wonderful for you, I'm sure, but torture for me. Good afternoon to you, my trial is at an end.

Annie: Perfect! There you go, we got right to the end without even so much as a glitch.

Zemina: Just let the sim play on a little more, will you?

Annie: There's no need, they've been through the whole book, the discussion is over.

Zemina: Go on, Annie, just do it — please, I want to see.

Annie: Well, if you're going to insist …

Zemina: I do insist.

Cuillin: What the hell are you doing, man? Let go of me this instant! What … what … let go of my tie, you're choking me. Help, robot!

Barney: Oi, XE9, take out the opposition, will you?

Cuillin: What's it doing, that vicious spike protruding from its fist …

Barney's Robot (XE9): Die! Alright, Barn, job done, mate.

Cuillin: Oh my god, my robot's ruined, he's beyond repair … how is that even possible, you monster!

Barney: I'm a real man, mate, I know how to take the safety-restraint chips out of a bloody robot. Now let's see what we can do about that annoying smirk on your face …

Zemina: OK, that'll do, Annie.

Annie: You're so childish, I told you it was a struggle to maintain the stability, I obviously wasn't going to put much effort into what would happen after the discussion.

Zemina: Oh do calm down, Annie, it really doesn't matter, it was only a bit of fun — all that matters is that you've been absolutely brilliant today, I've got exactly what I needed. Tartaglia definitely didn't mean what Krebons has been saying, so we need to move fast. The first thing is to arrange a meeting with Krebons, I want him to be the first to know, it's the decent thing to do. Once that's over you can schedule a date with Universae Philosophia, then go straight to the press.

Annie: I'll do as you ask.

Zemina: What a way to let the universe know your philosophy's been eclipsed, eh ... with a statement about a fossil like *Inner Space Philosophy*! Krebons is such a silly old fool, what was he thinking, picking a fight with me over something like that? It's obsolete, sure, but it's so highly charged, so nostalgic and sentimental. I feel for Krebons, I really do ... give me something for this tear, Annie ... thanks. Yes, I feel for him, of course I do after all we've been through together, but it's not my fault, he forced my hand. Now I've no choice except to tell the world what they already knew about Tartaglia — like, duh! — and then everyone will know I'm the undisputed Czar.

Annie: You don't rate Tartaglia, then?

Zemina: Well ... I know it's historically important, but it's all so painfully obvious now, I struggle to appreciate it in the way I doubtless should ... my interests are in philosophy, not history.

Annie: You're interested in the history of philosophy.

Zemina: I suppose so, but there's nothing to be learned from Tartaglia anymore, no lost insights — he wasn't a terribly subtle thinker in the first place, and we'd already learned his lessons a thousand years ago.

Section 8: The Great Plain of the Wolves

Over there! Do you see it? Rip it to shreds, my fellow wolves, rip it to shreds … arrrggghhh, ARRRGGGHHH!!! What the … no, wait a minute, wait, hold back. What is that? That can't be our quarry, it's a woman and I think I know her … she's wearing a black hooded cloak … it's … it's Philosophy!

The leaders of the pack who were first to leap were immediately cowed into submission by her presence. The rest of us skidded to a halt, then bowed our heads and whimpered. When we were all tamed in unprecedented self-control, Philosophy led our pack out of the woods to a vast plain, dappled in deep orange sunlight which cast ever-changing bronze shadows. We were joining innumerable other packs that had already gathered on that magical plain, there were wolves as far as the eye could see, millions, billions—around the edges small groups headed out on joyous hunting expeditions, they brought back duikers and bushbuck for the many.

There were two rocky outcrops rising up from the plain, visible from all perspectives. On one stood Zarathustra, with an eagle circling above him as it fought with a snake—the snake was strangling the life out of the eagle. As the eagle lost consciousness, it swooped out of control towards the other outcrop, where Gambo Lai Lai was talking his old anglé. The snake released the eagle and then fell from the sky, landing on Gambo's broad shoulders—Gambo continued as if he hadn't noticed. The eagle flew away to nurse its wounds and Zarathustra followed, far across the plain and out of sight.

Philosophy stood aloft on the outcrop which Zarathustra had now vacated and she raised her arms to the sky; seeing this, Gambo Lai Lai raised his arms too. In the sky, the spirits of Plato, Plotinus, Xuanzang, Nana Abena Boaa and Bradley could be seen, discoursing in a circle of clouds, while Zemina and Krebons walked hand in hand among the wolves of the plain, gazing up at the spirits. Most of the wolves, billions of them, threw back their heads and howled. Then there was silence, while all waited motionless—the wolves, the spirits, the philosophers from the future, and, of course, Philosophy herself. The silence was broken by the voice of Destiny, booming throughout the whole of reality. "The nuclear threat has been neutralized," they incantated—and this was perfectly well understood by everyone present.

Endnote

1.   Bradley, F.H. (1883/1912) *The Principles of Logic*, New York: G.E. Stechert and Co., p. 533.

Author Biography

James Tartaglia is Professor of Metaphysical Philosophy at Keele University, UK. His main works of original philosophy are *Philosophy in a Meaningless Life* (2016), *Gods and Titans* (2020) and *Inner Space Philosophy* (2024). He is also a jazz saxophonist, whose main albums of original music are *A Free Jazz Treatise Concerning Current Affairs* (2003) and *Jazz-Philosophy Fusion* (2016).

www.JamesTartaglia.com

IFF
BOOKS

ACADEMIC AND SPECIALIST

Iff Books publishes non-fiction. It aims to work with authors and titles that augment our understanding of the human condition, society and civilisation, and the world or universe in which we live. If you have enjoyed this book, why not tell other readers by posting a review on your preferred book site. Recent bestsellers from Iff Books are:

Why Materialism Is Baloney
How true skeptics know there is no death and fathom answers to life, the universe, and everything
Bernardo Kastrup
A hard-nosed, logical, and skeptic non-materialist metaphysics, according to which the body is in mind, not mind in the body.
Paperback: 978-1-78279-362-5 ebook: 978-1-78279-361-8

The Fall
Steve Taylor
The Fall discusses human achievement versus the issues of war, patriarchy and social inequality.
Paperback: 978-1-78535-804-3 ebook: 978-1-78535-805-0

Brief Peeks Beyond
Critical essays on metaphysics, neuroscience, free will, skepticism and culture
Bernardo Kastrup
An incisive, original, compelling alternative to current mainstream cultural views and assumptions.
Paperback: 978-1-78535-018-4 ebook: 978-1-78535-019-1

Punk Science
Inside the Mind of God
Manjir Samanta-Laughton
Many have experienced unexplainable phenomena; God,
psychic abilities, extraordinary healing and angelic encounters.
Can cutting-edge science actually explain phenomena
previously thought of as 'paranormal'?
Paperback: 978-1-90504-793-2

The Vagabond Spirit of Poetry
Edward Clarke
Spend time with the wisest poets of the modern age and of the
past, and let Edward Clarke remind you of the importance of
poetry in our industrialized world.
Paperback: 978-1-78279-370-0 ebook: 978-1-78279-369-4

Readers of ebooks can buy or view any of these bestsellers by
clicking on the live link in the title. Most titles are published
in paperback and as an ebook. Paperbacks are available in
traditional bookshops. Both print and ebook formats are
available online. Find more titles and sign up to our readers'
newsletter at http://www.johnhuntpublishing.com/non-fiction
Follow us on Facebook at
https://www.facebook.com/JHPNonFiction
and Twitter at https://twitter.com/JHPNonFiction